AF662079

Poems and Ponderings

Laxmi Narayan Gupta

DK PRINTWORLD
Publishers of Indian Traditions

ISBN: 978-81-246-1318-4
First published in 2025
© Author

All rights reserved. No part of this publication may be reproduced or transmitted, except brief quotations, in any form or by any means, electronic or mechanical, including photocopying, recording, or any information storage or retrieval system, without prior written permission of the publishers.

Printed and published by:
D.K. Printworld (P) Ltd.
Regd. Office: *Vedaśrī*, F-395, Sudarshan Park
(Metro Station: ESI Hospital), New Delhi - 110015
Phones: (011) 4172 2626, 98713 94815
e-mail: indology@dkprintworld.com
Website: www.dkprintworld.com

Preface

SEVERAL years after I had started my Hindi blog, I realized that I wanted to share my ideas with a wider audience. I wanted to reach my non-Hindi speaking friends both Indian and American. I started my English blog: laxmisponderings.blogspot.com. The first post was published on May 1, 2011 and is about the Hindu View of Creation. It included the way Hindus consider time, tremendously different from the Judeo-Christian view that God created the world around 6000 years ago. In the Hindu view, the creation is ongoing and the present cycle started some 14 billion years ago. I actually wrote my first English poem in the year 2000 to celebrate my wife's birthday. It is written in the style of Dr. Seuss, a childrens' writer. Next poem I wrote was to celebrate my retirement in 2009. Once the trend started, it continued and continues to this day. The blog came several years after I started writing poems in English. So the proper title of this collection should be: Poems and Ponderings. This is the title you are holding in your hands. Enjoy!

March 13, 2025 **Laxmi N. Gupta**

Thinking Outside the Box

While reading Today's Democrat and Chronicle, our local Rochester, NY daily newspaper, I came up with some ideas for fixing our broken economy by suggesting some extra sources of revenue for our state government.

I was reading the story about third party candidates for governor. One of the candidates is 35-year old Kristin Davis whose platform includes legalization of marijuana, gay marriages and prostitution. Kristin is the alleged madam of the escort service used by our ex-governor Eliot Spitzer.

While reading this story, I thought of so-called sin taxes on alcohol, tobacco and gambling. Why don't we extend our list to include prostitution and marijuana? I propose we legalize the prostitution and marijuana use and levy heavy taxes on both. Revenues raised by taxing prostitution can be used partly to make sure that prostitutes have regular health checks and don't pose a danger to public health. If sufficient funds are raised we can also use them for the control of sexually transmitted diseases in general and Aids in particular. Revenues raised by taxing marijuana use can be used for drug education and for funding 'Marijuana Anonymous' in the style of the prestigious Alcoholic Anonymous.

We might also establish a department of the state government to handle the control and taxation of all such sins. We might call it the Department of the Controlled Folly. I rather like this name as it has a Zen feel to it but I am open to other suggestions. We may not go far wrong with our illustrious ex-governor Eliot Spitzer as the first director of this new department.

– 22 October 2010

Big Bang or Big Bounce

There is an article in the New Scientist magazine of October 16, "Bouncy Cosmos makes inflation a sure thing." See:

> http://www.newscientist.com/article/mg20827825.200-big-bounce-cosmos-makes-inflation-a-sure-thing.html

As is well known that our universe is expanding and this expansion started 10^{-39} seconds after the big bang. According to this article if it is assumed that our universe is a recycled version of an earlier cosmos then the probability of super inflation a fraction of a second after the big bang (which is replaced now by a big bounce) becomes an almost sure thing according to calculations done by Abhay Ashtekar and David Sloan both of Pennsylvania State University.

So the picture seems to be that an earlier universe was crunched down and from its remnant emerged a new universe with a big bounce.

As a person of Hindu background, I noticed a couple of things. The current age of the universe is of the order of 10^{17} seconds. Now if you compute the number of seconds in a Kalpa that is made up of 1000 Chaturyugis (4 ages literally) with each Chaturyugi of (4.32) x 10^6 years. You get:

$$4.32 \times 10^6 \times 10^3 \times 365 \times 24 \times 60 \times 60 = 1.32 \times 10^{17} \text{seconds.}$$

I do not for a moment suggest that ancient Hindus were somehow cognizant of modern cosmology but it is curious how they came up with this number.

Also familiar to all Hindus is the idea of a partial destruction of the universe called Pralaya after each Chaturyugi. Much greater destruction, the Mahapralaya happens after a Kalpa.

So what the Hindu Cosmology seems to say that there is a small crunch after each 4.32 million years followed by a small bounce and a big crunch each 4.32 billion years followed by a big bounce.

– October 23, 2010

Rama, the Steadfast

This is the title of a book by John & Mary Brockington of the University of Edinburgh, published in the Penguin Classics series in 2006. The authors claim that there are 5 identifiable layers in the Valmiki Ramayana. Here they have taken what they consider to be the earliest layer based on the linguistic and textual analysis informed by "Their knowledge of Hindu beliefs and practices as they developed later" and translated into English.

Western scholars have believed for a long time that both the Bala Kanda and Uttar Kanda are later additions to the text. As for the Uttar Kanda it should be clear even to a casual reader of the Valmiki Ramayana. The verses at the end of Yuddha Kanda indicate that the recitation of the story has ended. To my unscholarly mind to accept the story begins with Ayodhya Kand is harder to accept for several reasons. The story begins too abruptly. There are no opening praises to deities (Mangalacharan) as is customary at the start of a book.

There are places where there is a break in the story because the translators are unable to identify the earliest text. They have inserted brief bridging passages in such places.

Ramayana so reconstructed makes an attractive compact story. Rama is depicted as a human with great but not supernatural powers.

Many of the flaws that we moderns see in the character of Rama now disappear. Rama is the only one of the four brothers who is married. So when in Aranya Kanda, he tells Shurpanakha that Lakshmana is unmarried, he is not lying. Also it takes care of the vexing question as to why Lakshmana does not take leave of his wife Urmila when leaving Ayodhya. Why does he never think of his wife in the fourteen-year exile? Why does Sita never mention Urmila who is her younger sister?

When Rama kills Vali no one including Vali questions his ethics. May be the ethical questions arose later and so were inserted in later versions.

There are no verses describing the meeting of Rama and Sita after she is brought to him after the killing of Ravana. So there is no Agni Pareeksha (Fire Ordeal). In this context, I would like to mention that, as the learned readers must know, there is a summary of Ramayana story in the Vana Parva of the Mahabharata. In this account when Rama is reluctant to take Sita back, Vayu, Agni, Varuna and Brahma urge him to do so as she is totally blameless and pure. Rama takes Sita back as a result with no Agni Pareeksha. It is conceivable that Agni Pareeksha was added later as the relatively benign attitude towards women in Vedic period hardened.

As Uttar Kand is not included, abandonment of Sita and killing of the Shudra Shambuk don't make appearance here.

I acknowledge with somewhat guilty conscience that I enjoyed this truncated version of Ramayana even though many of the favorite stories are missing from it.

– October 25, 2010

Some Thoughts On Our Trip to Spain

We recently visited Costa del Sol, the southern coast of Spain with side trips to Tangier, Morocco and the rock of Gibraltar.

One of the sites we visited was Alhambra in Granada. Alhambra was the last stronghold of Moors in the Iberian Peninsula. We were impressed by its size, beauty and abstract geometrical patterns charactersistic of Islamic art. Queen Isabella is supposed to have remarked that she did not conquer Alhambra but Alhambra conquered her. She left the place largely unchanged and we should be thankful of that. The mosque in Alhambra was converted to a church. Presumably Moors had converted a church to this mosque when they conquered the region in the 8th century. We visited several sites in southern Spain where churches were converted to mosques and then back to churches.

We Americans remember the year 1492 as the year when Columbus 'discovered' America, which he thought, was India. But another earth-shaking event occurred that same year. Moors were defeated by Ferdinand and Isabella, co-rulers of an area around Castile and thus an era of pluralism in which Christians, Muslims and Jews co-existed harmoniously ended and a new country was born. There was no country called Spain before 1492.

Moors were followers of the then new religion of Islam. It is said that they were about 80 percent Berbers and 20 percent Arabs. Present day Morocco is still about 60 percent Berber. Moors came to the Iberian Peninsula from Northern Africa in early eighth century CE. The Peninsula became part of a large Moor empire extending to present day Morocco, Mauritania and Libya. They established a largely tolerant multi-cultural pluralistic society. This society was more sophisticated than the other societies of Western Europe of the time and made great advances in art, music, literature and architecture. They have a left a large imprint on the cultures of Portugal and Spain. It is strange as Washington Irving; the first American ambassador to Spain remarked that Spaniards still largely think of Moors as usurpers. I first learned about Moors when I was in college from the excellent 'Glimpses of World History' by Jawaharlal Nehru, the first prime minister of the independent India. Nehru is full of admiration for Moors and their cultural contributions. Incidentally it is Nehru's birthday today; it is celebrated as children's day in India as Nehru was very fond of children.

What happened in Spain after Moors is truly tragic. Ferdinand and Isabella gave Muslims and Jews three months to convert to Christianity or leave Spain. Many converted. Nobody seems to know how many. We all know the bigotry that followed the departure of Moors. Spanish inquisitions and other horrors were carried out in the name of Christianity.

In these troubled times when many people equate terrorism with Islam, we should think of the great pluralistic society nurtured by Muslim Moorish rulers over a period of more than 700 years.

– 14 November 14, 2010

From Goethe & Schiller to Kalidasa in San Francisco

We recently visited the lovely Japanese Garden in San Francisco with our daughter and son-in-law. The garden is located in the Golden Gate Park. Just outside the garden we saw a statue of two great German literary figures Johann Wolfgang von Goethe and Friedrich Schiller on the same pedestal. I was not sure why they were placed together. I learned later, thanks to Google and Wikipedia that the two were associated for 17 years until Schiller died of tuberculosis at age forty-five. Together they founded the Weimar Theater that became a leading theater in Germany. Schiller started writing plays again-a practice he had given up- at Goethe's urging.

All I knew about Schiller was that his poem "The Ode to Joy" is the basis for the 4th movement in Beethoven's 9th symphony.

My knowledge of Goethe is also quite meager. I know that his magnum opus is Faust. I possess a translation of Faust in English that I have tried to read several times but have not made much progress. Either the translation is poor or my understanding of poetry is poor or both. The other thing that I knew about Goethe is some thing that many educated Indians know. Goethe read Sanskrit poet and playwright Kalidasa's play, " Abhigyan Shakuntalam" meaning "the Recognition of Shakuntala " and was very pleased with it. He wrote, "If you want heaven and earth combined in one name, I say Shakuntala and all is spoken." He also added a prologue to Faust in the fashion of Shakuntala in which the play is introduced at the beginning of the performance with a dialog between the director and actors.

Kaldasa lived between late 4th century and mid 5th century. He probably lived in Ujjain in Central India. He was one of the nine 'jewels' in the court of Chandragupta Vikramaditya. Only seven of his works are extant: three plays, two epics and two smaller poems. Shakuntala is his best-known play.

A synopsis of the plot is as follows. King Dushyanta on a hunting trip encounters Shankuntala in a hermitage while her adoptive father is away. They fall in love and marry secretly. King gives her a ring with his name inscribed on it and promises to send for her in a few days. As Shakuntala is pining at his departure, a fiery-tempered sage visits the hermitage and curses Shakuntala as she does not rise to greet him. In her despondent state she does not see him. The curse is that the person in whose remembrance she is so busy with will not recognize her. A friend of Shakuntala pleads with him and he relents so that the curse will be lifted once the object of her remembrance sees a memento.

Shakuntala is pregnant and when her adoptive father arrives he sends her to the king with some attendants. While crossing a river Shakuntala drops the ring given her by the king. Sure enough king has no recollection of her and she has no ring to show him. Shakuntala is grief-stricken and does not know what to do. At this moment her mother who is a heavenly dancer in the court of Indra, the king of heaven appears and whisks away her daughter. She gives birth to a son who is named Bharata and is being brought up in the hermitage of sage Kashyapa, the father of Indra.

Meanwhile a fisherman finds a ring in the belly of a carp. The ring has the king's insignia so he brings it to the king. On seeing the ring the king remembers Shakuntala and is full of remorse. At this time a messenger from Indra shows up and asks for the king's help in fighting demons who have become very powerful. King goes to help Indra and is victorious against the demons. He is triumphantly on his way back to earth in a heavenly chariot. On his way he goes to pay his homage to Indra's father. There he has a joyous reunion his wife Shakuntala and meets his son Bharata. This son Bharata becomes a mighty king in his time. The country he rules is called 'Bhaarata' after him. Bhaarata is the ancient name for the country that we now call India. In India the name is still used in the Indian languages.

– 5 December, 2010

A Remarkable Book

I just finished reading Rian Malan's, "My Traitor's Heart", published by the Atlantic Monthly Press. Ever since I retired in May 2009, I have been reading quite a bit. This is probably the most significant book I have read in past couple of years. The book was published in 1990 so many of you readers might have read it.

Malan was commissioned to write a book about the history of his family that has been quite prominent in South Africa. As he says (I am paraphrasing) whenever any thing significant happened, a Malan was there. He writes about his ancestor Dawid Malan in the 18th century, who ran away with a slave girl. Many years later, he resurfaces as a white supremacist without his black lover, "willing to die rather than accord black people equality before the law." He counts a prime minister among his more recent ancestors. About one hundred pages in the book, it takes a life of its own and even though his family figures in it, the book becomes about his own struggles to come to terms with the South African reality.

Malan is a South African born in 1954. This book is part autobiography and part reportage. It is a difficult but engaging read. Malan's father is an Afrikaner or Boer and his mother is English. As a young man he considers himself a leftist liberal. He does not have much contact with black people except for the family maid. He gets a job as a crime reporter. He covers a series of crimes mostly murders and in process visits black neighborhoods. He talks about the contradictions of South African society that make him run away from his native land. Here he describes why:

"I ran away because I was scared of coming changes, and scared of the consequences of not changing. I ran because I wouldn't carry a gun for apartheid, and because I wouldn't carry a gun against it. I ran away because I hated Afrikaners and loved blacks. I ran away because I was an Afrikaner and feared blacks. You could say, I suppose, that I ran away from the paradox."

After wandering around in Europe, he finally arrives in US in

1979. He does odd jobs, writes for Rolling Stones and other magazines and gives talks about South Africa. He notices that America is the most classless society he has ever seen. He sheds his leftist leanings in America. He misses the momentous happening in South Africa and goes back in 1986 and becomes a reporter again.

Malan covers many murders and interviews a lot of people. He describes predictably the horror of apartheid but also horrendous acts of violence that blacks commit against other blacks and the curious addiction of Zulus to internecine warfare.

The book ends with an account of a white family in Msinga, a Zulu area. Msinga is a wasteland. Malan calls it an ecological Hiroshima. Neil and Creina Alcock settle there. They opt to live like Zulus in a mud hut. They try to reverse the ecological disaster in a part of Msinga that they have bought. With great persistence, they have persuaded Zulus to cooperate in their venture to make the land green and productive again. Neil designs a water wheel and starts fertilizing land with cattle dung. He keeps a herd of 800 cattle. Gradually, greenery comes back and land is rejuvenated. For three years his experiment is successful but then he gets caught in a crossfire trying to make peace between two Zulu warring groups and is killed. Creina and her two sons keep living there but Zulus have refused to cooperate with the experiment and the land is barren again except for a small patch which Kreina keeps.

Her life becomes very difficult. She does not have a good grasp of the Zulu language and does not have Neil's commanding presence. She tries to keep the project going but it falls apart gradually. She even gets death threats for an offence she did not commit. But she refuses to leave. In an interview with Malan she says, "I think you will know what I mean if I tell you love is worth nothing until it has been tested by its own defeat. I felt I was being asked to try to love enough not to be afraid of its consequences. I realized that love, even if it ends in defeat, gives you a kind of honor; but without love, you have no honor at all. I think that is what I had misunderstood all my life. Love is to enable you to transcend defeat."

– March 22, 1911

Hindu View of Creation

According to Hindus, in an absolute sense, creation is without beginning and without end. In a relative sense, cosmos itself is periodically created and destroyed, similar to big bangs and big crunches of modern cosmological theories. The period called a kalpa lasts for about 4.32 billion years. A kalpa is also a day in the life of the creator god Brahma. The period between a big crunch and a big bang is also a kalpa. This is a night in the life of the creator god Brahma when cosmos exists only in a latent unmanifest form. A day of Brahma begins with sristi, the divine manifestation of unmanifest.

Each kalpa consists of 1000 Mahayugas with each mahayuga of 4.32 million years. Each mahayuga consists of 4 ages Satyuga, Treta, Dwapara and Kaliyuga. Virtue declines as we advance through these ages. The history of universe is seen as a biological process with continuous decline with advancing of time. Kaliyuga lasts for 432, 000 years, dwapara is twice as long, treta thrice and satyuga 4 times as much.

The creator god Brahma is not to be confused with Brahman, the supreme God, the energy of the universe. Life span of a Brahma is 100 Brahma years which works out to be about 311 trillion years. Incidentally, this is supposed to be the first day of the 51st year in the life of the present Brahma. After one hundred Brahma years, there is a total and complete dissolution of the three worlds. The cosmos is completely absorbed into divine and remanifests after 100 Brahma years.

At the beginning of creation the great God Vishnu is lying asleep atop the primordial serpent Ananta (meaning endless) on primordial waters when a lotus stalk arises from his navel with Brahma sitting atop a lotus flower. Brahma's job is to create. He is also called Prajapati, the lord of creatures. The Hindu view of creation is not similar to the view of creation in genesis where God fashions and builds a creature from earthly materials as a potter models clay and breathes life into it. Rather Brahma pours forth his own being in giving birth to creatures that inhabit the universe. Thus demons are born from his thigh and gods from his mouth in some accounts. In some accounts, by thinking alone, he creates sages who set out to produce offspring. After the initial creation the great god Vishnu asks his lovely wife Lakshmi to keep the creatures (jiva in Sanskrit) enchanted and bewitched by the world so they love and procreate and remain interested in the world. Lakshmi in this role is the divine Maya, the goddess who keeps the world (samsara, the world of coming and going) keep going.

– May 1, 2011

Because I Am Retired

Because I Am Retired,

I want no fame or fortune,
No laurels or brickbats,
No applause or hoots,
No recognition or accolades,
I am done with all that.

I want to read a book,
Listen to a song,
Watch a bird take wings or a flower bloom,
Stroll idly or hum a tune.

I want to do the dishes,
Do laundry,
Cook a meal,
Compose a poem,
Play with my grand kid,
Cuddle with my wife,
And try not to snore (Never works according to her).

I don't want to complain about my ailments,
My finances,
Property and income taxes.

I want to live and love,
Till my day under the sun,
Is done.

– June 19, 2011

A Love Song

My dear friend Dr. B.K. Gaur commented that my previous post was my first poem in English. He is almost right. I wrote a humorous love song in the style of Dr. Seuss on my wife's 50th birthday some years ago (it is not polite to say how many). It is here for you to enjoy.

– 21 June 21, 2011

A Love Song

Rejoice beloved have some fun.
Your fifty-first year has just begun.
I love you more than ever before.
You know, who can ask for more?
Love you through menopause and all.
They say love conquers it all.
Love you through Alaska and Yukon.
Love you, all through Hindustan.
Love is all that matters, honey.
You can bet on it all your money.
Love you, love you, honey bright.
Love you; love you, all the night.
Love you when the stars are bright.
Love you through the moonlit nights.
Love you in light, love you in dark.
Love has its own eternal spark.
Love you when you are fifty, honey.
Will love you at sixty, honey.
Such love withers not at the age of seventy.
Goes right through the age of eighty.
More than this we need not talk.
Love through the eternity is going to last.
Love is hot and love is cold.
Love is sometimes very, very bold.
Love is what makes the world go round.
Love is simple, love is profound.
Love is nice, love is warm.
Love can survive the greatest storm.
Love is gentle, love is kind.
Love can make you go out of your mind.
Love is complete, love is full.
Love can make you look like a fool.
Love is foolish, love is wise.
Love can make you lose your stride.

--- Laxmi N. Gupta

5/18/2008 5:49 PM

What Am I, a Believer or a Nonbeliever?

When I was in the first year of college, I became uncertain about many things which I had routinely believed as part of my upbringing. I was no longer certain of existence of God or gods, Karma and rebirth. It is customary in India, while writing letters, to state that the person you are writing to is well by the grace of God. I dropped this usage and started wring simply, "I hope you are well." When Asked about my beliefs, I started telling people that I am an agnostic.

From time to time, I almost became atheistic. But whenever that happened I became filled with a strange melancholy. I had forgotten about this phenomenon but it asserted again recently.

I read a novel, "The Tale of Carvaka" by a Manga Randreas. It is a much fictionalized biography of an ancient Indian philosopher who boldly asserted that there is no God, no soul, no Karma and no rebirth. I liked the book very much and wrote a review of it for the Amazon.Com.

Soon afterwards, I found myself strangely despondent. On analyzing my feelings, I found that I rather like the uncertainty of the existence of God, and afterlife and related ideas. I am not sure that all this is true but to deny boldly that this world and this life is all that there is fills me with a strange sorrow and unease.

As luck, God or chance would have it, I had ordered a book, "Two Strange Tales" by Mircea Eliade. I read the first of the two tales, "Nights at Serampore." In this tale the author and hist two friends are unbelievably transported to another time and place due to a Tantrik's power. Event though it is just a work of fiction, it relieved my melancholia. Things became uncertain again, just as I like.

I had a conversation with a Jehova's witness missionary many years ago. He asked me if I believed in God. I replied that it depends on what he means by God. If by God he means this strange universe full of mystery which can't be totally explained by religion or by science then I believe in God. His answer was, "So all this a mystery to you?" I said, "Is it not to you?" He said pointing at his bible that it is all written here. I jokingly asked him to go away as I like to have my mysteries. I did not realize that it was no joke but an existential truth for me.

– 28 September, 2011

Some Thoughts on Retirement

I have now been retired for over two years. I offer some thoughts in easing to retirement after a long working life. Perhaps some will find my reflections useful.

Starting right from childhood, we are taught to be future oriented by our parents, teachers and society at large. When children ask certain questions, we tell them, " You will know when you grow up." We ask them to get good grades, work hard and sacrifice now to assure a good future.

As adults we do things to get ahead, get promoted, buy a house, get married and so forth. There is always something to look forward to in future. We don't worry much about now as presumably we have a long life ahead.

Better things are always supposed to be in future. Many spend a lifetime for their ship to come in, so to say. Better days are always ahead of us. In future, we will be richer, wiser, happier and healthier.

I don't know about you but I don't feel much wiser now than when I was a teenager. Actually, I feel less wise now than then. I am less certain of things now. Before I knew what should be done to solve world problems. I was surer of my spiritual beliefs and surer of my place in the scheme of things. The things which grownups, in childhood, used to say, you will know when you grow up, I still don't know.

When you retire, future oriented thinking leads to unhappiness. It is hard to realize that your best years are behind you. Your health will only get worse; your faculties will only deteriorate and many of us will spend old age alone. You are for the most part are not going to achieve dizzying new heights; there are not going to be job promotions and salary raises any more.

What nobody tells you and prepare you for is that you have to learn to live in present moment. Enjoy today and what it brings. Look at a flower, laugh with a baby, and enjoy a show or whatever. Don't brood about past glorious or otherwise and don't worry much about the future. I am slowly learning to be happy in my retirement.

– 18 October 2011.

From 'Jya' to Sine and 'Shunya' to Zero

Here I would like to talk about the etymology of two mathematical terms Sine and Zero. Both ultimately come from Sanskrit but in a roundabout fashion.

First we take the etymology of Sine. Indian Mathematician Aryabhatta called it 'ardh-jya' i.e. half the chord (of a unit circle) and later abbreviated it to 'jya.' Arabs phonetically derived 'jiba' from 'jya' and then dropped the vowels to get 'jb.' It is a common practice in Arabic to drop the vowels. Later writers decided to put some vowels in to make the word meaningful. Thus they got the word 'jaib' which means bosom in Arabic. Latin writers translated it to 'sinus' from which comes the English word 'sine.'

Zero comes from Sanskrit 'shunya' again in a very curious fashion. Shunya means empty or void. Arabs translated it to 'sifr.' From 'sifr', somehow comes Latin 'zephirum' from which English 'zero' is derived.

Incidentally Arabic 'sifr' was introduced in German as 'cifra' from which comes English 'cipher.'

Reference

An Introduction to the History of Mathematics (Revised Edition) 1964, by Howard Eves (pages 20 and 198)

– December 15, 2011

Narada-Vishnu Dialog

This is a translation of a Hindi poem that I wrote recently. The translation is done by my dear friend Alaka Srivastava with editing done by her daughter Adraja. I have tweaked the translation slightly.

Background: In Hindu mythology, Narada is an itinerant saint traveling back and forth between heaven and earth, carrying news. On this particular occasion he is visiting Lord Vishnu with news from the Earth, the land of mortals.)

Narada Arrived at Vishnu's door
Lord stood and welcomed him
Narada, come in please!
Tell me about Mrityu Loka (the land of mortals)

Narada said:
Lord, Earth's situation is very strange
Your children are determined to kill Death.
Fatal diseases like Cancer and Heart attack
Human beings want to wipe them out.
They are limiting ways of dying.
Elderly population is on the rise.
They do die, but a slow death with suffering galore.
They suffer with crippling diseases like arthritis.
Diseases like Alzheimer's are increasing.
Difference between living and dying is decreasing.
Old people are taking care of even older ones.
The ratio of Young is decline.
Humans are set upon digging their own grave.

The Lord said: Narada, you have correctly spoken.
In the name of progress, humanity has sought devastation.
In order to take care of this universe properly which is my function,

Balance is needed.
Death is not an enemy of humanity.
Life and death go together.
It is said, they go hand in hand.
But, do not worry,
Wait for a century or two,
Humans will then understand.
They will change direction.
They will understand that it is necessary for the elderly to die;
It is necessary to increase the proportion of Young.
The Old do not have the energy to run the world.
They are no longer capable of hard work.
So, do not think of Death as an enemy
Think of it as a tool to manage and care for the Creation.

– April 1, 2012

Parallel Truths

I was listening to a lecture on Shakespeare's Twelfth Night by Peter Saccio, an eminent Shakespearian scholar. Saccio explains a bit of a dialog by Viola, disguised as Cesario to Olivia, " What is yours to bestow is not yours to reserve." Saccio explains that the beauty that Olivia possesses must be passed on that is to say that she must marry and have children to pass on this beauty. Saccio relates this to the parable of talents in the gospel of Matthew. A master with three servants is going away. He gives 10 talents (a coin or an unit of money) to the first servant, five to the second and one to the third for safekeeping. The first and second servant invest and double the amount whereas the third buries it. When the master comes back he praises the first and second servant and rebukes the third. Saccio claims that the origin of the word talent in most European languages is this parable. The parable is interpreted to mean that whatever talent you have is given to you by God and is to be returned to Him by developing it and using it for the benefit of fellow human beings.

While listening to this lecture, I was reminded of a Hindi phrase that is often used in Hindu prayers: Tera tujhko arpan, kyaa laage meraa. It means, "I offer to you (God) what already is yours; there is nothing that belongs to me." I have repeated this phrase many times without realizing its true meaning. The Christian parable and its interpretation clarified the meaning. Truth is not sectarian; it is universal.

– 17 April 2012

Musings

You don't see too many bumper stickers these days but I saw a good one yesterday. It said, "I was born ok the first time." It is obviously a dig at the Born Again Christians. This reminded me of the former Minnesota senator Eugene McCarthy who after his memorable presidential campaign in 1968 ran several forgettable campaigns for presidency. In one of these latter campaigns he remarked that of all the major presidential campaigns he was the only one who was born only once. Romney is a Mormon and I have no idea whether Mormons are born once or twice. May be a reader of this blog would enlighten me. As far as I know Obama was born only once.

Now Hindus have a notion of twice born but it only applies to the men of upper three castes: Brahmans (priests, teachers, and scholars), Kshatriyas (soldiers and rulers) and Vaishyas (traders, farmers and dairymen). It does not apply to Shudras who are workers of all kind. The upper castes have a sacred thread ceremony that is a sort of religious and spiritual initiation. It is considered as the second birth. Except for the Brahmans, the ceremony is a perfunctory one. For the Vaishyas (of which I am one), the ceremony takes place at the time of wedding. You will notice women are excluded from this ritual.

During my wedding the thread ceremony was not performed. It just so happened that the priest my father-in-law hired was not very good. I got married in the month of January and generally at that time of the year there are no auspicious days for a wedding. As I had only limited time in India, I asked my father-in-law to offer the priest a monetary inducement to find an auspicious day. The ploy worked. It would not have worked with a priest who knew what he was doing. So I am born only once. It is said that every man is born a Shudra. Only with the thread ceremony, one acquires a higher caste. So I am a Shudra, technically speaking, which is fine with me. Upper castes have all kind of dietary restrictions, which Shudras don't. So I eat pretty much any thing and anywhere. I am not saying that I would have followed the restrictions if I had the sacred thread.

Hindus are not supposed to eat beef even the Shudras. Many Hindus living outside India eat beef and I am one of them. I some time joke that American cows are not holy as they don't have 'the holy hump' as Indian cows do. Actually in Vedic times, even Brahmans freely ate beef. Shatapatha Brahman, a text dating to about 900 BCE, says, "Beef is the most excellent food." Somewhere along the line injunction against eating beef came. It is speculated that it happened due to Buddhist influence. Now one can ask why the injunction does not apply to goats, sheep, water buffaloes and chicken. Modern Hindus say that it is because cow is the most useful animal. It produces milk and oxen are used to plough the land and are used as beasts of burden. Buffalos perform all these functions but not an ounce of sanctity is attached to them. Actually most milk in India is from the water buffalo. Indian cows yield very little milk. But no body sings songs in praise of mother buffalo or mother goat.

A western scholar whose name I do not recall has speculated as follows. Due to success of Buddhism, there arose a revulsion against ritual sacrifice and as cow was the most common sacrificial killing, a ban against cow slaughter was the most effective way to minimize ritual sacrifice. My own speculation is that it was perhaps Krishna who was a cowherd in his boyhood. He had special affection for cows and as he became very influential and was recognized as an incarnation of Vishnu, he might have made this injunction. I can find no textual source to support my thesis.

I have to get ready for a trip to see our grandson so this associative game has to stop.

– July 5, 2012

A Mythological Tale of Lust and War

Hindu mythology is expounded in a vast collection of books called Puranas, literally meaning ancient tales. Such tales are called pauranik or puranik. Hindu stories of gods, demons and humans are somewhat similar to Greek myths. In Greek stories gods intervene in human affairs much more than in Hindu stories. Before telling the story, I have to give a brief account of the basic set up of heavens. Highest Gods are the Gods of trinity: Brahma, Vishnu and Shiva. They reside in the highest heavens. Below them is the lower heaven presided by Indra. The lower heaven is called Swarga and the gods residing there are called Devas. The demons or Asuras reside in nether regions. Devas and Asuras are constantly at war as Asuras have a claim to Swarga and want to dethrone Indra.

Brihaspati, the guru of Devas and presiding deity over the planet Jupiter has a very beautiful wife Tara. The moon god Soma is enchanted by Tara and kidnaps her. This is a momentous event that shakes up heavens and nether regions. Alliances are formed. Most but not all Devas are on the side of Brihaspati. Soma is assisted by some Devas and most Asuras. A war ensues. This war is called Tara-Kamaya, a war prompted by desire for Tara. The war is so fierce that the creator God Brahma is afraid that the entire creation may be destroyed. He intervenes. The war is stopped and Tara is restored to Brihaspati.

It turns out that Tara is pregnant. A son named Budha is born. The child is very handsome and both Brihaspati and Soma claim him. At Brahma's behest, Tara declares Soma to be the father. Then an argument ensues as to what is more important field or seed. Brihaspati claims that field is his so the son belongs to him. Soma claims the seed is his so the son belongs to him. At this point, accounts differ. In some accounts Soma gets the son; in others Brihaspati. I may point out here that in ancient Hindu society, husband of a woman is entitled to all her progeny, no matter who the biological father is. So most probably Brihaspati and Tara got the custody of child Budha who grew up to be the presiding deity of the planet Mercury.

Budha married Ila, a daughter of Manu, the first man. Ila and Budha had a son named Pururavas. Some wonderful stories are associated with Pururavas, which I reserve for another time.

Bibliography

A Classical Dictionary of Hindu Mythology by John Dowson

Puranic Encyclopaedia by Vettam Mani

– August 14, 2012

A Story of Gender Transformation in Hindu Mythology

Readers will recall from the previous post:

> http://laxmisponderings.blogspot.com/2012/08/a-mythological-tale-of-lust-and-war.html

that Budha, son of Soma and Tara married Ilaa, a daughter of Manu, the progenitor of human race. Budha and Ilaa had an illustrious son named Pururava. Mahabharata, the story of great war has a curious sentence: Ilaa was both Pururava's mother and father.

This post is about Ila/Ilaa. Ila is male and Ilaa female.

Manu and his wife prayed to gods Mitra and Varuna for a son. However because of an error made in the prayer, a daughter named Ilaa was born. The parents prayed again and gods rectified the error and the gill was turned into a boy Ila.

In time Ila became an illustrious king. Once prince Ila went hunting and inadvertently entered an area where goddess Parvati sports with her husband Shiva. Only females are allowed in this area. Even shiva has to assume a female form. If any male enters this region he is transformed into a female. So Ila is transformed into a charming female Ilaa and wanders around. During her wanderings, she meets Budha, himself a dashing figure. They fall in love and marry. They have a son named Pururava whose story will be told in the next post.

Ilaa prays to Lord Vishnu who turns her into a man again. As a man he regains his kingdom and has three sons.

– August 21, 2012

PS: Ila's retinue of soldiers, naturally all males was also turned into females when Ila was. These were called Kimpurushas or Kinnaras (what? Men) and settled in Himalayan foothills by Budha. Modern day eunuchs (Hinjaras in Hindi) in India have adopted the name Kinnaras as a measure of adding respectability.

There are many versions of this story but they all involve the theme of gender transformation and sometimes ambiguity of gender.

Bibliography: In addition to the bibliography in the previous post:

The Concise Ramayana of Valmiki by Swami Venkatesananda State University of New York Press.

Story of Pururava and Urvashi

Pururava is a son of Budha and Ilaa. As a son of a mortal (Ilaa) and an immortal (Budha), he is a mortal. He is a grandson of Soma (Moon) and the first king of lunar dynasty.

Heavenly nymph (Apsara) Urvashi had to come down to earth as a punishment to some offense to gods Mitra and Varuna. On earth she met Pururava who fell in love with her. Urvashi agreed to live with Pururava provided he met certain conditions. Urvashi had a couple of pet rams that should always remain by her side and she should never see Pururava naked.

Gods in the heaven of Indra and Gandharvas, heavenly musicians and close associates of apsaras, the heavenly dancers were anxious to have Urvashi back in heaven. So gandharvas went disguised as robbers and stole Urvashi's rams. Pururava was naked in bed so at first he did not respond for the fear that Urvashi will see him undressed. Later he roused himself and went in search of robbers. Gandharvas brought a flash of lightening and Urvashi saw Pururava naked so the charm was broken and Urvashi went back to heaven.

(This is a painting of Urvashi leaving Pururava by famous 19th century painter Raja Ravi Varma.)

Pururava distraught with grief at the loss of Urvashi roamed the earth. Once he saw Urvashi at Kurukshetra bathing with four other apsaras. Urvashi told him she was pregnant and asked him to come back. Urvashi gave him a son on the second trip and spent a night with him. This sequence was repeated. She spent a night with him each year and bore him four more sons.

Myth of Pururava and Urvashi goes back to Rgveda (1500 BCE). According to some scholars Pururava represents the sun and Urvashi the morning mist. Just as morning mist disappears on the sight of sun Urvashi vanishes from the sight of Pururava.

Kalidasa's play Vikramorvashi (Vikram and Urvashi) is based on this story. Vikram meaning valor is Pururava. Kalidasa changes the story somewhat. Urvashi is living on earth with her lover Pururava. She is summoned to heaven to perform in a celestial play. She is so much smitten with Pururava that she makes mistakes in the performance and ruins the play. She is banished from heaven but cursed to return the moment her earthly lover sees her newborn child. After a series of mishaps, she is united with her earthly lover on earth.

– 27 August 2012

A Story of Gender Transformation from Greek Mythology

Once Tiresias of Thebes was walking in the forest when he saw a copulating serpent couple. He put his staff between the copulating couple and was immediately turned into a female. He lived as a woman for seven years. After seven years he encountered the same serpent couple copulating again. He put his staff between them and was turned into a man again.

It just so happened that Olympian God Zeus and his wife Hera (divine couple of Greek myths, somewhat like Vishn̄u and Lakshmi or Shiva and Parvati of Hindus) were arguing as to who has more fun during sexual intercourse male or female. Zeus thought women have more fun and Hera men. They put the question to Tiresias who was in an ideal position to settle the issue, as he had been both a man and woman. Tiresias ruled in favor of Zeus. Hera was furious and turned Tiresias blind. Now in Greek mythology a curse of a deity can't be undone so Zeus gave Tiresias the gift of prophecy. Tiresias made many famous prophesies. In particular, he tried to warn Oedipus not to try to find his parents.

Joseph Campbell talks about this episode in his, "Mythic Worlds, Modern Works." He mentioned this story in a seminar once. During a break between sessions, a woman approached him and said, "I know why Hera was so mad." Campbell asked her to explain. She said, "From now Hera could not say to Zeus, 'I am doing this for you, darling.'"

Bibliography

Joseph Campbell: Mythic Worlds, Modern Times: On the Art of James Joyce edited by Edmund L. Epstein 1993 Harper Collins.

– September 2, 2012

Swami Vivekananda's 1893 Speech

Dear Readers,

On this day, 119 years ago, Swami Vivekananda delivered a stirring speech to the World Parliament of religions. It will be an understatement to say that it had quite an impact. Here is the speech in full. In my mind, it still ranks with the greatest speeches ever delivered.

The historic Speech of Swami Vivekananda to the World Parliament of Religions on September 11, 1893

"Sisters and Brothers of America,

It fills my heart with joy unspeakable to rise in response to the warm and cordial welcome which you have given us. l thank you in the name of the most ancient order of monks in the world; I thank you in the name of the mother of religions; and I thank you in the name of the millions and millions of Hindu people of all classes and sects. My thanks, also, to some of the speakers on this platform who, referring to the delegates from the Orient, have told you that these men from far-off nations may well claim the honor of bearing to different lands the idea of toleration.I am proud to belong to a religion which has taught the world both tolerance and universal acceptance. We believe not only in universal toleration, but we accept all religions as true. I am proud to belong to a nation which has sheltered the persecuted and the refugees of all religions and all nations of the earth. I am proud to tell you that we have gathered in our bosom the purest remnant of the Israelites, who came to the southern India and took refuge with us in the very year in which their holy temple was shattered to pieces by Roman tyranny. I am proud to belong to the religion which has sheltered and is still fostering the remnant of the grand Zoroastrian nation. I will quote to you, brethren, a few lines from a hymn which I remember to have repeated from my earliest boyhood, which is every day repeated by millions of human beings:

As the different streams having there sources in different places all mingle their water in the sea, so, O Lord, the different paths which men take through different tendencies, various though they appear, crooked or straight, all lead to thee.

The present convention, which is one of the most august assemblies ever held, is in itself a vindication, a declaration to the world, of the wonderful doctrine preached in the Gita:

Whosoever comes to Me, through whatsoever form, I reach him; all men are struggling through paths which in the end lead to me.

Sectarianism, bigotry, and its horrible descendant, fanaticism, have long possessed this beautiful earth. They have filled the earth with violence, drenched it often and often with human blood, destroyed civilization, and sent whole nations to despair. Had it not been for these horrible demons, human society would be far more advanced than it is now. But their time is come; and I fervently hope that the bell that tolled this morning in honor of this convention may be the death-knell of all fanaticism, of all persecutions with the sword or with the pen, and of all uncharitable feelings between persons wending their way to the same goal."

Eleven years ago today, some narrow minded religious fanatics created havoc in this country. On this day, Swami Vivekananda's message of tolerance and diversity is timely and appropriate.

– September 11, 2012

How Savitri Outwitted the Lord of Death

Once upon a time there was a princess named Savitri resplendent like sun. Her splendor discouraged any suitors. Her father, the king wanted her to find a suitor. She set out to find one. She found one in prince Satyavan who was at present living in forest with his blind father and mother. Blind king's kingdom was taken away from him by force by an old enemy.

When Savitri returned from her trip to find a husband, sage Narada was visiting. He said that savitri had chosen wrongly as prince Satyavan had exactly one year to live. But Savitri had her mind set to marry only satyavan and no one else.

Her father agreed and in due course Savitri and Satyavan were married. Savitri gave up her royal comforts willingly and dutifully served her in-laws and husband. But the fateful day was fast approaching. Three days before the day Satyavan was supposed to die, Savitri engaged in austerities and rituals to please gods.

On the day Satyavan was to die he set out for the forest with his axe to fetch wood and fruits. Savitri insisted on accompanying him. In the forest satyavan chopped wood and gathered fruit. Then he lay down in Savitri's lap with a horrific headache and was soon unconscious. Savitri saw a resplendent man in yellow robes. His eyes were red and he had a noose in one hand. He told Savitri he was Yama, the lord of death and had come to take Satyavan's soul with him. He extracted a thumb-sized person from Satyavan's body and set out south towards his abode.

Savitri followed Yama, praying to him and uttering words that pleased Yama, the lord of Dharma. He asked her to return and as he was pleased with her agreed to grant her a boon except the life of her husband. Savitri asked for her father-in-law's sight to be restored. But she still pursued him. Yama agreed to grant her another boon except for Satyavan's life. She asked for the restoration of her father-in-law's kingdom. But she still pursued Yama. Yama promised another boon with the same exception as before. She asked for sons for her father, as he had no male heir.

Savitri still pursued Yama uttering honeyed words. Yama granted another boon except for the life of Satyavan. She asked for a son for her with Satyavan. In his hurry to get rid of her, Yama granted the boon but now he was caught in a dilemma. He asked Savitri to ask for another boon without the usual exception of Satyavan's life. Yama was pleased to grant it.

Satyavan came back to life. He and Savitri enjoyed many years of marital bliss together.

– September 20, 12

A Poem by the 15th Century Indian Saint Poet Kabir

A fish is thirsty in the midst of water;
What a laugh! says Kabir.
Forest to forest you wander
Overlooking what was right at home.
What use it is to go to Mathura and Kashi
Life is dreary without knowledge of the Self.

Notes

1. Mathura and Kashi are Hindu holy places.
2. I wish to thank Dr. Corinne Dempsey for help with the translation.

Here is the original for those who read Hindi.

पानी बिच मीन पियासी
मोहें सुनि सुनि आवत हाँसी
घर में वस्तु नजर नहिं आवत
बन बन फिरत उदासी
आतम ज्ञान बिना सब सूना
क्या मथुरा क्या काशी

– October 3, 2012

Om, Hail to Goddess Turkey!

Happy Thanksgiving to all my readers.

Several years ago, I wrote a poem in Hindi called Turkey Aaaratii:

http://www.kavyakala.blogspot.com/2005/11/blog-post_17.html

I offer here a translation for non-Hindi readers:

Om, Hail to Goddess Turkey!
Rewarded is the one, who eats you,
His hunger is assuaged.
It matters not that you lose your life.
Om, Hail to Goddess Turkey!

How do we sing this sad tale of yours?
How do we describe your selfless sacrifice?
Om, Hail to Goddess Turkey!

Franklin had wanted you to be the national bird.
By a sad twist of fate
You became the national sacrifice
On the Thanksgiving Day.
Om, Hail to Goddess Turkey!

Nation gives thanks by trussing, baking and
Devouring you.
O, Great Goddess, tolerate
This wretched hypocrisy.
Om, Hail to Goddess Turkey !

Whosoever sings this great glory of you
Is rid of all sorrows,
Their desires all fulfilled.
Om, Hail to Goddess Turkey!

– Thanksgiving Day, November 22, 2012

Who Were Tilangas?

When I was very young, perhaps 4 or 5 years old, my mother used to utter a phrase when things happening in the outside world upset her. The saying in Hindi is:

> अब आई राज तिलंगन कै
> बनि आई नंगी नंगन कै

Roughly translated it means, "Tilanga's are ruling now. Shameless crooks can do whatever they desire."

I did not know who were Tilangas and why they were so bad. It remained even after I retired. But then I bought a copy of William Dalrymple's The Last Mughal. For those who are not familiar with the work, it is the story of Bahadur Shah 'Zafar', the last Mughal emperor of India. He was an emperor in name only as his rule did not even extend all over Delhi, his capital. The East India company ruled over much of India. A rebellion broke out in 1857. It was called the Sepoy Rebellion by the British. Sepoy is a mispronunciation of Hindi Sipahi, meaning a soldier in Hindi. Independent India calls it the First Struggle for Independence. Zafar was the titular head of the rebellion. The rebellion developed in the ranks of British Indian army. It started in Bengal and rebel soldiers marched towards Delhi. These soldiers were largely from Bihar and eastern Uttar Pradesh. They were a rag tag group, ill-prepared and ill-equipped. Delhi folks did not much like them and called them 'Tilangas' or 'Purbias.' Now, Purbia is clear enough; it means an easterner. According to Dalrymple, Tilanga means a person from the Telangana region of modern Andhra Pradesh. This is the region that was ruled by Muslim rulers called Nizams. British recruited a large number of troops from the region. Both Purbia and Tilanga essentially indicated foreignness of the troops whom the Delhites were forced to support in terms of food and lodging; hence the resentment.

– January 10, 2013

A Poem To Share

I came across this poem. I thought I would share it with you. It has a wonderful sense of irony. Notice in how many different ways the word 'nice' is used. The poem is universal in the sense that you can replace English with any nationality and it still works. The idea is that we are nice and others are not quite as nice. Enjoy!

The English Are So Nice! - D.H. Lawrence

The English are so nice
so awfully nice
they're the nicest people in the world.
And what's more, they're very nice about being nice
about your being nice as well!
If you're not nice, they soon make you feel it.

Americans and French and Germans and so on
they're all very well
but they're not really nice, you know
They're not as nice in our sense of the word are they now?
That's why one doesn't have to take them seriously.
We must be nice to them, of course,
of course, naturally--
But it doesn't really matter what you say to them,
they don't really understand--
you can just say anything to them:
be nice, you know, just be nice--
but you must never take them seriously, they wouldn't understand
just be nice, you know! oh, fairly nice,
not too nice of course, they take advantage--
but nice enough, just nice enough
to let them feel they're not quite as nice as they might be.

– January 31, 2013

You and I, a Love Song

On this Valentine's Day, I offer a love poem that I wrote in Hindi some years ago with the original and an English rendering.

मैं और तुम, एक प्रेमगीत
You and I, a Love Song

मैं चातक हूँ, तुम स्वाती हो।
*I am the Chatak bird and you are the waters of Swatii.**

मैं दीपक हूँ, तुम बाती हो ॥
I am a lamp and you are its wick.

मैं बड़वानल की ज्वाला हूँ।
I am a flaming fire

तुम कालिन्दी की धारा हो ॥
And you are the cool current of Kaalindii river.

मैं हिमगिरि का उच्च शिखर हूं।
I am a high peak of the Himalayas

तुम उस गिरि की गहराई हो ॥
And you are its unfathomable depth.

मैं समीर हूँ, तुम तरंग हो
You are a wave and I am the wind propelling you.

क्यों न सखी, हम अन्तरंग हों ॥
Why shouldn't we be intimate, love?

मैं गुलाब हूँ, तुम सुगंध हो।
I am a rose and you are its fragrance.

तुम मेरे जीवन का सुख हो ॥
You are the joy of my life.

मेरे मन के मरुथल में प्रिय।
In the desert of my life dear,

सुन्दरि, तुम इक रसधारा हो।
You are a current of nectar, my love!

– 14 February, 2013

* There is an Indian folk lore that Chatak birds drinks rain water only at a specific time of the year signified by certain configuration of stars.

How New Yorkers View the World

I thought you would enjoy this New Yorker magazine's cover from way back in 1976, showing a New Yorker's jaundiced view of the world. Cover is by Saul Steinberg and is titled, "View of the World from 9th Avenue."

An English Rendering of a Meera Bhajan

A Friend recently requested me to render the following Meerabai bhajan into English. It is given here in Latin script for those who understand Hindi.

Pyaare Darashan Di Jo Aae
Tum Bin Raho Na Jaae

Jal Bin Kamal, Chandr Bin Rajani
Aise Tum Bin Suni Sajani
Aakul Byaakul Phirun Main Birahan
Biraha Kalejo Khaae. Pyaare Darashan Di ....

Kyon Tarasaao Antarayaami
Aan Milo Krripa Karo Swaami
Meera Daasi Janm-Janm Ki
Padi Tumhaari Paaen. Pyaare Darashan Di..............

Here is my translation

Beloved, come and let me behold you.
Unable I am to live without you.

As a lotus out of water, as a night without moon
So my love, I am desolate without you.
Pangs of separation anguish me and make me agitated.
Pain of separation is devouring my heart. Beloved-----
O my lord, who dwell in all hearts
Why do you make me suffer from longing for you?
Have mercy on me and show yourself to me.
Meera, your servant for life after life
throws herself on your feet. Beloved-----

– Feb 2, 1914

A Request to Rama

Rama, you are called, "The Ideal Man."
You set up the codes of conduct for
An ideal son,
An ideal friend,
An ideal husband,
An ideal Foe,
Etc, etc.....

As an ideal husband
You refused to accept
Your kidnapped wife.
Even if Ravana had raped her,
How was it her fault?
By fire trial, I wonder
If your intention was to be rid of her.
Then you brought her home
Only to exile her while she was pregnant
Incensed by some silly remarks made by a foolish laundry man,
Just so your 'honor' will remain intact.
What kind of ideal husband
Are you, "The Ideal man?"

When your righteous followers, keepers of virtues
Throw out their wives, daughters or sisters out of
their homes
After they have been brutally raped.
They are victimized again.
Sometimes even worse happens
They are murdered, burned to death
To save the 'family honor',
I wonder if they are emulating you, Rama.
What kind of justice punishes
The victim and not the culprit?

Rama, you are supposed to be God incarnate
Can you tell me who is guilty of
killing these innocent women?
I am just a poor human
But you are God himself.
Why don't you reincarnate
And right the wrongs of
Your previous incarnation?

– March 26, 2014

PS: This is a translation of a Hindi poem I wrote in November, 2009 and published in my blog:
Kavyakala.blogspot.com.

Preamble to Sita's Fire Trial

As a background to my previous post, I am posting these excerpts from Griffith's translation of Valmiki Ramayana. Please read carefully and decide whether or not you approve of Rama's conduct.

If Rama is the great God then Sita is none other than the great Goddess too.

Canto CXVII.: Sítá's Disgrace

He saw her trembling by his side,
And looked upon her face and cried:
'Lady, at length my task is done,
And thou, the prize of war, art won,
This arm my glory has retrieved,
And all that man might do achieved;
The insulting foe in battle slain
And cleared mine honour from its stain.
This day has made my name renowned
And with success my labour crowned.
Lord of myself, the oath I swore
Is binding on my soul no more.
If from my home my queen was reft,
This arm has well avenged the theft,
And in the field has wiped away
The blot that on mine honour lay.
The bridge that spans the foaming flood,
The city red with giants' blood;
The hosts by King Sugríva led
Who wisely counselled, fought and bled;
Vibhíshan's love, our guide and stay--
All these are crowned with fruit to-day.
But, lady,'twas not love for thee
That led mine army o'er the sea.

'Twas not for thee our blood was shed,
Or Lanká filled with giant dead.
No fond affection for my wife
Inspired me in the hour of strife.
I battled to avenge the cause
Of honour and insulted laws.
My love is fled, for on thy fame
Lies the dark blot of sin and shame;
And thou art hateful as the light
That flashes on the injured sight.
The world is all before thee: flee:
Go where thou wilt, but not with me.
How should my home receive again
A mistress soiled with deathless stain?
How should I brook the foul disgrace,
Scorned by my friends and all my race?
For Rávan bore thee through the sky,
And fixed on thine his evil eye.
About thy waist his arms he threw,
Close to his breast his captive drew,
And kept thee, vassal of his power,
An inmate of his ladies' bower.'

Canto CXVIII.: Sítá's Reply

Struck down with overwhelming shame
She shrank within her trembling frame.
Each word of Ráma's like a dart
Had pierced the lady to the heart;
And from her sweet eyes unrestrained
The torrent of her sorrows, rained.
Her weeping eyes at length she dried,
And thus mid choking sobs replied:
'Canst thou, a high-born prince, dismiss
A hign-born dame with speech like this?

Such words befit the meanest mind,
Not princely birth and generous mind,
By all my virtuous life I swear
I am not what thy words declare.
If some are faithless, wilt thou find
No love and truth in womankind?
Doubt others if thou wilt, but own
The truth which all my life has shown.
If, when the giant seized his prey,
Within his hated arms I lay,
And felt the grasp I dreaded, blame
Fate and the robber, not thy dame.
What could a helpless woman do?
My heart was mine and still was true,
Why when Hanúmán sent by thee
Sought Lanká's town across the sea,
Couldst thou not give, O lord of men,
Thy sentence of rejection then?
Then in the presence of the chief
Death, ready death, had brought relief,
Nor had I nursed in woe and pain
This lingering life, alas in vain.
Then hadst thou shunned the fruitless strife
Nor jeopardied thy noble life,
But spared thy friends and bold allies
Their vain and weary enterprise.
Is all forgotten, all? my birth,
Named Janak's child, from fostering earth?
That day of triumph when a maid
My trembling hand in thine I laid?
My meek obedience to thy will,
My faithful love through joy and ill,
That never failed at duty's call--
O King, is all forgotten, all?'

To Lakshman then she turned and spoke
While sobs and sighs her utterance broke:
'Sumitrá's son, a pile prepare,
'My refuge in my dark despair.
I will not live to bear this weight
Of shame, forlorn and desolate.
The kindled fire my woes shall end
And be my best and surest friend.'
His mournful eyes the hero raised
And wistfully on Ráma gazed,
In whose stern look no ruth was seent
No mercy for the weeping queen.
No chieftain dared to meet those eyes,
To pray, to question or advise.
The word was passed, the wood was piled
And fain to die stood Janak's child.
She slowly paced around her lord.
The Gods with reverent act adored,
Then raising suppliant hands the dame
Frayed humbly to the Lord of Flame;
'As this fond heart by virtue swayed
From Raghu's son has never strayed,
So, universal witness, Fire
Protect my body on the pyre,
As Raghu's son has idly laid
This charge on Sítá, hear and aid.'
She ceased: and fearless to the last
Within the flame's wild fury passed.
Then rose a piercing cry from all
Dames, children, men, who saw her fall
Adorned with gems and gay attire
Beneath the fury of the fire.

– April 3, 2014

Krishna Meets Radha

Who are you, fair maiden, asks Krishna?
Where do you live?
Who are your parents?
Haven't seen you in Braja before.
Why should I come to Braja?
I play in my own yard.
But I have heard about
A son of Nanda, who is in the habit of
Stealing butter and curds.
What can I steal from you?
Let us go together and play.
Surdas says Krishna the supreme lover
Puts lovely Radha at ease by his sweet talk.
This is the translation of a Bhajan by Surdas(16th Century, North India). Here is the original for those who read Hindi.

बूझत श्याम कौन तू गोरी
कहाँ रहति काकी है बेटी, देखी नहीं कहूँ ब्रज खोरी
काहे को हम ब्रज तन आवति, खेलत रहति आपनी पौरी
सुनत रहति श्रवनन नंद ढोटा, करत रहत माखन दधि चोरी
तुम्हरो कहा चोरि हम लैहैं, खेलन संग चलो मिलि जोरी
सूरदास प्रभु रसिक शिरोमणि, बातन भुलइ राधिका गोरी

– 10 July 2014

Some Thoughts on Retirement and/or Aging

The main problem as I see it that all through our life we have been conditioned to think of future and promises it has in store for you. When you are young, parents constantly goad you to think of future. They urge you to get good grades so you get a good job and have a prosperous future. They rejoice if you suceed in studies, sports, and other activities. When you have a job you look forward to future promotions, pay raises and any other accolades that come your way.

When you have retired and are getting old, future is not so rosy. But you are faced with illness, surgery, bereavements and many other unpleasant phenomena. I think this is why many older people become religious so some deity or prophet will look after them and they have heaven or nirvana to look forward to.

As for myself, faith left me or I left it long time ago. God, liberation and heaven have lost their emotional charge. I can conceive of an impersonal God which is some sort of power or energy that animates the physical world and living things. I don't know if such a God listens to prayers. Afterlife does not make much sense to me either.

I am presently exploring if secular pursuits such as art and literature can give one solace. Also I am trying to become more oriented to life and its pain and pleasures right now and don't worry about future, wheelchairs and nursing homes. If it is going to happen so it will.

– July 22, 2014

Where Does Nirguna Live?

I am presenting another Bhajan (a devotional poem) by legendary Krishna devotee Surdas. First some background. After Krishna has left Braja, Gopis (milkmaids) are pining for him. Krisna sends a messenger, his friend Uddhava to urge the gopis to turn their minds to God without form and attributes, called Nirguna Brahman. Gopis question him about this Nirguna as follows. First the Bhajan is given in Hindi, followed by an English translation.

निरगुन कौन देस को वासी।
मधुकर कहि समुझाई सौंह दै, बूझतिं सांचि न हांसी॥
को है जनक, कौन है जननि, कौन नारि कौन दासी।
कैसे बरन भेष है कैसो, किहिं रस मैं अभिलाषी॥
पावैगो पुनि कियौ आपनो, जो रे करेगौ गांसी।
सुनत मौन ह्वै रह्यौ बावरो, सूर सबै मति नासी॥

Where does Nirguna live?
Please explain, we beg you.
We are not asking this in jest.
Who are his parents?
Who is his wife and who is his maid?
Is he black or white?
What does he look like?
What are his pleasures?
If you tell us a lie
Providence will punish you for this sin.
Uddhava could give no answer to Gopis,
His intellect rendered speechless.

– July 27, 2014

Tears That Can't be Shed

There are some tears that can't be shed.
Some secrets that can't be unveiled.
Some windows that can't be opened.
Some thoughts that don't transfer to paper.
Some words that can't be brought to tongue.
Some wounds that fester unhealed.
Some blots that can't be wiped clean.
Some strings that remain muted.
Some songs that remain unsung.
Some buds that never bloom.
Some rivers that are lost in sand.
Some loss that can't be recovered.
An ache that pricks the heart.
An ulcer that remains unhealed.

– November 8, 2014

Longing

Have met you after so long
Seems like a miracle!
You are as enchanting as ever
I tremble with worry and joy.
Long for you still
But do you?
Smoldering still here is old fire,
Hope you too have some kindling afire .
Would like to ask
But worry you might say no.
Better to cherish hopes untrue
Than be shattered by tidings true.
Strange are the ways of love;
Who knows one day
It may flower again.

– December 2, 2014

Juices of Life

Life does not have the previous zest.
Food does not taste as good as before.
Arms lack strength
And feet are tired.

It is as if all things have lost some luster.
Even the lightening seems to be dimmer.
The movie of memories has become bleary.
Life has become somewhat dreary.

Sadness is not as heart-wrenching
And happiness is not as keen.
There is no love or laughter like before;
No attachment or hatred as of yore.

Gita says detachment is the goal of life.
That is when Nirvana is in sight.
I think this happens
When the juices of life are running dry.

It is not a goal to which I aspire.
O God, likely controller of my life,
Give me back, if you please,
My life of love, hate and desire.

– January 27, 2015

Mutability

"This existence of ours is as transient as autumn clouds. To watch the birth and death of beings is like looking at the movements of a dance. A lifetime is like a flash of lightning in the sky, rushing by, like a torrent down a steep mountain." ~The Buddha

There are two beautiful poems by Percy Byshe Shelly, called Mutability and Mutability 2. I would like to share them with you.

Mutability

We are as clouds that veil the midnight moon;
How restlessly they speed, and gleam, and quiver,
Streaking the darkness radiantly!—yet soon
Night closes round, and they are lost for ever:

Or like forgotten lyres, whose dissonant strings
Give various response to each varying blast,
To whose frail frame no second motion brings
One mood or modulation like the last.

We rest.—A dream has power to poison sleep;
We rise.—One wandering thought pollutes the day;
We feel, conceive or reason, laugh or weep;
Embrace fond woe, or cast our cares away:

It is the same!—For, be it joy or sorrow,
The path of its departure still is free:
Man's yesterday may ne'er be like his morrow;
Nought may endure but Mutability.

Mutability 2

The flower that smiles to-day
To-morrow dies;
All that we wish to stay
Tempts and then flies.
What is this world's delight?

Lightning that mocks the night,
Brief even as bright.

Virtue, how frail it is!
Friendship how rare!
Love, how it sells poor bliss
For proud despair!
But we, though soon they fall,
Survive their joy, and all
Which ours we call.

Whilst skies are blue and bright,
Whilst flowers are gay,
Whilst eyes that change ere night
Make glad the day;
Whilst yet the calm hours creep,
Dream thou—and from thy sleep
Then wake to weep.

Source: The Poetical Works of Percy Bysshe Shelley, Volume 4 (1839)

– March 23, 1915

Tears in your eyes

Tears in your eyes I can not bear.
Don't shed those invaluable pearl drops,
Keep and safeguard them with care
Because these are not just water my dear.

When you weep my heart weeps with you.
It rends my heart feeling guilty for what I may have done.
I promise I will do all
To bring you happiness; your sorrow undone.

when you laugh my heart dances with joy.
Delight and bliss I deeply enjoy.
May you be happy and full of laughter;
That is all I wish here and hereafter.

– 21 February, 2015

Confessions of a Book Worm

I confess to having a life-long love affair with books. In Joseph Campbell's words books are my bliss. Not too long ago, an acquaintance in India said that I must have been ambitious as a kid. He thought so because in spite of coming from a very modest background I managed to come to US, get a Ph.D. and became a professor. Actually I was not ambitious at all. I remember when I was in 5th or 6th grade, I dreamed of having a little bookstore where I will read and sell books all day.

As a child I had little interest in sports. Most summers I used to go to my paternal aunt's house. They had a room full of books. I spent most of my day there. They ran a general store on the first floor of their home. They bought old newspapers, magazines and books. These were used to pack packets for the goods sold. I used to sit in the shop and read the magazines and books before they got utilized for making packets. I did the same at our family store.

There is an amusing memory from my childhood. I was in 6th grade and 10 or 11 years old. School was about 2 miles away from home. I used to walk to school with some boys. A market was held in the village where the school was every Tuesday and Saturday. My father along with an employee used to bring his shop to the market. His wares were spread out in front of a mosque. There was a tamarind tree close by. A christian missionary used to preach under the tree which offered little protection from the hot sun. I used to admire his forbearance. He used to denounce Hindu superstitions and exalt virtues of Christianity. Most people paid scant attention to him. People came, listened for a few minutes and walked away. I don't know if he ever converted any body. He used to give my father missionary literature in Hindi translation . I used to read this literature before my father used them to make packets of cumin seed and other stuff. This was my first introduction to Christianity. I read it until I got to the story of loaves and fishes. Then it dawned upon me that what Jesus did were miracles but what Hindu saints and gods did were superstitions.

For a village grocer, my father owned a rich collection of books. Many but not all were on Hindu mythology and religion. He had Upanishads, Ramayana, Mahabharata, Bhartrihari's Shataktrayam and a whole bunch of others. Bhartrihari's book has three chapters: Love, Renunciation and Ethics. Each chapter has one hundred (shatak) couplets. Bhartrihari has been compared to Shakespeare in his understanding of human emotions, humor, pathos and pithiness. There was even a biography of Eamon de Valera in my father's library. Strangely missing were works of fiction except for the ones used in school by my uncle or older brothers. I read at least portions of all of the books at home. My father had very little formal education but he was self-taught.

In my village, no newspapers were available then. About once a week my father or my eldest brother used to go Kanpur, the nearest city for business reasons. I used to wait eagerly for them to return and bring the paper.

In High School, a friend of mine and I used to sit next to each other in English class. We used to read novels under the desks and discuss them. Professor thought that something funny was going on so he separated us. In 11th grade, we were assigned to write an essay on the First Person Singular. The professor liked it and commented, "Written with gusto." He also circulated it for my classmates to read. I was proud as a punch. In high school, I read a lot and saw a lot of Bollywood (the designation was not as yet invented) movies. My reading was rather indiscriminate: mysteries (Earl Stanley Gardiner's Perry Mason was a favorite), serious literature such as Dostoyevsky's The Idiot, Julius Caesar of Shakespeare, short stories of Maupassant and so on. Probably the first horror story I ever read was Maupassant's The Horla. It gave me creeps and I even developed a fever. Bram Stoker's Dracula was next but it did not horrify me as much. I read Pandit Nehru's Glimpses of World History when I was in college. Indian education at college is devoid of any liberal arts component, at least for science students. I found Nehru's book to be splendid. Late Turkish prime minister

Bülent Ecevit was once asked what one book he would like to have with him if he were stranded in a deserted island. Glimpses of World History was his answer. In this book or perhaps Discovery of India, Nehru talks of Stefan Zweig's Letters of an Unknown Woman (or some title like it). I read it and found it very moving. Most of these books I borrowed from a neighborhood library. The library allowed only two books to be borrowed at a time.

My father and uncles were small shop keepers who bought old newspapers, old magazines and books and used them to make packets of goods sold. Once I found an American marketing textbook, I found interesting. Another was a memoir by a Russian defector to west, describing the horrors Stalin brought upon the Russian people. It also talked of Gulags later made generally known by Alexander Solzhenitsyn's novels. The Author's name was Victor Kravchenko. This book deterred me from communism which was very much the fashion of the day in high schools and colleges. I also discovered an American book of nursery rhymes. One of the rhymes, I remember was: Now baby has a trumpet and Billy has a drum. There were also pictures to go with rhymes. There were also Hindi books and magazines to be harvested from this trash treasure trash. I still remember some of the poems, jokes and stories learned from these sources. When I first came to US, it bothered me that all the newspapers, magazines and books were thrown out in trash. In India you sold them to street vendors who then sold them to grocery stores and like.

I also read many Hindi books. Now days, students in Hindi speaking parts of India don't read much Hindi and seem to be almost ashamed of it. In my school days, Hindi was taken seriously as it was guaranteed to be the national language as guaranteed by the constitution of India. Language riots in mid-sixties made sure that it would never happen. This lead to a let down and English medium schools mushroomed every where. Any body who could afford the tuition started sending their kids to these schools.

I continued to read through my college days but not as voraciously because academic work was heavy and I had started to tutor some students as money was tight. My father had died and there was not much money I could get from my home. Actually the pressure was on me to get a job.

Whatever I have learned about the world has been mostly from the books. Even now reading is my most pleasurable activity. I dare say books have served me well over the course of years. After my cataract surgery in December 2005, my vision did not return to normal for almost nine months. I was like a fish out of water without being able to read. I played a lot of Sudoku in those months.

After I got married my wife thought of my library as her competitor for my attention with some justification, I think.

Amongst the inanimate objects, I love books the most. They make me happy, sad, excited and alive by opening a new or long lost world to me.

– March 25, 2015

Die Not before You Are Dead

Die not before you are dead.
Live with zest to the very last breath.

Alas! Death is always knocking at the door.
Drink, Drink till there is no more.

Be humble when times are good.
Despair not when tables are turned.

Humor and courage go a very long way.
Smile and endure till the end of your play.

Die today or live for years.
Bear it all always with good cheer.

No regrets when your time ends.
A dream, a play, a mirage it was my friend.

– April 30, 2015

Long and Short of It

For almost all of my life, I have liked to kid around and don't take life too seriously. But a wise man advised me to take life seriously. Actually a British lady of Indian origin has written a book titled 'Life is Not All Ha-Ha-Hi-Hi.' I believe her name is Mira Sial. So i decided to take life seriously and became quite miserable as a result. Then another piece of wisdom came my way that to have a long life you should not take life too seriously. Since given a choice, I would rather live long than short, I went back to my old ways.

There are a couple of stories regarding time that come to mind. These are of Indic origin as am I.

Story of an One-Horned Bull

Once upon a time there lived a very old bull with one broken horn. Some people (or bulls, I am not sure) asked him how old he was. Here is what he answered, "I am older than earth. Sun and moon were born after me. I carried spices over the mountains for many years. Once while climbing a mountain I collided with a rock and thus broke a horn." It is possible that the old bull was just talking bull as is natural for a bull.

Story of a Very Old Holy Man

Once there lived a holy man named Lomasa. He had no fixed abode and no clothes to speak of. As a protection from the elements, he covered his head with a 'Karaahi' (more popularly known in west by its Chinese name 'Wok.'). Once when asked about his strange way of life, he replied, "Life is short why bother with possessions. Just take Lord's name and pass your days." Then he was asked, how old he really was. Now things get really hairy.

Hindus have this fantastic idea of time-spans. An eon lasts for 432 Billion years which counts as a day of the creator god Brahma. The world is almost but not completely destroyed at the end of an eon. This is followed by an equally long night of Brahma when nothing happens.

Then a new eon (day) begins. A Brahma lives for one hundred years. This is followed by a deluge and another Brahma takes over.

A 'Loma' or 'Roma' means a single body hair in Sanskrit. The holy man was not named Lomasa for nothing. In answer to the question of his age he replied, "I have had a short life. Each time a Brahma dies I lose a Loma. As you see this small hairless patch on my body, I have only seen twenty Brahmas come and go." End of the story.

Seriously, may all of you have a long life not taken too seriously.

– May 16, 2015

Gita, A Nontraditional, Cross-cultural Perspective by V. V. Raman

I had the privilege of proof-reading the manuscript of:

"**Bhagavad Gita, Non-traditional, Cross-cultural Perspective.**" by my friend and colleague **Dr. VV Raman**. Here are some thoughts about this work.

It is unlike any other commentary on Gita that I have ever seen. It is not a mere translation and its elaboration. It is much more than that. It does provide a word-for-word translation of the original. Then proceeds to its elaboration, parallels in other religious traditions such as Christianity, Islam, Buddhism and Sikhism. Dr. Raman is very familiar with all these traditions. He is a Tamil Brahmin who grew up in Calcutta, did his doctoral work in Paris, France, resided in Algeria for a time and then taught at the Rochester Institute of Technology in Rochester, NY for many years. He elucidates that the truth is not unique to any one tradition but is experienced by mystics and perceptive people in all cultures and religious traditions. This is not to say that all religions are the same. Each culture has its own genius and peculiarities but there are also broad parallels among them.

He also gives poetic parallels ranging from Elizabeth Barrett Browning to William Butler Yeats. It is somewhat uncanny to see that a poet completely unfamiliar from the Indic tradition, seems to express deep Vedantic truths in his or her poems.

Being a physicist Dr. Raman frequently explains deep philosophical concepts with scientific examples. For example, he explains a rather difficult concept of Gunas by comparing it to the concept of bonds in organic chemistry. He also points out where some philosophical ideas come close to modern scientific ideas without claiming that ancient Indic people possessed a knowledge of Relativity and Quantum Mechanics as some have ridiculously claimed.

Dr. Raman makes it abundantly clear that unlike many swamis he is not a self-realized soul so he may not the deeper truth of Gita. He is attempting to interpret Gita for an ordinary person in a way which is useful in the modern world. Frequently he explains what Gita is saying literally. Then he goes on to explain why the literal interpretation is impractical today and points out an alternative interpretation which is useful to modern men and women.

Gita emphasizes selfless action. Raman interprets it as selfless action in the service of humanity. He interprets yajna not as a fire ritual but sacrifice in the service of humankind. The idea of lokasamgraha in chapter three, supports such an interpretation. It is also in line with the interpretation of modern commentators as B.G. Tilak and Mahatma Gandhi.

In many places Gita emphasizes equanamity in all circumstances and seems to advocate an impossible ideal. Raman dares to differ and says that there is nothing wrong in enjoying life's pleasures and being sad when tragedy hits but one should not be overwhelmed by pleasure and pain.

All in all, this is a fine work and a reader will be rewarded by many insights and a unique perspective on one of the world's great scriptures.

– May 31, 2015

Death Casts a Shadow

Death casts a shadow on us all.
All our efforts are for nothing at all.
Bodies that we wash, dress and adore
One day will be food for worms or flame.

What good does an eulogy do
To the one who has died?
What good are wealth, honors and fame?
Victory and loss are all the same.

Criminals, saints and scholars alike
Equal in death comrades them all.
A perfect democracy enjoyed by all.
No winners and no losers at all.

Why does then hate, lust and greed abound?
When all heads eventually kiss the ground.
Since death is stalking us all
By loving kindness embrace them all.

– June 26, 2015

Fear of Death

Prospect of death presents no joy
Except perhaps to a suicide bomber
Enjoying his martyrdom
With a vision of lovely maidens in heaven.

But I got a bit side-tracked
From what I wanted to say.

Now I see friends and relatives of my age dying,
Putting a fear of death in me.

But then I thought
It would not be so bad to die now.

I would not have to bear
The grief of my loved ones dying before me.
No horrors of nursing home living.
Also I would not have to be a burden
On my family in my even older age.

No one knows what happens after death.
If I go to heaven, great
If not, no need to worry about it now.
If there is no heaven or hell then certainly there is
Nothing to worry about.

If there is God he will take care of every thing.
If not nothing to worry about.

After all every one has to die some day
Whether it is today or years from now
It does not make much difference
In the cosmic scheme of things.

Thinking this way has eased my fear of death
Not entirely but a little.

– July 9, 2015

Being Dead Can't Be That Bad

So many of my friends are dying these days
That I read the obituary column every day.
Glad my name is not there yet.

Suppose one day I find my name
In the obituary column
It could mean That
I have died
But can still read the paper.

So being dead can't be so bad after all
If I can still read the paper.

– July 25, 2015

A Happy Life

Life has no meaning
No purpose
And no goal.
Nevertheless seeking of
Meaning and purpose
Have given us
Philosophy and religion.
Goals are good for keeping
The engine of Civilization running
But they have no deeper meaning
In the larger scheme of things.
As the ultimate goal is death
Which nobody really wants to reach
But all do any way.

Seeking of meaning
Purpose and goal
Philosophy and religion
Have created a lot of havoc
fanaticism, misery and grief.
Some make up their
Gods of stone and clay
and worship them.
Others create their idols
of beliefs, doctrines and creeds.
Each claims to be
better than the rest.

People kill each other
in the name of religion
Or this 'ism' or that 'ism'.
Even animals generally
Don't kill of their own kind

At least not on the scale
In which humans do.

No religion or 'ism' really
Has A leg to stand on
In the sense of having helped us
To live in harmony and peace.

Better to think of life
As a lila or play
Or a stage as the bard famously said.
Where we play our bit part
And then depart.
The best we can do is to play our role
As well as we can.
There were eons before we were born.
There would be eons after we are gone.

Nothing to be sad or glad about it.
That's how it is.

Happy life is authentic and sincere
Not weighted down by guilt ordained
By religion and politics.
To be content in all situations
Or at least not blown away by adversities
And not letting success go to one's head.
And treating every one
With compassion and understanding.

Come to think of it
This too is a bit of philosophy.
A paradox, that is true!
Make what you make of it
While I bid my adieu.

– July 27, 2015

Have You Ever Wondered

Have you ever wondered
How many lives does the grim reaper
Claim that are incomplete, unfinished
Like an incomplete sentence?

Do all lives end unfinished and incomplete
Or some actually reach completion and/or perfection?

How do you take the measure of a life;
Does any one know?

Is a life that is complete and finished
Necessarily meaningful?

Bhishma of ancient lore had the power to chose
The Hour of his death.
So one can say that his life was complete
But was it meaningful?

Nietzsche thought a meaningful life
Is a work of art
Like a painting or a sculpture
Or a well-crafted novel.
But the ending of this novel
Can't be controlled by its author.
Nietzsche himself died in a mental asylum.
Was his life meaningful and complete?

People of faith find meaning and perfection in their God.
But what if God is just a concept
Devised by humans.

So many questions
But no answer that rings true.

– 19 September 2015

Strange Are The Ways

Strange are the ways of old age
Drugs are having a ball.
Yes Sir, Drugs are having a ball!

Take as many drugs as you want
In the end you will die.
Yes Sir, no body is getting out of here alive.
Even then drugs are having a ball.
Oh Ya! drugs are having a ball!

Strange are the ways of old age
Diseases are having a ball.
Flourishing are
Asthma, cough or TB
Heart attack, blood pressure and epilepsy.
Cancer is thriving lustily.
Oh Ya! Diseases are having a ball!

Brave are the ones
Fighting disease.
Pain and suffering are having a ball.
All is suffering said Buddha.
He sure knew a thing or two.

Since all are going to die
Why not just sing and dance.
Enjoy! while you can.
Crying and wailing is of no avail.
Live till you die.
Patients are having a ball.
Oh Ya! patients are having a ball!

– 22 September 2015

I Don't Know How

I don't know how the leopard got its spots
But I do know how it got stuck in a pot.
He was thirsty and very distraught.
No water to be found where ever he sought
Until he came across a pot.
His thirst will be quenched
At least that is what he thought.
There was water in the bottom of the pot.
He put his head inside the pot.
So narrow was the neck of the pot
Poor fellow! his head was stuck inside the pot.

See the story below:

http://www.bbc.com/news/world-asia-india-34409635

If you really want to know how the leopard got its spots a la Kipling , read below:

http://www.boop.org/jan/justso/leopard.htm

Ignore some politically insensitive language. He was writing in 19th century, after all.

– October 1, 2015

A Sequel to Previous Post

If you want a scientific explanation of leopard's spots, go here:

http://www.theguardian.com/science/2010/oct/20/leopard-spots-kipling-just-so

Why?

Why?

Flowers bloom
Birds sing
Wind blows
Rivers flow
Grass grows
Sun shines
Fires blaze
lightening flashes
Storms brew
Rain pours
Oceans raze
Snow falls.
Futile to ask
Why.
All this happens
because all this does.
Every moment
Our world renews
Man alone
A reason construes.
Creation flows
Without interruption.
Man and man alone
Seeks a reason.

– October 11, 2015

PS: Except for some minor changes, this poem was written in November 1992. I don't know any better now than I did then. So much for the old adage that as one becomes older, one gets wiser.

Musings on Non-Linearity

What is wrong with this picture of evolution of humans? It shows that humans have descended from a monkey-like creature in a linear fashion. So it says humans have evolved from monkeys. This is entirely false. Evolution says no such thing. It says that sometime in ancient past humans and monkeys had a common ancestor. No species is more evolved than another. Each extant species is most evolved in its line of descent; a leaf in the tree of evolution of species. That is to say that evolution of species is non-linear.

A similar situation prevails in anthropology. Early American anthropologists Henry Rowe Schoolcraft and Lewis Henry Morgan studied native American Indians. They believed, as was customary those days (19th century) that all civilizations move on the same time-line, progressing from community ownership to private ownership, from polygamy to monogamy, from polytheism to monotheism and so on. So it was thought that American Indians were currently at a primitive stage but in time would progress to be just like Euro-Americans. This line of thinking, called recapitulation, was largely arrested by the work of Franz Boas (1858-1942). Boas, early in his career, went to study Inuits in Baffin island in northern Canada. The expedition did not go well and Boas and his companions were lost and taken care of by native Inuits. Boas was tremendously overwhelmed by the generosity and civility of Inuits. Here is what he said:

> I often ask myself what advantages our 'good society' possesses over that of the 'savages' and find, the more I see of their customs, that we have no right to look down upon them ... We have no right to blame them for their forms and superstitions which may seem ridiculous to us. We 'highly educated people' are much worse, relatively speaking ...
>
> – Franz Boas to Marie Krackowizer, 23 December 1883

Boas became the first major American anthropologist at Columbia University and trained most of the first generation anthropologists. He maintained that cultures do not recapitulate on their way to universal westernization. In other words no culture can be claimed to be more evolved than any other.

Lame Deer, Lakota Sue medicine man (1900-1976) saw straight lines, squares and cubes typical of modern life as wrong kind of symbols emphasizing separation and division. American indian symbol of life is a circle. As you can see plants, humans, and animals are all nonlinear. You don't see a square leaf or a cubical pig.

Mathematicians have always known that nature is non-linear. But linearity is easier to tackle mathematically so they devised tools such as calculus which approximates for example a small piece of a curved surface by a plane.

Modern humanity believes in continuous progress for ever. I see it as another obsession with linearity. It will be better to recognize that endless progress is not possible. Civilizations flourish and then decline or even die. Things may move in circles rather than lines.

– Laxmi N. Gupta

– October 21, 2015

References

The American Mind: Allen C. Guezlo, The Great Courses.

The Meaning of Life: Jay L. Garfield, The Great courses

Why Wish to Keep on Living

Why wish to keep on living
And why worry about dying?

Moment by moment night will wither
Why wait for morning star to arrive?

Leisurely my Love would be coming
But why should I be anxioulsy waiting?

Why worry about Love's deceptions
Why keep an account of their sins?

Moths keep dying on a flame any way
Why does my Love then sigh on my demise?

– November 9, 2015

PS: This is a translation of an Urdu poem (a ghazal) that I wrote in 2005. It is somewhat difficult to convey the special romantic feeling, the original has.

Rama in a Rock

Don't seek Rama in an idol my friend
Rama resides in your heart.
Rama in your heart
Put Rama in the idol, my friend.
Rama in the idol
Like a lotus in mud
Mere touch of Rama's feet
Brought lovely Ahilya
Back to life from a desolate rock.

Beauty is not in body
It is in your heart, my friend
Beauty in your heart
Puts beauty in body, my friend.
Beautiful pearl comes from
An ordinary oyster shell.
And diamond from
A coal mine, my friend

Rama is not in the world, my friend
Rama is in your heart
Rama in your heart
Put Rama in the world, my friend

Rama in the world
And the whole world is in Rama
Rama is in this world
And all worlds are in Rama

Rama in your heart
You are Rama, my friend.

– 19 November, 2015

Love's Lunacy

Love's lunacy
Dear Krishna, I want.

Fill my cup, O Love of Mine
With Sweet ever lasting Wine.

Senseless be I
Till the curtain drops.

Meera's madness
Is what I want.

Right and wrong
I care not.

That knowledge to Pundits
Dear Krishna, you grant.

Mad, crazy love
Is what I want.

Let my Passion
For ever last.

Love's lunacy
Dear Krishna, I want.

– 29 November 2015

PS: This is the translation of a Hindi poem I wrote in 2005. Here is the link for those who read Hindi:

http://kavyakala.blogspot.com/2005/12/blog-post_15.html

It is not really a complete translation. Hindi-Urdu-Farsi word 'Musti' has connotations that go beyond divine madness. It also means a carefreeness. This and other elusive connections are not captured by my translation. But it has a breezy quality that the original does not.

Infinite Grace

O! compassionate and merciful God
Hallowed be Thy name.
In your infinite grace
You gave me aches and pains
Of arthritis in many of my limbs
So that I am never bored.

Boredom is worse than death
And truly what are a few aches and pains?
A real man who does not eat quiche
Can certainly handle them.

You also gave me the itch
That never goes away.
Now, what is more satisfying
Than scratching an itch until it bleeds?

You blessed FDR and LBJ
To have the wisdom
Of providing oldsters like me
Social Security and Medicare.
Along with my TIAA I can pay my myriad
Physicians, therapists and labs.

I am blessed with the opportunity
Of providing part of
Expensive tuition at private schools
For the children of my physicians.

Dear God, your compassion overwhelms me.
Which one of your blessings
Can I deny?

– December 30, 2015

A Leaf

A leaf falls from a tree.
An ordinary event as ordinary could be.
Think deeply and you will see.
things are not always as they seem to be.

This leaf embodies a profound mystery.
Lies in it the soul of the tree.
Without it the tree couldn't be.
Neither would the wind that caressed it so lovingly.

Neither would the clouds that soared joyously.
Neither the ground on which the tree stands firmly.
Neither would you who watched it dropping from
the tree.
And without you the world couldn't be!

– January 18, 2016

What, Where and When?

Where do I want to go?
What do I want to do?
When will I understand
What this is all about?

Elusive remains
The desired place
The desired thing
The desired Understanding.

After I get some place
O! this is not at all
Where I want to be.

After I start doing some thing
I begin to wonder
If this is what I really want.

Understanding offered
By books and Gurus
Does not satisfy.

I can not rest
I can not act
And I don't understand.

Some people find God
Divine love
The unity of all things
Or a mystical experience.

To one who has lost faith
Or had none to begin with
It all seems like delusion.

Is delusion the price

We have to pay
To be happy, contented
And secure?

In a world where
Every thing is foggy
And nothing is clear
I just drift along.

Is this all
There is to life?
No meaning, no purpose
No goal
No wisdom.

You can ask
Why must we have a goal?
Why must we seek God?

Why do we suffer from such anxieties?
You ask.

Of course meals have to be made
And dishes to be done.
Taxes to be paid
And bed to be made.
Laundry to be done
And floor to be swept.

I must have my cup of tea
After chores are done.
At least this much is clear.

Aha! That's where
Zen offers a glimmer of hope.
Just do one thing after the other.
Sit in Zazen and watch your breath.

You don't have to go any where

Do any thing special
Or have any special understanding.

After all where ever you go
There you are!
As the good doctor
Jon kabat-Zinn says.

I can add that
Whatever you are doing
Is just what you do
Just whenever you do it.
Drink your tea.
Do your chores.
Nothing to gain.
Nothing to loose.
Nothing to get hung about
As Beatles sang.

You ask
When am I going to
Get enlightened?

Zen says
You are already enlightened.
You are already Buddha.
But you are also you
And Buddha is of course Buddha.
Harbor no duality
And all is just as it is!

– February 8, 2016

Eternal Dancer

All Creation is dancing
Your eternal dance swaying with love
Every leaf and blossom
Every atom in creation
Full of devotion
Permeatend by Your love.

Devotees worship You
Poets sing Your praises
It is Your beauty in them
Lovely maidens adorn.

Every vine, every tree in every forest
In every home, in every town
It is You Goddess, dancing with abandon
Your eternal dance.

In every discussion, every discourse
Every affirmation, every refutation
In anger, in pleasure, in manifestation
In desolation and destruction
In body and soul
You, the queen of my heart are ever present in all.

In lovely lips, in tender embraces
In timeless beauty of ephemeral faces
In lingering sweetness of lovers' breath
You dwell in all and like strings in a lute
Play every heart.

All time, all places near and far
Like Krishna's flute
You, my lovely enchantress enthrall them all.

– 19 March, 2016

A Curious Coincidence

There is a passage in Brihadaranyaka Upanishad (Circa 700 BCE) which expounds the unity of Atman (individual self) with the universal self (Brahman). Then it goes on to say that gods (Devas) don't like men to know this because gods regard men as their property like cattle and can not bear to loose even a single man to self-realization and thus loose his utility to gods.

Brihadaranyaka Upanishad, Chapter1 Verse 10

As having a lot of livestock is useful to a man, so each man proves useful to the gods. The loss of even a single head of livestock is painful: how much more if many are lost. The gods, therefore, are not pleased at the prospect of men coming to understand this.

'This' here refers to freedom arising from self-realization i.e. the realization of 'Brahman.'

Now fast forward to 5th century BCE Greece. In chapter Phaedo of Plato's Dialogs, Socrates is chatting with his friends and disciples before he drinks hemlock. Disciples question him whether he is not sad or depressed at the prospect of death being so near. Socrates replies that to the contrary he has prepared all his life for this day. His disciples then ask him then why he didn't commit suicide. Socrates responds by saying that men are like gods' livestock and just as you wouldn't like if one of your cows ran away, gods don't like to loose their men to suicide.

Dialogues of Plato, Phaedo, Socrates:

There is a doctrine whispered in secret that man is a prisoner who has no right to open the door and run away; this is a great mystery which I do not quite understand. Yet I too believe that the gods are our guardians, and that we are a possession of theirs. Do you not agree?

I don't venture to know if this is a sheer coincidence or there is more to it.

– 24 March, 2016

Life and Death

Why do we live
And why do we die?
Question has been asked
Through the ages.

Krishna taught Arjuna
In the midst of a battle field
Self is not born
Nor does it die
Deathless, eternal
Is this self
This, he said, renders this question
Of life and death meaningless.

But this ancient question
refused to die
Of Krishna's irrefutable logic.

Buddha said
There is no self
Self is the biggest illusion.
He said
There is no life or death
For the one that does not exist.

But Buddha's wonderful teachings
Did not heal the sorrow
Of human kind.

Jesus says, take refuge in me
Forget all sorrows
And gain eternal life.

But humans still fear death
And life still seems meaningless.

Descartes and Marx claimed
Humans are like machines.
As the machines eventually break down
So do humans.
Self and God are constructs
To fool the naive.

The question of life and death
Still remains unanswered
All answers appear hollow.

Existentialism of Sartre and Camus
Does not ultimately satisfy.

Meaningless are virtue and sin
Meaningless all rituals and worship
Meaningless seem yoga and meditation
Meaningless are God and Devil
Meaningless seem religiosity and human conceit.

Meaningful is only this burning Question
Why do we live and why do we die?

– April 7, 2016

Despair of a Mosquito

(Scientists have developed a genetically modified mosquito that can't spread malaria.)

What did you gain, O human!
Causing me such inhuman hurt?
Taking away malaria from me, you brute!

A mosquito without malaria
Is like a preacher without scripture
A temple priest without a temple
Or, a mullah without a mosque
An elixir that confers not immortality.

Without malaria a mosquito
Is like a living dead;
Its ego undergoing suffering untold.

What did you gain, O human!
Taking away a mosquito's raison d'être?
Death will still get you, my friend.

You made DDT to kill us all.
We died but kept our mosquito-hood withal.

But now our mosquito-hood is at stake
A death even more horrible than malaria
You might get in its wake
By causing ecological damage so great.

A mosquito bereft of all joy without malaria
Is like a patient of ED with no Viagra.
I resent my lot but am patient
May still outsmart you in the end.

– April 10. 2016

An Ode of a Mosquito

Woe to you human
For untold crimes against mosquito.

Admittedly we suck your blood but always gently
Just to keep alive but you snuff out our lives
Violently and mercilessly.

Even if we just buzz innocently
You kill us with your palm or a swatter.

You call yourselves humane
But we mosquitoes know the real you
Cruel and viciously brutal.

All the creatures agree
That human is the most vicious
Animal of all.

We mosquitoes even when we die
Do you a good turn.

You may have read or heard the story of a mosquito
Who helped solve a crime at the cost of its life.

A man stealing a car was bit by a mosquito
Who was swatted by the man
With its corpse left in the car.

Cops found the car suspect denied stealing it
But the dead mosquito's DNA analysis revealed
the man's blood in mosquito's gut.

Thief got nailed
But the mosquito who lost its life
To help solve a crime
Alas! Remained unsung.

– April 19, 2016

When Life Deals You Lemons You Make a Lemonade

I would like to thank my detractors (they know who they are) to inspire today's post. It is a collection of quotes of writers and artists who were distressed by the behavior of their critics.

Sit back and enjoy:

> As for literary criticism in general: I have long felt that any reviewer who expresses rage and loathing for a novel or a play or a poem is preposterous. He or she is like a person who has put on full armor and attacked a hot fudge sundae or a banana split.
>
> – Kurt Vonnegut, Palm Sunday: An Autobiographical Collage

> Some people insist that 'mediocre' is better than 'best.' They delight in clipping wings because they themselves can't fly. They despise brains because they have none.
>
> – Robert A. Heinlein, Have Space Suit – Will Travel

> Asking a working writer what he thinks about critics is like asking a lamp-post what it feels about dogs.
>
> – [Time Magazine, October 31, 1977]
> – John Osborne

> I've been all over the world and I've never seen a statue of a critic. – Leonard Bernstein

> Still the voices of your critics. Listen intently to your own voice, to the person who knows you best. Then answer these questions: Do you think you should move ahead? How will you feel if you quit pursuing this thing you want to do? And what does your best self advise? What you hear may change your life." – Steve Goodier

> It is a thing of no great difficulty to raise objections against another man's oration, it is a very easy matter; but to produce a better in it's place is a work extremely troublesome. – Plutarch, Parallel Lives

I would like to add an Indian folk saying: Elephants keep walking while dogs keep barking.

I personally like John Osborne's quote but perhaps it is better to follow Steve Goodier's advice.

– April 28, 2016

Unending Love

I seem to have loved you in numberless forms,
numberless times...
In life after life, in age after age, forever.
My spellbound heart has made and remade the
necklace of songs,
That you take as a gift, wear round your neck in your
many forms,
In life after life, in age after age, forever.

Whenever I hear old chronicles of love, its age-old pain,
Its ancient tale of being apart or together.
As I stare on and on into the past, in the end you emerge,
Clad in the light of a pole-star piercing the darkness of time:
You become an image of what is remembered forever.

You and I have floated here on the stream that brings
from the fount.
At the heart of time, love of one for another.
We have played along side millions of lovers, shared in the same
Shy sweetness of meeting, the same distressful tears of farewell-
Old love but in shapes that renew and renew forever.

Today it is heaped at your feet, it has found its end in you
The love of all man's days both past and forever:
Universal joy, universal sorrow, universal life.
The memories of all loves merging with this one love of ours –
And the songs of every poet past and forever.

– Rabindra Nath Tagore

(May 4 is Audrey Hepburn's birthday. This was her favorite love poem recited by Gregory Peck on camera after her death.)

Love vs. Food

Fools are they
Who get entangled in webs of love
Far safer are love affairs with food.

Much more important than love is food
Vedas consider it nothing short of divine.
Without love you may die
But without food
You will Surely die.

Love only brings misery
Romeo and Juliet, Laila and Majnu
Hir and Ranjha
All bear testimony to this grim reality.

If you must love something
Love food and drinks.
Delicious rasamalai,
Succulent dahi-bada
Samosas and kachoris
Chocolate Ice Cream
Mango lassi and single malt scotch
Are foods and drinks fit for gods.

Having taken your fill
Of delicious foods and drinks
You will die happy.

– May 12, 2016

A Doubt

If you are lonely
Follow the path of Buddha.
Buddha says there is no self.
If self does not exist
Nobody is there to feel lonely.
Nobody is there to sleep or eat
Or love or hate either.

It is all illusion.
But whose illusion is it?

Buddha says
There is no permanent self.
Which means the self
That was you yesterday
Is not the same self today.

This makes sense
But leaves a lingering doubt
I may not be
Completely the same as yesterday
But I am not totally different either
From what I was yesterday.
So some thing in me
Must survive from day to day.

– May 16. 2016

Wondrous All

Who fills flowers with fragrance
And sky with stars?

Who makes the silent music of heavenly spheres
And audible music that fills music halls?

Who makes flowers bloom
Birds sing, rivers flow
And lions roar?

Who fills music
In inert instruments that pleases
Even a savage beast?

How do we discriminate between beautiful and ugly
And what makes us
Choose beauty over ugly?

Who makes possible the grand phenomenon
That is our universe
The glory and cruelty of it all?

Who makes possible
The culture, art, civilization
And myriad other things?

Whose riches is spread in front of us
Shared by one and all?

Those of religious bent say God does it all.
I think saying God does it
Means we don't really know who does it.

I prefer to keep an open mind
And rejoice in the wonder
That is this ALL.

– May 19, 2016

Beggar's Bowl

Listen O people this ancient tale
From the hoary past of human kind.

A beggar with a begging bowl in his hand
And a mysterious smile on his lips
Approached a mighty king.

The beggar addressed the king thus
O mighty warrior I have come with great hope
Please fill my bowl to the brim I ask thee of nothing else.

King answered worry not you mendicant
I will have your bowl filled in a moment
Just tell me what do you want
Diamonds , precious stones, jewels or gold.

The beggar answered, O king I am not picky
Just fill it with whatever you please but fill it so there
is no more room.

The king called upon his men and asked them to fill the bowl
With gems, pearls, diamonds, gold and precious stones.

Lo and behold
Miraculously the bowl could not be filled to the top.

King's treasury was empty
But the bowl was only half full.

King was amazed and asked the beggar
Where he acquired this magic pot
And why it could not be filled.

Beggar replied O great King
This pot is made of human greed and that is why
This is never going to be full.

– May 24, 2016

Who is He?

Formless is He
But all forms are His.

He has no abode
But all abodes are His.

He has no name
But all names are His.

He does no work
But all work is done by Him.

He owns nothing
But all things belong to Him.

All the world thinks of Him
But He is beyond thought.

He was never born
But all births are His.

He never dies
But all deaths are His.

He never uttered a word
But all words are His.

He never wrote a things
But all writings are His.

How do we bow at His feet, He has no feet?

How do bow at his feet, All feet are His?

– June 13, 2016

PS: This poem goes back to 2005 when I was somewhat of a theist. It expresses essentially the Vedantic view of the ultimate reality. To call the ultimate reality 'He' is perhaps not correct but all words are inadequate for this purpose any way.

Bully

Love me, love me
I am a bully
I too need compassion.

I am a school bully
I bully school boys
I snatch their lunch money
And offer protection.

I am a mafia bully
I threaten small shopkeepers
Charge weekly dues
And offer protection.

I am an art critic bully
I buttress my ego
By fair and foul critique
Of artists more creative than me
And offer condescension and humiliation.

Love me, love me
I am a bully
I too need compassion
Just compassion may not suffice
I need redemption.

– June 21, 2016

Yayaati Syndrome

There is a story in the Indian epic, Mahabharata about a king Yayaati who reached old age but his lust for good things of life: wine, women, and song, was undiminished. Also unabated was his appetite for food, hunt, and victories in warfare. He still wanted to enjoy all good things of life but alas his vigor and youth were gone.

In those days, magical things were possible. For instance, if both parties were willing one could exchange one's old age with the youth of a young man. Now Yayaati had five sons. Yayaati called his sons one by one but all except the youngest refused the exchange. Yayaati disinherited all but the youngest son.

After the exchange Yayaati enjoyed his borrowed youth for good many years, only to realize that his desires were not only undiminished but had increased. Realizing his folly he gave back the youngest son's youth back to him and accepted his old age. He gained wisdom in the process that old age and death are inevitable. Indulging your passions does not diminish them. Just as pouring ghee in fire does not extinguish it likewise indulgence only whets your appetite and makes you want more.

Many of us seniors are also caught in the same problem that Yayaati faced. Our desires are still burning in us but our faculties are declining causing us much sorrow and feelings of deprivation. We have to realize that decline of one's youth and vigor is inevitable. We must face and accept it like old stoics or karma-yogis in the sense of Gita. Also knowing that death is inevitable, we should stop fretting about it.

As someone said, "We seniors live in eternal now. The Past is forgotten and there is no Future so there is no other choice." Take each day as it comes and enjoy it. Be grateful to see another sunrise.

– June 24, 2016

Dispelling of Despair

When heart grows weary
And spirit sags
When clouds appear
And clarity is lost
When desires arise
Without focus
When despair is felt
And doom seems impending
When all seems lost
A ray of light creeps in
From behind the dark clouds
Dispelling the gloom and doom
Soothing the forlorn heart
Uplifting the spirit
Dispelling the clouds of despair
And spirit soars once again.

– June 27, 2016

A Dialog between Man and God

Once so happened
That God and Man
Came face to face.
What came after
Was exactly what
I was afraid of.
Fierce debate ensued
About who made whom.

God said
Every body and every thing
Has a maker
And I am yours.
This is an irrefutable fact.

Man countered
Dear God, forgive me
For saying so
But your logic is bad.
If every body has a maker
Then some body must
Have made you
And your maker
Must have a maker too
And so on.

There is only one solution
To this enigma, my Lord,
You are simply my imagination.
Where will you be without me?

No temples, no mosques, no churches
Or gurudwaras for you. My Lord.
No worship, no puja, no sacrifice

Or service for you My Lord.
Please don't be angry
But no recognition for you
Without me My Sweet Lord.
You exist because of me.

God said, you talk too much.
May be I am your imagination
So you win
But hurry it is time for you
To do my evening puja.

Your life has no meaning without me
If you abandon me
You will be like a rudderless boat
And soon you will come back to Me.

May be I am your imagination
But you are too fond of me
To let me go.
You are nothing without me
And in this No Thing
Lies the mystery of you and me.

– 13 July 2016

PS: This is a translation of one of my recent Hindi poems. Hindi poem was moderately well-received. So I decided to translate it into English for a broader audience.

I apologize for using 'man' for a generic human but 'human' did not seem right in this context

Who Enjoys Sex More: Men or Women?

This question worthy of consideration by Kinsey or Masters and Johnson is asked and answered in the Hindu epic Mahabharata dating approximately to 500 BCE. The answer comes in the form of a charming and intriguing story.

Once there was a great and righteous king who was nevertheless unhappy as he had no sons. He performed a sacrifice to Agni, the fire god who blessed him to have several sons. But Indra felt slighted because he as the king of gods must get his share of any sacrifice performed by humans.

Indra tried hard to find fault with the king's behavior but found none. Once when the king went on a hunting expedition, Indra saw a way to punish him. He made the king lose his way and separate from his hunting companions. King was tired, hungry, thirsty and woefully lost. Suddenly he saw a beautiful lake. He plunged into the cool waters of the lake but when he emerged from the waters, he was transformed into a woman! Such tales of transformation by entering into waters are common in world mythology.

The king was perplexed but in the end decided that honesty is the best policy. He found his way home and told his spouses and sons what had happened. He asked his sons to enjoy the kingdom jointly and he departed to a forest. In the forest, he met a handsome ascetic and married him. The king transformed into a woman bore several sons. Now He(she) had two sets of sons, father to one set and mother to another. She took the latter set to meet the earlier and asked both sets of sons to enjoy the kingdom together and she herself retreated to the forest to be with her ascetic husband.

Indra was annoyed that his trick not only did not work but increased the king's enjoyment of life. He sowed the seeds of discord amongst the two sets of sons and soon they were at each others' throat. Eventually, all of them perished. Now the old king was extremely unhappy mourning the loss of his sons when Indra appeared in front of her and told her the cause of his misery. King apologized profusely and said that he intended no slight to Indra. Indra was pleased with the apology and offered to grant her a boon. She could choose one set of sons to come back to life. King chose the set of sons she bore as a mother. When asked why she explained that a mother has a greater bond with her children than a father. Indra was pleased and made both sets of sons to come back to life.

Indra further offered king another boon. This time, he offered to restore king's gender but the king refused. Indra was perplexed and asked the king why he did not want to become a man again. King replied that it is because women derive a greater sexual pleasure in union with men.

So there you have it. The answer is women.

– July 22, 2016

PS: The story comes from the Anushasan Parva of the Mahabharata as Bhishma's response to a question of Yudhisthira.Name of the king is: Bhangashva

Tavern

Tavern is open my friend.
No payment is required.
Just drink to your heart's desire.

Drink till you get drunk
Is all the payment required.

In all other sports
You pay and play.
Here you first play
Then pay.

Those who get drunk
Love and laugh.
Those who drink not
End up loveless and distraught.

So drink and enjoy
Or, abstain and cry.

This drink of life my friend
comes in many colors and blends,
Pure or blended
Mixed or unmixed
Rosy, red, white or pink.

Drink as much as you dare.
Barkeeper is always there,
His supply endless mon cher.

For those who drink without love
A drink is a poison for sure.
But elixir of life it is
For those who imbibe it with love.

– July 24, 2016

A Buddhist Parable

This is a Jataka story. Jataka stories refer to the previous births of Shakya Muni Buddha. In this birth Buddha was a prince called Five-Weapons because it was prophesied that he will be proficient in five weapons.

When the prince was sixteen years old, his father the king sent him away to a teacher from whom he was supposed to learn the five weapons. In due time the prince having finished his education was returning to his kingdom. He had to pass through a forest where lived a fierce ogre who killed any body who happened to be passing by. The descriptions of ogre are indeed quite picturesque. He was as big as a summer house, his nose was like a beak, blotchy skin and so on and so forth. He was also green, I guess, like The Incredible hulk but far more fierce. The prince was warned about the ogre but he had no fear.

This ogre was named Sticky-Hair as every thing that touched his skin stuck to his body hair of which he had an abundance. The prince came face to face with the ogre who threatened to kill and eat him. The Prince said, "I am prince Five-Weapons and I will surely kill you. Prince attacked him with arrows but they just stuck to his body. Prince then attacked him with a sword, a spear and a club successively but all the weapons stuck to ogre's hair. The prince was not phased and said, "I will smash you with my bare hands. " He attacked the ogre with his right hand which stuck to ogre's hair. He kept attacking with his left foot, left foot, right foot and finally his head. So the prince was stuck to the ogre in five places.

But the prince was unafraid. The ogre was amazed so he asked the prince, " I am about to kill and eat you. How come, you are not afraid?" The prince replied that death is inevitable so there is no point in fearing it. But he warned the ogre that if he eats him, a thunderbolt in his belly would certainly kill him. The ogre reconsidered and decided not to risk it.

The prince taught the ogre the precepts of Buddhism. The ogre gave up his evil ways and travelers paid him homage from that time onwards.

Joseph Campbell quotes this story in his book The Hero with a Thousand Faces. He offers the following explanation. The five weapons are five senses and the thunderbolt is the weapon of wisdom. The ogre represents the phenomenal world. So long we cling to the world through our senses we are stuck but we can kill this clinging with the thunderbolt of wisdom and be free.

– August 1, 2016

I don't Love You

This poem is a translation of my recent Hindi poem:

https://kavyakala.blogspot.com/2016/08/blog-post.html

I love your smile
And your laughter even more
But I don't love you!

I like the way you dress
I like your style.
I like your glowing countenance
Resplendent like a precious stone.

But I love you not
You ask, pray, why?

Because you don't like my loving
And I don't want to do any thing
That does not please you.

Your happiness comforts me.
My Love may interfere
With your happiness and my comfort
And may even upset you.
I can't risk it
And that's why, my Love,
I can't love you!

– Aug. 9, 2016

Poetry and Pain

Hear dear readers, I want to explore
What relation do pain and poetry bear?
Of course, bad poetry can cause you pain.
And poetry sure can emerge from grief and pain.

All is Sorrow, so Buddha says.
How true! I say as I age.

Pain comes to all, rich and poor
Old and young, king and beggar
A scholar and a dolt.

No monarchy here in the reign of pain.
Democracy here supremely reigns.

Pain makes us human.
Vulnerable and humble.
Fellowship of pain in which we toil and tremble.

Pain mental or physical can make your spirits sag.
Everyone is hurting no one is spared.

My hands and wrists
Are hurting with arthritic pain.
I thought I must gain
Something out of this pain.

Hence dear reader
I have subjected you
To this ditty about pain.

I hope this has not caused
You too much suffering and pain.
I must stop here
My hands have begun to complain.

– September 1, 2016

Love, Lawn and, Wisdom

Love, Lawn, and Wisdom

Why so quiet and morose, my son
Our lawn is not mowed, tell me why dear one?
Neighbors will complain
That our unkempt lawn
Will drive their property value down.

Dad, I can't hide it from you,
I met a girl of beauty so pristine
My heart aches for her
Wanting to make her mine.

Her smile is like a flash of lightning.
Her teeth are the color of fresh snow.
Her eyes are big and enchanting.
Her hair is lustrous and shining.

Her speech melts to mush my heart.
Her sweet gaze has bored a hole in my heart.
From where gushes forth my love.
Tell me dear dad
What should I do?

Son, I have seen more than you.
Nothing will cure your lovesick heart
Than cutting grass, I tell you.

Son, teenage love is like
The grass in our lawn
in spring so lush, and green
But come summer
Extreme heat will make it wither.

Like summer grass
Your love may wither.

Is she as fond of you
As you are of her?

I am going to tell you stories
Of gods and kings and common folk
Love for whom became a grief stroke.

Ancient sage Narada wooed a princess
Pure of heart and full of beauty
No chance he had
With the visage of a monkey,
Courtesy of Lord Vishnu.

You know the story
Of Nala and Damayanti
Many ordeals
That love them brought.
They succeeded but at
What a terrible cost!

Romeo and Juliet
Shiri and Farhad
Hir and Ranjha
All distraught
Tragic end their love them got.

So listen, my dear son
Cut the grass
And meditate on love and loss
Wisdom will come to you
With each swath.

Those who cut grass with affection
Are not brought to grief through love
Even by loveliest maidens.

– September 16, 2016

Narada-Vishnu Dialog

Narada, a celestial sage
Troubled by human suffering
Visited Lord Vishnu,
Recumbent on Ananta
The infinite snake,
In the milky ocean.
To seek a solution.

Lord Vishnu greeted Narada and asked this question.
How does it go with the mortals you visit often?

Narada replied,
Dear Lord, these earthly mortals
Imagine, they want to conquer death!

They want to eradicate
All terminal diseases
Cancer, heart attacks,
TB, asthma, or what you please.

Day by day, it's harder to die
People living longer with miserable lives
And diminished vigor.
Dementia sufferers their identity lost.

Ratio of old to Young is on the rise.
Old taking care of even older;
Is that wise?

It appears Dear Lord, in my opinion
Humankind is sowing the seeds
Of its own destruction.

Dear Lord answered,
Very true, Narada
All you say.

In the name of progress
Humans will soon regress.
You can't have never-ending
Progress in longevity or prosperity
Or for that matter any earthly entity.

Opposites must balance
For things to run smoothly.
Life and death, good and bad
Prosperity and poverty
Virtue and vice, pride and humility
One without the other
Is an impossibility.

Death comes with life
It can't be otherwise.

But Dear Narada
No need to worry.
In a few decades, Change
Will assert itself in a hurry.
Unwise this craze to keep on living
Old must die to make a place for living.

Bereft of vigor and stamina
Their juices not flowing
Old can't keep the world going.
Young are needed
To keep things running.
Death is not a foe
Just an agent to make the world flow.

– October 5, 2016

Despair

When the heart grows weary
And spirit sags,
When clouds appear
And clarity is lost,
When sorrow arises
And heart aches,
When shadow of
Impending doom hovers over soul
Then from some region unknown
A bright ray of sunshine appears
Dispelling clouds of gloom and doom,
Soothing the aching heart,
Calming turbulent emotions,
Despair dispelled.

– November 18, 2016

Forebodings

Heart soars no more.
Spirit is damped.
The World is very unsettled.
The danger is imminent.

Small mean-spirited
Rule larger and larger parts of the world.
A homicidal maniac
Rules over the Philippines.
Arab Spring has ended
With wars, violence.
Tyranny has returned.

Even the US, a bastion of democracy
Has elected a bigot, a narcissist
A reality show star, a liar
And tax-cheat as its leader.
This moron thinks he has been
Elected emperor of the United States
So he is going to rule by tweets, threats, lies,
And unscrupulous means.

Right wing fringe in Europe
Is stirring as well.
Nazis, Fascists, and goons
Are coming out of bulwark.

Aryan Nation, Alt-Right, KKK
And myriad hate groups
Are raising their ugly head.

These may be just Forebodings
Harbinger of unimaginable
Horrors to sweep the land.

Ban Muslims
Ban Mexicans
Put uppity minorities back
In their proper place.
Cries of 'Make America great again'
Which perhaps is code for
'Make America white again.'

I hope I am wrong
But I fear repression, racism,
misogyny, mayhem
And much worse
To come.

People of good sense
Please raise your voices
Against this menace.
In the words of Dylan Thomas
Do not go gentle into that good night
We have no choice but fight.
There is no easy way out.

– December 8, 2016

Cartoon for the Day

A Berkeley Breathed Cartoon Appropriate to the New Age of Ignorance:

"Ignorance brings chaos not knowledge."-
quotes, funny, cartoons, jokes on biscuits

Rejoice!

Rejoice, Rejoice, you crooks
One of you is now ruling the roost.

Glory hallelujah! White men will rule again.
Happy days are here again.

Blacks will be sent back to their kin
To Africa where mighty Gorillas grin.

Racism will be the order of the day.
Misogyny will be made legal any day.

3G have been endorsed by our leader.
Grabbing, grasping and groping
Are now OK, my dear.

Latinos, pack your bags and be ready.
Deportation orders are almost ready.

Welfare for poor will soon be curtailed.
But for billionaires, it will be the order of the day.
It will be called tax reform by the way.

"Crooked" Hillary is gone.
Rude, crude, and crooked Donald,
Righteous in the eyes of fellow goons and misguided
Is sadly very much in.

Gun lobby rejoices with our wonderful leader
Time to kill anybody anywhere
with a gun or a semi or a rifle
My friends is here.

Muslims, abandon your hopes to come here
Prepare to register those who are already here.

Idiots like Giuliani and Christie
Thought they will make political hay
But wise Donald has them on the bay.

Our wise leader will abolish welfare.
Money saved will be used to make nuclear hardware.

Rejoice, rejoice, my friends, I say.
Great White Father will have his way.

– December 24, 2016

My Modified Bodhisattva Vow

Providence gives you pains that you must endure.
For certain maladies there is no cure.

I feel angry, sad and melancholy
For the most part, it is my own folly.

Knowing that your anger hurts only you I still get angry.
Knowing that certain things you can
Do not much about,
I still worry, fret and knock about.

Buddha said long ago to see
Things as they really are
Without coloring them with your likes and dislikes.

I vow to do as Buddha says
But still try to do whatever I can
To make things slightly better
And alleviate suffering whenever I can.

– December 27, 2016

Lead, Kindly Light

Another favorite hymn of Mahatma Gandhi was: Lead, Kindly Light, a Christian hymn.

1. Lead, kindly Light, amid th'encircling gloom;
Lead thou me on!
The night is dark, and I am far from home;
Lead thou me on!

Keep thou my feet; I do not ask to see
The distant scene--one step enough for me.
2. I was not ever thus, nor pray'd that thou
Shouldst lead me on.
I loved to choose and see my path; but now,
Lead thou me on!
I loved the garish day, and, spite of fears,
Pride ruled my will. Remember not past years.

3. So long thy pow'r hath blest me, sure it still
Will lead me on
O'er moor and fen, o'er crag and torrent, till
The night is gone.
And with the morn those angel faces smile,
Which I have loved long since, and lost awhile!

Text: John Henry Newman, 1801-1890
Music: John B. Dykes, 1823-1876

Song of Life

Sing me a song, O Singer
To weave my life together.

Joys and sorrows of yesteryears
Bring me all together.

Hopes and aspirations for tomorrow
Sing them all, dear singer.

Kith and kin, friends and lovers
Foes and detractors
Make me remember dear singer.

Pearls, beads, and trinkets
In the necklace of life
Seem to be coming asunder.

Sing me a song, O singer
To bring them all together.

– January 21, 2017

Feelings without Context

Feelings have a context
Meeting is happiness
Departing is sorrow.

Laughter, Love, and loathing
Are all directed
Towards tangible things.

What happens often
In the tumults of life
The tangible is forgotten
But feelings remain.

Feelings without context
Like clouds in a clear autumn sky
Fly away leaving abstractions
A little pain, a little smile
Some sweet, some sour.

With passing of time
Even these are gone
Leaving only a memory
Of these feelings.

Even these leave eventually
Leaving only a feeling
That something is lost.

– February 7, 2017

Diamond Sale

You standing there
As a question-mark, dear
How can I refuse?

Pearl drops in your proud eyes
How can I ignore?

You win this one my dear
I am happy to loose.

Diamond rings are
On half-price sale
Sure, I will be glad to get
You one, my love.

– February 14 (Valentine's Day), 2017

Wait

You came for me with fragrant blossoms.
You left without seeing me thinking I was asleep.

I saw only your back
And felt a whiff of scent.

I called but you did not hear.
You left without a word not even a smile.

Why my dear
I ask why?

Now I pine and wait for you to come again.
How long, Love for how long?

– February 15, 2017

Desperation

Walking on a dark moonless night
On an unfamiliar road
There is a tiny lamp in distance
Its light reaching me just barely.

Still looking for a ray of inspiration
With a dimming hope.

What should I play
What notes should I sing
What lamps should I light
Whom should I garland
With the desires of my heart?

Who is coming my way
To take me in arms
And make everything right?

– February 28, 2017

King

I waited and waited
But you came not.

Since you like fancy words
I was a victim of ennui.

Ennui provoked hunger
So I started eating without you.

Then I partook of
Our sacred Champagne
The most expensive
We ever had.

Got sleepy
So locked the door
And went to sleep.

Woke up at night
Got up
And watched a Japanese Movie.
Samurais and their swords
Put me to sleep.

Now I intend to renounce everything
And abandon all desires
Including you, Love!

This decision has freed me
And make me feel like a king.

Now I only pray
That this mood of mine endures
And may you be happy too.

– March 15, 2017

What Need?

What need to cling to life?
Why desire an end to life?

Moment by moment the night will wither
What need to wish for the morning star to rise?

My Love will come in her own time
Why do I then count the hours?

Why should I care if my Love is guilty
What need do I have to keep an account?

Moths keep dying for the love of flame
Why do you sigh Love on my demise?

– April 1, 2017

Trump Doctrine

Mild manners have not succeeded
So give bullies a chance.

Diplomacy has not worked
So give belligerence a chance.

Political correctness has not succeeded
So give intolerance a chance.

Love folks has not worked so give hate a chance.

Good manners have not worked
So give rudeness a chance.

Racial equality has not been fruitful
So give racism a chance.

Gender equality does not work give misogyny a chance.

Experts have failed
So give hacks a chance.

Light has not worked
So give darkness a chance.

Moderation has not worked, folks
So give extremism a chance.

Traditional wars have not worked
So give nukes a chance.

Facts have not been working
So give alternative facts a chance.

Real news has not helped us
So give Fake News a chance.

Democracy has failed us
So give Fascism a chance.

– April 6, 2017

The Sweet Delusion

It is OK if you don't love me
Just don't say it, Love, I plead.

It is OK if you don't love me
Just pretend that you do, please.

Hoping you love me
I will happily pass my days.

Let this be our secret, Love
Never for the world to know.

I don't mind your deceit, Love
Trapped happily in your net.

Keep me captive, I don't mind
It is not the freedom that I seek.

Promise you would love me
Raise your deceit a notch, please.

Help me keep this lovely illusion
Let not the color of my glasses fade.

What good will your truth accomplish
Except to take away my happy illusion.

Just keep me intoxicated by your charms
Even if false and insincere.

Truth is highly overrated dear
Much more blissful is the sweet delusion.

– April 24, 2017

Books I Have Enjoyed Reading

As I have already confessed I am a book worm:

https://laxmisponderings.blogspot.com/2015/03/confessions-of-book-worm.html.

Friends often ask me what I recommend for them to read. So here I am listing some of the books I have enjoyed reading, in no particular order. Here we go.

1. Sacred Games by Vikram Chandra
   This very long novel (over 900 pages) is rich and detailed. It illustrates well the moral and ethical dilemmas faced by everyday people in modern Indian urban landscape. There is a universality to the theme, in the sense that similar scenarios can be anywhere.
2. Novels of Haruki Murakami
   I especially loved 1Q84.
   It is hard to say why I like Murakami. His novels are magical (magical realism) but not quite like Gabriel Garcia Marques'. Murakami's works are set in modern day Japan. Even when events are magical, the characters are ordinary people you can be friends with.
3. My Name is Red by Orhan Pamuk.
   Pamuk's 2001 novel is set in 13th or 14th century Turkey. It involves with master miniature painters. It is historical fiction but unlike any I have read before. It is also a Whodunit.
4. A New Life by Bernard Malamud
   This is the first and only Malamud novel I have read from start to finish. It is wonderful, funny and breezy. I thought I have found a wonderful writer but found that this is very atypical Malamud. His other works are heavy, somber and ponderous.
5. Olive Kitteridge by Elizabeth Strout
   I feel I know Olive. She is very real and so are other characters

in the book. I like her other books too but this one remains my favorite.

6. Short Stories of Isaac Bashevis Singer
   I think his short stories are wonderful often involving folk tales, superstition, supernatural and intimate details of Jewish life.
7. Interpreter of Maladies by Jhumpa Lahiri
   I like her other works too but this collection of short stories remains my favorite.
8. Tortilla Flat by TC Boyle
   Amodern classic about limits of liberal tolerance and our common humanity with the, "Other" especially relevant in this intolerant era of macho nationalism a la Trump.
9. The Remains of the Day by Kazuo Ishiguro
   A serious study of British "Service" class.
10. Novels of Jane Austen
    Pride and Prejudice remains my favorite.
11. Wuthering Heights by Emile Bronte
    A hauntingly beautiful British romantic novel.
12. American Gods by Neil Gaiman
    Gods of various lands have come to America with the immigrants and have been largely abandoned so they make a living by doing whatever a God can. Charming and fantastical.
13. The Poisonwood Bible by Barbara Kingsolver
    This novel is about a missionary family in Congo. Father has typical missionary attitude, bringing civilization to heathen but as is not unusual, his children are much more in tune with the local culture.

Well, this makes it a baker's dozen. If you readers find it of any use, let me know and I will post a sequel.

– April 30, 2017

Books That I Have Enjoyed Reading 2

This is a continuation of the previous post. I decided on new numbering rather than continuing the old one.

1. Novels of Marissa Pessl:

   i) Special Topics in Calamity Physics

   Things are not always as they seem to be. I don't want to reveal the plot. Exquisitely plotted, a real shocker.

   ii) Night Film

   Even more unusual than her first novel. In the center is an avant-garde film maker Cardova whose identity remains a secret for much of the novel. Even at the end you are not quite sure of who he is.

   Either you are going to love Ms. Pessl as I do or you will detest her. Incidentally both of her novels involve father-daughter relationship.

2. The Yiddish Policemen's Union by Michael Chabon

   Suppose the new state of Israel collapsed in 1948 and jews of Israel were given a 60-year lease to settle in Sitka, Alaska. End of lease is approaching. A whodunit and love story is set in this background. A tour-de-force.

3. Novels of Tom Robbins

   A Robbins novel is a weird, wonderful and uncanny creation. If you are not a deadly serious type of person, pick one and have fun. Two that come to mind are Half Asleep in Frog Pajamas and Skinny Legs and All.

4. Mystic River by Dennis Lehane

   A great read with profound insights.

5. Novels of Tony Hillerman and His Daughter Anne Hillerman

   Set in Navajo country, these are mystery novels steeped in

Navajo mythology.

6. Rabbi Small Novels of Harry Kemelman

   Rabbi solves mysteries by using Talmudic logic.

7. Plays of Bernard Shaw

   Shaw is very witty and his satire is biting. I have been in love with his plays since my college days. Man and Superman, Pygmalion and St. Joan are some of the plays I have thoroughly enjoyed.

8. Novels of Rex Stout

   Duo of Nero Wolfe and Archie Goodwin is great fun.

9. Mark Tully

   Tully was BBC bureau chief in India. After 25 years in BBC, he retired and settled down in India. He writes movingly about India. He has a marvelous short story collection, The Heart of India. He has written non-fiction too. One that I have read is India's Unending Journey.

10. Glimpses of World History by Jawaharlal Nehru

    I read this book when I was in college. Most of what I know of world history is an elaboration of this book. Beautifully written in form of letters from a father to his daughter(Indira). He wrote it while serving a prison sentence, courtesy of British Raj. Late Prime Minister Bulent Ecevit was once asked what book would he take with him if he knew he might get stranded in a deserted island. His answer was Nehru's Glimpses of World History.

I think that is it for now. There may be another sequel but not very soon.

– May 2, 2017

Scratch an Itch

Scratch an itch, what a pleasure.
Scratch too much what a bummer.

Partying all night, delightful raveling
Hangover next morning is not very pleasing.

Kabab, biriyani, and pulao in plenty
Heavenly pleasures when the wine is handy.
Overindulge and pleasure turns to misery
A trip to a doctor is now necessary.

Wine, women, and song
Make life worth living.
Overindulge and life is a suffering.

A well-tuned lute
Creates music so pleasing.
But out of tune, it
Creates noise so jarring.

Moderation in all things
Is worth cultivating.
Follow the middle way
Is Buddha's teaching.

– May 22. 2017

The Books I Have Enjoyed Reading 3

1. The Way Things Were by Aatish Taseer

Aatish is the son of an Indian woman journalist and a Pakistani politician. They had an affair while both were in London. Aatish is somewhat of a Sanskrit affectianado. His novel is about a Sanskrit scholar named Skanda, writing about his parents. He is doing a translation of Kalidasa's Kumarasambhava (The Birth of Kumara). Kumara also happens to be another name for Hindu god Skanda. The novel really is about his parents. His father, also a Sanskrit scholar, has just died and he has to travel to India (from the US) to meet his mother who was divorced from his father. The novel also deals with complex relations between conservative and liberal forces (cultural and political) in India.

2. Novels of Carlos Castenada

If you don't worry about whether these accounts are true, these novels are great fun to read. These novels deal with an alternate view of reality as expounded by Don Juan, a Yaqui Indian 'sorcesor.'

3. Transformation of Myth Through Time by Joseph Campbell

Campbell's conversations with Bill Moyers on PBS in print form.

4. The Emperor of All Maladies by Siddhartha Mukherji

A thorough history of cancer and its treatment. Never boring.

5. The Way of Zen by Alan Watts

I have found it to be the most insightful book on Zen and I have read several.

6. A History of Sanskrit Literature by Arthur McDonnell

A truly wonderful book if you have any interest in this subject.

7. Indo-Aryan and Hindi by Suniti Kumar Chatterji

A treasure-trove of information on Indo-European languages, written by one of the most important Indian linguists.

8. Myths and Symbols in Indian Art and Civilization by Heinrich Zimmer

I can't think of a better introduction to Hinduism and related arts.

9. Dubliners by James Joyce

This is Joyce for mere mortals. I have never gotten beyond the second chapter of Ulysses.

10. Novels of Barry Hughart

He has three novels: Bridge of the Birds, The Story of the Stone and Eight Skilled Gentlemen. All are based in ancient China. Great comic writing but also full of ancient Chinese lore.

11. Mystery Novels of Eliot Patison based in Tibet

I learned much about Tibetan culture and Buddhism from his novels and also the tremendous destruction of Tibetan culture by Chinese communists.

12. Guns, Germs and Steel by Jared Diamond

A really profound work. Hard to summarize.

13. The Hobbit and The Lord of The Rings Trilogy by JRR Tolkien

One of the greatest mythological stories ever told.

14. Kurt Wallander Mysteries by Henning Mankell

Great novels of police procedural and a brooding detective.

15. Mystery Novels of Arnaldur Indridason featuring Inspector Erlendur

These novels are great not only in their plots and execution but also in their deeply sympathetic depiction of human relations.

16. Inspector Vish Puri Novels by Tarquin Hall

Set in New Delhi. Narrated with great gusto.

17. Things Fall Apart by Chinua Achebe

Deals with traditional tribal society in West Africa. What made it work and what led to its downfall. Great work of a master.

18. This Earth of Mankind by Pramoedya Ananta Toer

Leads credence to the belief that we Indians were colonized by British and not the Dutch who were absolutely horrible in Indonesia. Ordinary citizens were treated as property and not as fellow humans.

19. The Good Earth by Pearl S. Buck

I read it when I was a teenager. It made a deep impression on me.

20. Moment in Peking by Lin Yutang

A sprawling novel of China in 1930's. Great insights, written by a respected philosopher of East and West.

21. Macbeth by William Shakespeare

For some reason, I find Macbeth to be the most accessible play of Shakespeare.

22. The Crucible by Arthur Miller

I read it in 1967, shortly after I had moved to the US. It moved me deeply.

23. Death of a Salesman by Arthur Miller

A classic.

24. Mystery Novels of Tana French

All set in Ireland. I like her first, "In the Woods" the best.

25. Grapes of Wrath by John Steinbeck

One of the first books I read after coming to the US.

26. To Kill a Mocking Bird by Harper Lee

Deeply moving.

– May 24, 2017

Trump Cabinet Agenda (Reading Between the Lines)

I thought my readers might want to notice some changes sought by the new administration:

EPA is now effectively EDA (Environment Destruction Agency) headed ably by Scott Pruit. I think it was more important to keep Rush Limbaugh's support than to protect the environment.

2. Justice Department under Attorney General Jeff Sessions will soon have a division of uncivil rights to safeguard Trump and his cronies' rights to lie, cheat and bully.
3. Department of (Mis) Education under Betsy Devos. will make sure to destroy public education.
4. Department of Energy under Rick Perry will perhaps try to dismantle the department as he has urged in past. Black Lung disease will also be rehabilitated and rightfully so.
5. Treasury Department under Steve Mnuchin will write tax code friendly to that most deserving group of people, the billionaires. Trickle down will take care of the rest of us.
6. Department of Health and Human services under Tom Price will make sure that maximum numbers of undeserving slobs(just some twenty-three millions) don't get health insurance. Many of them will get their just rewards for voting for Trump.

You, readers, are invited to point out other glorious changes to make America great again.

Are you not already tired of winning? I am.

– June 5, 2017

A Reading List for Composers

My friend Robert Morris is a composer and professor at the Eastman school of Music. Here is a reading list he has compiled for composers. I thought it may be of interest to the readers of my blog.

Some books recommended for composers by Robert Morris

Anderson, Walter Truett, **Reality Isn't What it Used to Be**: Theatrical Politics, Ready-to-Wear Religion, Global Myths, Primitive Chic, and Other Wonders of the Postmodern World. (San Francisco: Harper and Row, 1990) — A popular, up-beat account of the sociology and anthropology of contemporary, postmodern American culture.

Basham, A. L., **The Wonder That was India,** (New York: Evergreen (Grove Press, 1959) —An introduction to the (vast) intellectual and artistic heritage of Indian cultures.

Brown, G. Spencer, **Laws of Form,** (New York: Julian Press (Crown), 1977) — The logic underlying our penchant to make distinctions at the most fundamental level of thought. Formal and elegant, but understandable by those with little experience in math or logic.

Crim, Keith, ed. **Abington Dictionary of Living Religions,** (Nashville: Abington, 1981) — A single-volume, almost up-to-date encyclopedia of the world's major and less well-known religions.

David and Herst, **The Mathematical Experience,** (Boston: Houghton Mifflin, 1982) — A chatty review of mathematicians, what they do and how, and their philosophies and opinions.

Flew, Anthony, ed. **A Dictionary of Philosophy,** (New York: St. Martin's Press, 1979) — A concise and very useful dictionary of basic and technical concepts in western (and some eastern) philosophy.

Geddes, Gary, ed. **20th-Century Poetry and Poetics**, (Toronto: Oxford University Press, 1969) — A selection of important 20th-century poetry (mainly by Americans) with essays by poets on writing and aesthetics.

Gleick, James, **Chaos: Making a New Science,** (New York: Viking, 1987) — A well-written layperson's introduction to mathematical chaos theory and its impact on science, art, and our world views.

Gleick, James, Genius: **The Life and Science of Richard Feynman,** (New York: Pantheon, 1992) — A biography of the famous physicist interlaced with considerations of the nature (and (im)possibility) of the concept of genius in the late 20th-century.

Goodman, Nelson, **Languages of Art,** (Indianapolis: Hacket Publishing, 1976) — A major philosopher's take on the use of symbol systems and notations in the arts including music.

Hayes, J.R., ed. **The Genius of Arab Civilization**: Source of Renaissance, (Boston: The MIT Press, 1983, 2nd ed.) — An introduction to the (vast) intellectual and artistic heritage of Arabic cultures.

Hofstadter, Douglas R., **Gödel, Escher, Bach: an Eternal Golden Braid,** (New York: Basic Books, 1979) — A engaging intellectual fantasy on the fundamentals and metaphysics of computer science, artificial intelligence, and logic and their connections to the author's (much less sophisticated) ideas about music.

Kosko, Bart, **Fuzzy Thinking,** (New York: Hyperion, 1993) — An introduction to a controversial branch of applied mathematics called fuzzy logic: thinking and problem-solving that rejects, for instance, the notion that a double-negative is the same as the positive.

Kostelanetz, Richard, ed. **Esthetics Contemporary,** (New York: Prometheus Books, 1978) —A set of essays by major artists, writers, composers, and philosophers on late 20th-century aesthetics.

Lee, Sherman E. **Far Eastern Art,** (Englewood Cliffs, N. J.: Prentice Hall, 1973) — A comprehensive survey of painting, sculpture, and architecture (and its secular and religious roles) in Asian cultures.

Lentriccia and McLaughlin. **Critical Terms for Literary Study,** (Chicago: University of Chicago Press, 1990) — Short essays on major concepts in recent writings in literary criticism including postmodern thought.

Levy, Steven, **Artificial Life:** A Report from the Frontier Where Computers Meet Biology, (New York: Vintage Books, 1992) — A popular introduction to (bottom-up) algorithmic systems that have the formal properties of living things.

Lucie-Smith, Edward, **The Thames and Hudson Dictionary of Art Terms,** (London: Thames and Hudson, 1984) — Useful for identifying and understanding concepts and terms in the visual arts.

McGowan, John, **Postmodernism and its Critics,** (Ithaca and London: Cornell University Press, 1991) — The influence of 19th-century philosophical idealism, skepticism, and social theory on postmodernism, and how the model of the artist as an opponent of commercial culture has evolved up to the present (by a professor once in the humanities department at Eastman).

Michaels and Ricks, eds **The State of the Language,** (Berkeley: University of California Press, 1980) — British and American observations on English as the register of cultural values at the beginning of the 80s.

Newton-Smith, W. H., **The Structure of Time,** (London: Routledge & Kegan Paul, 1984) — A highly technical but rewarding analysis of our concepts of time.

Nørretranders, Tor., **The User Illusion**: Cutting Consciousness Down to Size, (London: Penguin Books, 1991) — A scientific approach to the limits of consciousness, which are held to be far greater than hitherto assumed.

Preminger, Alex and T.V. Brogan, **The New Princeton Encyclopedia of Poetry and Poetics**, (Princeton: Princeton University Press, 1993) — Exactly what the title says: 1383 pages of information on poetry in all major languages, American, European, African, and Asian.

Quine, W.V., Quiddities: **An Intermittently Philosophical Dictionary,** (Boston: Belknap Press (Harvard), 1987) — A world-class philosopher's witty yet deep commentary on key concepts in philosophy presented in a dictionary format.

Rokeach, Milton, **The Open and Closed Mind,** (New York: Basic Books, 1960) — An undoubtedly out-of-date, but extremely stimulating discussion of the psychology of prejudice and dogmatic thinking (including many reflections on the nature of creativity).

Rucker, Rudy, **Infinity and the Mind**: The Science and Philosophy of the Infinite, (Toronto: Bantam Books, 1982) — A fascinating, challenging, and eminently readable account of the main issues and problematics in modern (infinite) set-theory.

– June 15, 2017

Darkness

Vedas, Bible and Quran
Scriptures all
Delight in light
And decry dark night.

I think they miss the point
Dark night is
The womb of all light.

That's why your dreams
Are colorful and bright.
Lovers rendezvous in dark night.

When night is dark
And rivers flood
Krishna, the dark one
Human form assumes.

In dark fair Radha
Dances to black Krishna's flute.
In total abandon.

Darkness covers
My dreary old town,
Mystery, romance
And awe abound.

Lovely Hypnos brings
Sweet dreams at night.
Turning mundane
Into sweet delight.

Primeval Cosmos,
A dark abyss
Lord Vishnu sleeping on a
Dark serpent named Infinite,

His eyes flutter
His dream the Cosmos be.

Contemplate deeply
On darkness sometime
Take in all its shades and creases.

Meditate in deep dark night
Bringing all its colors to light.

– July 5, 2017

Divine

Divine is spread on the dewdrops
Divine is the bird sitting on the tree top.
Divine is the compassion in your heart.
Divine peers through the lovers' hearts.

Divine is the music
That makes spirit soar
Mends broken hearts
And does much more.

Beggar near the temple gate
Is divine, I am sure.
Whether the stone image inside
Is so, I am unsure.

A stone image needs
Consecration to come alive
No such ritual is needed
For the lowly worm crawling outside.

Worshipping idols
Is certainly fine
Loving kindness to fellow creatures
I think, is more divine.

Saints have found
Divine through the ages
By realizing Her presence
Everywhere in all shapes and sizes.

– July 7, 2017

A Female Past Birth of Buddha

Shakya Muni Buddha achieved Buddhahood as a culmination of many previous virtuous lives. These stories are called Jatakas. In practically all these stories the future Buddha is a male but there are a few in which he is a female. Here is one such story.

In one of his previous births, Buddha was a beautiful princess named Rupavati (meaning one who is beautiful). Once out on an errand at a time of famine, Rupavati encountered a starving mother with a small child. The woman was about to kill her child and eat it. Rupavati tried to talk her out of it. She asked the woman to look around the house to find some food, ask a neighbor and so on. When nothing worked, Rupavati asked the woman for a sharp knife with which she cut off her breasts and gave them to the woman to eat. She told the woman that with her flesh she is buying her child and so she should keep the child safe until she comes back with some food.

Rupavati goes home. Her husband is aghast at the side of her and asked who did this to her. She narrates the story and asks the husband to prepare some food for the woman and child.

The Husband before preparing the food, speaks some words of truth: Such a marvelous act of virtue has never been seen or heard before. If such is indeed the case, let both of your breasts reappear. And they did!

In time after many more biths, Rupavati was born as prince Siddhartha who became our Shakya Muni Buddha, the Buddha of our present kalpa(the aeon).

– July 29, 2017

Clothes in a House of God

What clothes should I wear
In a house of God?
I bring this question
To all the worshipers of the Lord.

Here is what Christian priests demand
Wear your Sunday best to honor the Lord.
Don't forget to take your hat off
In the house of the Lord.

Many Hindu temples demand
That males wear only a Dhoti with shirts off.
Ladies please your western clothes lay off.
Cover your heads, O devotees, please
In the presence of the Lord.

Sikhs insist whoever you are
Please don't bare your head to our Lord,
Represented by our holy book
The very image of our Lord.

Friends, I have been busy
Thinking how to resolve
This knotty question
Once for all.

I have come up
With this radical thought
We check our clothes in,
On entering any house of God.

After all we all came naked
From the house of the Lord.
What is there to hide
From One who can see it all?

What is there to impress our Lord
With all our finery?
What does He care for your
Suits, fine hats, and, jewelry.

He knows all and sees all
Just bare your bodies and souls
To almighty Lord
And sing, "Praise the Lord."

– August 4, 2017

Narada-Vishnu Dialog

Sage Narada who roams
The three worlds
Bringing news and gossip
Back and forth
Between gods and men
Men and demons
And demons and gods
Paid one of his periodic visits
To Lord Vishnu,
Recumbent on the serpent
Ananta, the infinite
In the milky ocean
With Lakshmi gently
Massaging his legs.

The Lord rose and
Welcomed the sage
And inquired how the folks
In the world of mortals
Were doing.

Narada replied, " O Lord,
People in the world of mortals
Are acting strange
They think death is
The enemy and
Must be overcome.
Your children, O Lord,
Want to eliminate all fatal diseases
Like Cancer, Heart-Disease
Cholera and TB.
So it is getting harder and harder
For people to die.

Population of old people is going up
And debilitating diseases like arthritis
Alzheimer's and dementia are on the rise.
Some people though technically alive
Are worse than dead.
Old people have to care for
Their parents who are even older.
I think, my Lord, Man is intent
On cutting the very branch
On which He is sitting."

The Lord spoke, "Narada, you
Are certainly right.
Man is seeking destruction in
The name of progress.
He does not realize that endless
Progress is not possible.
For the creation to work smoothly
Proper balance is necessary.
Death is not an enemy of humankind.
Life and death are like two sides
Of the same coin. One without the other
Is not possible.
But Narada, do not despair
In due course, may be a century
Or more, Man will realize that
Change is necessary.
Old depleted of their juices
Can't run the world.
Young full of vigor and energy
Must replace Old
Who must die
To make room for Young."

– August 11, 2017

God-Man Dialog

On a fine morning, one day
God and Man came face to face.
I was afraid of this happening one day.
A monumental debate soon ensued
Who made whom was the question pursued.

God said every thing and person
Has been created by someone.
So I made you is true
All your scriptures agree with me, not you.

Man said, Dear lord, I suspect
There is a deep flaw in your argument.
If everything and person is made by someone.
Pardon my saying that
You must have been made by someone
And that someone must
Have been made by someone else
And ad infinitum, as mathematicians state.

So I say, my Sweet Lord, you are my creation.
There will be no devotees in
Temples, mosques, or churches without me
Actually who would have built them but me.
If you, dear Lord, pardon my saying so
No one would recognize you if I don't do so.
No one will worship, adore, or pray to you.
Without me, dear Lord, where will be you?

God said, OK, you win
But don't delay my Service, my son.
Without me, meaningless is your life.
If you abandon me, after some time
You will seek refuge and

Find it only in me, I promise.

May be, I am just your imagination
But you have no choice my son
But engage in my worship and devotion.
You are nothing without Me
Is your own conviction.

You are nothing without Me
And I am not there without you.
Try as much as you wish
You can't be rid of me because
Without me you face an abyss.

– August 20, 2017

PS: I offer my apology for using the word, "Man" for a human being. Using, "Human" seemed awkward and I was not sure if, "Woman" would work either.

Even sickness is good

Even sickness is good
If it doesn't kill you
And doesn't last long.
Your spouse looking at you,
With concern and care
Oh! What a delicious
Moment to savor.

You can be lazy when you are sick.
You can read fiction
Even if trashy
And not feel guilty.

Even hard times are good
If they don't last too long.
You learn resilience and nurture bonds
That are strong.

Even temporary parting from
Your beloved is good.
Absence makes hearts go
Fonder, the wise have said.

Even tears are good.
They lighten your heart
Making bearable
Your sorrows untold.

Even Trump is good
If impeached and soon convicted.
It would show how strongly
To fairness, justice, and diversity
Our institutions are committed.

– September 2, 2017

Unintended Gifts

This thought came to my head unexpected
What if all my ailments suddenly disappeared
What will I do, my Lord, what will I do

So much of my life revolves around
Physicians, chiropractors, counselors
Therapists, acupuncturists and healers
Of psyche, Self and No-Self,
I will go mad without them.

So this is my prayer for the day,
Thank you Lord for these ailments
Of body, mind, and soul.
They provide me a social life
Above and beyond my social gatherings
Of food, drinks, gossip, and movies.

My ailments broaden my horizons
and besides give me a chance to help
My healers send their kids
To Harvard, MIT, Oxford, and Cambridge.

Some of these kids
Will become future healers
Who will take care of the next generation
Of suffering humanity.

How many these unintended
Gifts of yours My, Lord I Can deny?
My Cup Runneth Over
O Lord with Thy grace and mercies.

– September 20, 2017

Self vs. No-Self

My Buddhist teachers proclaim
No self, no problem.
But the problem persists;
Self keeps barging into No-Self
Creating havoc.

I imagine a dialog,
No-Self says to Self
Scram, you don't exist.
You are so vain, you think
This poem is about you.

Self says, Not so fast
If Self doesn't exist
How can No-Self?
How is one to know what it is?

So I keep running
Between Self and No-Self.
Like, "Torn between two lovers
Feeling like a fool."

I envision Existence like
A stream with Self and No-Self
As its two banks.
Poor I-whosoever that may be-
Keeps swinging between them.

Self likes attachment
No-Self likes detachment.
Self is hot; No-Self is cool.
Self likes Samsara
No-Self likes Nirvana.

Self is like a flame
And No-Self is its extinction.
My Mahayana teacher says,
Samsara is Nirvana
And Nirvana is Samsara.

Explain how is that, dear teacher
It leaves me befuddled
And unsure of
A solid ground.

May be, the teaching means
That there is indeed
No solid ground
To stand on.

– September 21, 2017

Irritation

An irritation in an oyster shell
Creates a luscious pearl.
An irritation in the heart of a poet
Creates a wondrous poem.

A butterfly flapping its wings in Brazil
Can cause a tornado in Texas.
One careless word
Can start a war.

One carelessly thrown matchstick
Can burn down a whole forest.
One drop of water
Can make the difference
Between life and death.

One act of kindness can
Alleviate suffering.
One act of love
Can change the world for better.

A single loving glance can
Begin a lifelong love story.
One tear of your beloved
Can rend your heart.

Drop by drop a pitcher fills.
A journey of thousand miles
Begins with a single step.

– October 8, 2017

Desire

When a mother scold a child
Child still clings to her.
When lovers quarrel
They still don't want to part.

If what your heart desires
Is not good for you
Even then you can't let it go
Clinging brings sorrow
You know but you still hanker
For what can't be had.

If you perchance get what you want
You eventually get weary of it
And want something or somebody else.
Happiness slips away
And can't be grasped.

Such is the nature of desire
The more you get,
The more you want.
The thirst is never quenched.

It is a bottomless well
The more you sink
The more you still have to go.

Best thing is to enjoy what you have
And hanker not for more.
Hankering and clinging
Bring only sorrow.

But clinging and wanting
Seem so sweet and comforting
Bewitching and endearing

It is hard to let go.

So I still hanker
And I still cling.
Such are the bonds of Samsara
That keep us tethered and bonded.

O Mind, when would you
Quit this wicked delusion
And wake up to
The Wisdom of Buddhas?

– November 10, 2017

Unrequited Love

The One who was never mine
Became the Other.
The moment I woke up
The dream was gone.

Lightning flashed.
The world shattered.
Wouldn't have been better
The on-going deception?

The dream, the illusion
The aspirations and desires
Embodied in the dream
More material by far than
The wicked reality that crushes them.

Alas! my friends
Done in by the truth
Dreams and illusions
I would rather have.

You, my Love
Who will never be mine
Would never even know
What made me perish.

– November 25, 2017

Love vs. Food

Don't ever fall in love, my friend,
Stay away from It's deadly trap
Fall in love with food instead
To keep you happy and fulfilled.

Want of love
May or may not kill you
But want of food
Surely would.

Love will only bring you sorrow
It's ways you can not mend.
Romeo and Juliet, Heer and Ranjha,
Shiri and Farhad You know,
All came to a sad end.

There is no greater folly
Than human love
No greater wisdom
Than to know this is true.

If you must love
Love a luscious chocolate cake
It will make you happy
Make no mistake.

If you die for love
You will die unhappy and sad.
If you love glorious food
You will die happy and not sad.

– December 15, 2017

Hope Springs Eternal

I wrote tomes in your praise
But you paid no heed.
Repeated entreaties
You blithely ignored.
A kind word for me
You never uttered.

I long to be yours
But you keep your distance.
I keep asking you to visit,
But you never do.

I open my heart to you
But you never listen.
The more I try to come near you
Farther you go away from me.

I love only you
But you never return my love.
I keep writing love letters
That you never reply.

I don't want to live
Without you, Love
But I can't die because
You may come around.

I am waiting for
That to happen
As hope springs eternal
They say.

– December 16, 2017

Wait

All my attempts have come to a naught.
Meeting you Love, was not my lot.

Hoping you will come, I can't sleep nights
When will your lovely form be in my sights?

Day and night I wait for you to arrive.
Why not my Love, you a meeting contrive?

O Clouds, you go the world over.
Why don't you take this message to my Love?

If you are so kind to come and see me
My heart will bless you with delight.
If not, probably you best know why
What can I do? Just wait and die.

– December 27, 2017

Imaginary Number By Vijay Seshadri

The mountain that remains when the universe is
destroyed
is not big and is not small.
Big and small are

comparative categories, and to what
could the mountain that remains when the universe
is destroyed
be compared?

Consciousness observes and is appeased.
The soul scrambles across the screes.
The soul,

like the square root of minus 1,
is an impossibility that has its uses.

PS: I found this wonderful poem referred to by Satya Nadela of Microsoft in a Linked-in article. I hope you enjoy it.

– December 29, 2017

A Poem by Surdas

This is a poem by Surdas, a sixteenth-century saint poet of India. It talks about the tragic consequences of romantic love as uttered by someone who has loved and lost.

प्रीति करि काहु सुख न लह्यो।
प्रीति पतंग करी दीपक सों, आपै प्रान दह्यो॥
अलिसुत प्रीति करी जलसुत सों, संप्रति हाथ गह्यो।
सारँग प्रीति करी जो नाद सों, सन्मुख बान सह्यो॥
हम जो प्रीति करि माधव सों, चलत न कछु कह्यो।
'सूरदास' प्रभु बिनु दुख दूनो, नैननि नीर बह्यो॥

– सूरदास

None who loved ended up happy.
Moth loved the flame
That scorched it to death.
Black bee loved the lotus flower
Only to become its prisoner at the onset of dusk.
Deer lured by lovely music
Only to be Pierced by hunter's arrow.
I loved Krishna with all my heart
But he left without a word.
Surdas says, without Krishna
My sorrows are doubled
And my eyes shed tears.

– January 11, 2018

Another Gem from Surdas

मधुबन तुम क्यौं रहत हरे। बिरह बियोग स्याम सुंदर के ठाढ़े क्यौं न जरे ॥
मोहन बेनु बनावत तुम तर, साखा टेकि खरे।
मोहे थावर अरु जड़ जंगम, मुनि जन ध्यान टरे ॥
वह चितवनि तू मन न धरत है, फिरि फिरि पुहुप धरे।
सूरदास प्रभु बिरह दवानल, नख सिख लौं न जरे

O flower tree, why are you still green
And standing erect when Krishna is gone?
Why did the pain of his parting not incinerate you?
Standing under your shade, leaning on a branch
He played his flute, charming
The objects movable and immovable, animate and inanimate
And making holy men lose their concentration.
O flower tree, how come,
You don't miss that lovely sight of Krishna
And keep on bearing flower after flower?
Surdas says, why hasn't the fire of separation from Krishna
Burned you down from bottom to top?

Translator's Notes

1. 'Madhuban' actually means a garden rather than just one tree. I thought that translating it as a single tree made the translation more coherent.
2. Well-known Urdu poet Nida Fazli, on hearing this song was so struck by its simplicity and plain telling that he adopted it as his own style.

– January 18, 2018

A Very Stable Genius

Glory to that very stable genius Trump
Stock market is going up, up and up.

What if a few million shit-holes
Lose health insurance
They did not deserve it
In the first place.

What if environment is going to hell
If a catastrophe comes that is swell,
You will die in this shit-hole of universe.
You will die rich, be sure of it.

Gentlemen and rogues, please enjoy yourself
Grab, grope and fondle to your hearts' content.
Just don't ever admit any wrong-doing
Having no conscience makes world worth-living.

Glory to the patriots of KKK and their ilk.
Fascists and racists coming out of bulwark.
Help me make America great again
By banning Muslims and pesky immigrants.

Rejoice my friends, I have started
To clean the swamp of filthy liberals
And populate it with my cronies and criminals,
Steadfast in their loyalty to VSG that is me.

Remember folks this irrevocable truth.
Any news against me is bound to be fake.
Trust only Fox news and Sean Hannity
Avoid the NY times, the Washington post
And CNN, the most unholy trinity.

There are freedoms galore in our land
All thanks to my genius, my dear friend.

Freedom to hate, freedom to discriminate
Freedom to tamper and tinker with truth
And call lies, the alternate truth.

Folks, don't you love my lovely ladies?
Humble Melania knows her place
Daughter Ivanka, what a piece of ass!
Sarah Huckabee Sanders and Kelly Ann Conway
Will lie through the teeth for my sake, hombre.

There is no end to my glorious misdeeds.
Enough for today, so me thinks.

– January 22, 201

Shenpa (Dedicated to Pema Chodron)

Have you noticed
How fragile is our ego
Hurt by slights
And buoyed by praise?

How easy it is
To lose our cool
Only to regret later
And feel like a fool.

Notice how we get stuck
And push and pull
Only to get
More and more stuck.

Getting caught thus
Buddhists call Shenpa
Or getting hooked
As says, dear Pema.

Force of habit makes
You tug and tug
Alas! the tug just makes
The hook more snug.

If you feel an itch
Scratch, scratch, what a bliss!
Bleeding from scratches
What a bummer!

Had you not scratched
The itch would have
Soon subsided
And suffering prevented.

Teaching to deal with Shenpa

Is to acknowledge it first
Then don't tug
But do something different.

Nothing is permanent
As is well-known
Shenpa will soon pass
Left on its own.

Make it A lifelong practice
The teaching says.
Shenpa will not touch you,
If you practice this way.

– February 13, 2018

Amerussia

Vladimir Nabokov,
one of the greatest literary giants
The world has ever seen
Wrote a novel named, "Ada"
In which much of the action takes place
In a land, he called, Amerussia.

As the name suggests
He envisions a land
That combines America and Russia
In one great nation.

It appears that our
Very own very stable genius
May have taken unwittingly the first steps
Towards making the vision of
The great novelist's come true.

People with small vision
That includes me
Don't understand the gravitas
Of such lofty notions.

The great Vladimir Putin of Russia
Late of KGB and in the tradition of
The great Russian tzars
With the cunning of a Rasputin
Made our very own
Want to be emperor Trump, the Great
An offer he couldn't refuse.

He provided money, hackers, Fake news
False ads and treachery
To help Trump get elected our president

And thus to have their own man
At the helm of our government.

Trump like a lap dog of Putin
kowtows to him
And treats him with great reverence.
He claims to have asked Putin if he interfered
In our elections and Putin reportedly
Said, "Of course not, Donald."

And Donald is so grateful to Putin
For saying it, that he quotes Putin
And praises him
Every chance he gets.

Sometimes, it appears to me,
and I hope I am wrong, as if
Trump is the regent of Putin in the US
And Amerussia of Nabokov
Is almost here.

Lenin and Stalin must
Be rejoicing in hell
Getting a little respite
From the raging fires of hell.

– February 17, 2018

Treasure Under Trash

A treasure is buried under trash.
A diamond is covered by rubbish.
A lotus grows out of mud.
After misery comes much bliss.

Sweet is so much sweeter
After you have tasted bitter.
Pleasure is more pleasurable
When you have known pain.

So don't be put off
By the look of things
Dig deeper
And you may find treasure.

Life guarantees nothing
Neither pleasure nor pain.
It's all luck of the draw
As they say, my friend.

– March 3, 2018

One More Song from Surdas

बिनु गोपाल बैरिन भई कुंजैं।
तब ये लता लगति अति सीतल, अब भई विषम ज्वाल की पुंजैं।
बृथा बहति जमुना, खग बोलत, बृथा कमल फूलैं अलि गुंजैं।
पवन, पानी, धनसार, सजीवनि दधिसुत किरनभानु भई भुंजैं।
ये ऊधो कहियो माधव सों, बिरह करद करि मारत लुंजैं।
सूरदास प्रभु को मग जोहत, अंखियां भई बरन ज्यौं गुजैं। – सूरदास

Without Krishna, even vine groves have turned into our enemies.
Before these vines used to be cool but now they feel
like terrible flames of a nasty fire.
The Yamuna keeps flowing, birds keep singing, lotuses
keep blossoming, and bees keep buzzing
But without Krishna, it all seems useless.
A breeze, cool water, camphor and life-giving rays of
moon, all have become
Like scorching rays of sun.
Udhava, please tell Krishna that our separation from
him is like a knife wounding and crippling us.
Surdas says, Gopis' eyes have become red like coral beads.

Background

After Krishna leaves Braja for Mathura, milk-maidens called gopis are pining for him. Krishna sends his friend Uddhava to console gopis and ask them to forget Krishna and devote themselves to the worship of the formless and attribute-less Brahman. Gopis are not at all convinced. This song is part of gopis' answer to Uddhava.

Acknowledgement

I gratefully acknowledge the help my friend Dr. Vijai Dixit rendered in translating this song. Any mistakes in the translation are of course mine.

– March 8, 2018

A Persisting Ache

There is a persisting ache in my heart
A fear that is only vaguely felt
A longing that is not to be fulfilled
A life incompletely lived.

Time is short
Unclear how not to waste it.
In the grand scheme of things
What chance do I have?

I am bounded by my own self.
Do not know how
To break these bonds
And be free.

Be free and make the spirit soar
How to overcome pain and anxiety
And be secure in your skin
Does anyone know how?

They said when you grow up
You will know
I have grown old
But still, know nothing.

Socrates said knowing
that you know nothing
Is the beginning of knowledge.
But he knew Nothing as he said.

– March 30, 2018

Divine

Divine is spread over the tree tops.
Divine is within you and me.
Divine are all the sentient beings.
One life divine flows through them all.

Divine is the lion that roars in the jungle.
Divine is the frog that croaks in a pond.
Divine is the mighty king who rules and judges.
Divine is the crook who cheats and steals.

Divine is the life itself
That flows through all.
Divine is the light
That falls on all
From a lowly worm to a mighty king.

Divine is the only actor
In the cosmic play,
Playing all the roles
From beggar to king.

We make distinctions
In conventional life
But in the final analysis
All life is One
And that One is divine.

– April 23, 2018

Insecurity

Why is my heart so insecure?
If my beloved doesn't smile at me
I think she loves me no more.

If my jokes don't make her smile
I think she must think
That I am a bore.

Why must I crave for
An amorous glance
Knowing that cards are stacked
Against a full romance?

My heart is a flutter
My nerves are in a jitter
What's wrong with me
Why can't I pull myself together?

O, my weary heart
Pull yourself together.
Why are you setting up yourself
For sorrow and tears once more?

– April 30, 2018

We Are Seniors

No child-resistant caps, please
We are seniors.
We have grown old
To become child-like.
So child-resistant is also senior-resistant.

Old and young are
Both are vulnerable and insecure.
But children are lovely
And Old are ugly!
Need I say any more?

Youth have little money.
They look forward to future.
Seniors have money
But there is not much future.

Youth can enjoy the pleasure
But have little leisure.
Old have plenty of leisure
But aches and pains
Make mincemeat of pleasure.

Seniors live in the moment
Because they have no recourse
Youth are urged to forego the pleasure
For a future no-one knows.

You, dear readers, make your choice
But remember with pleasure comes pain
All decisions are regret-prone.
Moment by moment our life drains.

– May 6, 2018

A Bout With Gout

I had a bout with gout
A nasty brute.
It sapped all my strength
Got me exhausted to the boot.
But I am back, friends
With renewed vigor and might
To write poetry again with delight
To use social media
for battling injustice, racism
And our despicable Don
He isn't the only one
Who can use Twitter.
This fight will go on
Till Don bites the dust
And a new dawn is here.

– May 18, 2018

Donald and Boehner

If Donald met Boehner and took his advice.
Mixed some weed with diet coke, what a delight!

Donald might mellow and grant DACA some relief
He might pity poor immigrants
And not tear poor children from mamma and daddy
Putting them in a foster home, what a tragedy!

He might see that chain immigration that has helped
His wife's folks
Would also keep helping H1B visa-holder's folks.

Compassion wrapped in a brownie may be the way to go.
Laced with a little 'bhang' may loosen his terrible ego.
May be it will awaken little Buddha within
And in the end, it may even save his skin.

A little weed Donald will not kill you.
It might save the country and you, from you.

– May 21, 2018

Some Hindu Religio-Philosophical Ideas

I have been giving some thought to the differences between Abrahamic and Hindu religious-philosophical ideas.

First, in the West, we talk of mind-body dualism. In the East, we assume that mind-body is essentially the same entity, not two. The duality is between the mind-body and the Self, often identified somewhat incorrectly as the soul.

When Hindus talk of non-duality, the Self or the Consciousness is primary and the mind-body springs from it in a number of steps as outlined in the Sankhya philosophy.

Sankhya has this idea of conservation. In Gita, Krishna states that, " Whatever exists can never not be and what does not exist can never be."

In the Hindu view of thinking, if a tree falls in the forest and there is no sentient being to observe it then it didn't happen. If there is no conscious being to observe the world there is no world to observe. The world is nothing but the play of consciousness. Just think of time, if nothing ever changes, there is no time.

In the Hindu view, there is no absolute beginning or end of the world. The world is periodically created and destroyed and this has been going on for ever.

At the end of an eon, the universe shrinks to a point which is immensely dynamic, a fusion of Shiva (consciousness) and Shakti (nature). This point begins to expand and creation begins again.

Creation for Hindus is not similar to a creator fashioning a creature out of clay and blowing life into it. Instead, it is Shiva-Shakti or Brahman expanding to become the universe. The word, "Brahman" comes from the root, "Braha," which means to expand. Sometimes metaphor of a spider weaving a web from its own substance is used.

The idea of rebirth is central to all Indic religions, Hinduism,

Buddhism, Jainism, and Sikhism. Closely associated is the concept of Karma. Karma does not mean fate or destiny as is sometimes mistakenly assumed. Karma literally means action. It is the concept of, "As you do so shall you reap," taken very seriously and systematized.

– May 27, 2018

Love

To love is to lose
Your heart and rejoice.
Love is not a win-win
It is rather a lose-lose.

If you think you have won in love
You have indeed lost.
To accede defeat is valor.
Drop your weapons and surrender.

As Kabir says,
To gain entry into
The house of love
The price is your head.

He also says,
The avenue of love
Is too narrow to allow two
Love is the merger of I and you.

– June 12, 2018

Resonance

A devotee sings a hymn
Wishing fervently
It resonates with God.

Earthly dancers dance to a beat
They hope resonates with
The great cosmic dance.

A Lover whispers sweet nothings
Into the ears of beloved
Hoping it resonates with her heart.

A bridge collapses
When soldiers' march
Resonates with its frequency.

A chef prepares a dish
Desiring it would
Resonate with patrons' taste buds.

Investors spend a life time
To get in tune with
The vagaries of the market.

A composer composes a symphony
Hoping it reverberates
In the hearts and minds of listeners.

A person spends a life time
To get in tune with its deepest longings
Sometimes succeeding.

The great game of resonance
Is being played all over
Just open your eyes and ears.

– June 14, 2018

IS God = Man?

This post is more or less an appendix to a previous post, "Some Hindu Religio-Philosophical Ideas." Here I want to discuss some differences the way most Hindus view divine and the way Abrahamic religions do.

Hindus believe that all religions are valid in the sense they are all different paths that lead to the divine. Hindus assume that followers of Abrahamic religions do the same and are perplexed on finding out that it is not so.

Abrahamic faiths deal with man's relationship with God. God is conceived as a father figure. God created all creatures and a creature can never equal its creator. This difference is dramatized in the famous Michael Angelo's painting on the ceiling of Sistine Chapel, shown here.

By contrast, Hindus may start with a dualistic relationship with the divine but the goal is to ultimately realize the identity of the man with the divine. The famous utterances from Upanishads make this point:

"तत् त्वम् असि" = Thou art that.

"अहम् ब्रह्मास्मि" = I am God.

These sayings are not to be taken as beliefs but are realized through, "साधना" i.e. practice.

Satya Sai Baba, once famously said, " I am God and so are you. The difference is that I know it and you don't."

Tulsidas says, "सोइ जानइ जेहिं देव जनाई। जानत तुमहिं तुमहिं होइ जाई॥" That means: "Only those know You whom You make Yourself known but once they know You, they become You."

In Christianity and Islam, the ultimate goal is to live in heaven in proximity to God. In Hinduism, the ultimate aim is to merge with God. This is called Moksha or Nirvana.

– June 24, 2018

Shame

Everywhere you see
Death, destruction, and cruelty.
Whatever happened to Faith, hope, and charity?

Babies separated from parents
In the name of justice and law
Justified by a bible quoting bigot
Trump blaming Obama, the height of hypocrisy.

O America, Don't you hear
These babies crying for their moms and dads?
The cruelty of this horrible man
Putting our nation to shame.

A regime headed by a con artist
He and his family members busy
Enriching themselves at the public expense
How come, they feel no shame?

Americans, are you sure
You are not in fact ruled by Russians?
Trump meeting Putin, seeking his counsel
On every chance, he can.

The president maligns our allies
Like Canada and Germany
And heaps praise on Kim Jon-Un, a murderous enemy.

Wake up America
Before it is too late.
Throw the rascals out
Don't forget to vote.

– June 29, 2018

Texts and Norms

The Central thesis of this essay is that as the societal norms change, religious and cultural texts change to reflect the new norms. I will illustrate it with examples drawn from Indic sources.

The story of Shakuntala and Dushyant is told in the epic Mahabharata. Here Shakuntala speaks Sanskrit like all other characters. The Mahabharata text was composed around 400 BC. Now fast forward to around 400 CE to Kalidasa's Abhijnan Shakuntalam. Here all women characters except courtesans speak Prakrita. So Shakuntala here does not speak Sanskrit.

After the Mahabharata war, Ashvatthama enters Pandava camp and kills five sons of Draupadi as they are sleeping. He gets caught. In the Mahabharata composed between 200 BCE and 200 CE, Draupadi wants him killed but in the Bhagavat Purana, composed around 600 CE, Draupadi opposes killing him as she does not want his mother to suffer as she is suffering after losing her sons.

In Valmiki Ramayana, composed between 200 BCE to 200 CE, Ravana kidnaps Sita, actual real Sita, not a shadow Sita as in later Ramayanas as Adhyatma Ramayana (1000 CE) and all subsequent Ramayanas. This reflects the hardening of chastity standards for women.

In Valmiki Ramayana, Rama is not aware that he is an incarnation of Vishnu. When after defeating Ravana, Sita is brought to him, he rejects her because he suspects that she must have yielded sexual favors to Ravana. Devas appear in the sky and remind Rama that he is Vishnu incarnate and such behavior is unworthy of him. In Adhyatma Ramayana and Tulsidas' Ramacharitamanasa, Rama and many others, including Ravana, know that he is an incarnation of Vishnu.

Another curious thing to note is that contrary to the traditional belief that Dharma (moral and ethical conduct) declines with time. In Satyuga, the bull representing Dharma stands on all four legs, declining to three in Treta, to two in Dwapara, and only one in our depraved age of Kaliyuga. But one observes that as we trace the Dharma from 500 BCE on, generally speaking, moral and ethical standards tighten.

– July 16, 2018

Putin's Pet

Putin plays his fiddle.
To whom he plays is not a riddle.
His charge dances to his tune.
To this tune, he is hardly immune.

We Americans have been dumb
He says wisely.
We will dance to your tune
And not act foolishly.

We were wrong
And you were right
We will do your bidding
And everything will be a delight.

Your spies are
Welcome to our shores.
Hacking websites
And leaking emails.

You and I, comrade
Have the same goal.
Power, sex, and money
By means fair or foul.

You want to dismantle Nato
I will render my help.
I will withdraw my support
And make them yelp.

We will replace Nato
By an alliance of strong.
You and I with Duterte
El-Sisi, and, Jinping.

– July 23, 2018

Waste of Time

What is a waste of time
In your eyes, friend?
Give it a thought
And listen to what I say.

Some say, it is the time
When you are not
Making money.
Time is money, as they say.

Some say it is the time not spent worshipping
The divine and not
Praying and chanting.

Some say it is the time when you are not serving
Your fellow humans and
Giving back to the community.

Some say it is the time when you are not being creative
And wasting your potential
On trifles and vanities.

I say it is the time when there is no joy
In your life and
Sadness pervades your being.

I say it is the time when you are mired in self-pity.
You are wasting your time
Asking, "Why me?"

Happiness is the ultimate virtue
That springs from your being.
Be joyous and bring joy
To miserable and suffering.

– August 3. 2018

A Higher Loyalty

A superb book by James Comey, FBI director fired by President Trump as he would not let General Flynn and collusion of Trump people with Russians in 2016 presidential elections. It is important to read this book to understand Trump's behavior similar to mafia bosses and a culture of personal loyalty rather than loyalty to the rule of law. Comey is a very good writer who can make a scene come alive. His personal courage and ideals shine through in contrast with the lawlessness of Trump and his cronies.

– August 9, 2018

Painful Patterns

Why do we weave painful patterns
That have only given us grief in past?
Instinctual behavior that has let us down
Time and time again.

Why are we given to anger,
Destroyer of good sense and wisdom?
We know by experience that
Anger never solves a problem.

Dishonesty and greed have destroyed
Many a promising lives.
But urged by temptations
We get caught in the snare of evils.

We accuse others of insensitivity to us
Whereas we are blithely insensitive to others.
We try to gain sympathy by pretending to be victims
Forgetting those we have victimized.

If we want to reduce sorrow and pain
To us and our fellow beings
We have to be loving and kind
Trite as it may seem.

– August 12, 2018

A Confession

Who is the person that has
Done most harm to me?
Answer perhaps not surprisingly is me.

My need to have the last word
Has often let me down
And made me unhappy.

Lack of flexibility
And a tendency to be obstinate
Has often caused me grief.

When I don't behave well
I am unhappy afterwards
But too proud to seek forgiveness.

On occasion my anger
Has created havoc
And disturbed the peace.

When I feel hurt and fire back
Result is hurt all around
And no-one is a winner.

When the hurt is too deep
Love is torn asunder
And no-one benefits.

Grant me the wisdom
To be sensible, sensitive,
And to have compassion.

– August 15, 2018

World Is Going to Pot

The world is going to pot
Wha's I am to do.
From China to Turkey
From Russia to the United States
Spoils are going to
Crooks and despots.

These indeed are times
That try your soul.
When fair is foul
And foul is fair
As witches in Macbeth say.

Truth is not truth
Says Rudy Giuliani
Truth is what serves
His master, the master crook
And rogue of the worst sort.

Truth always wins
Out in the end
As they say.
Is it indeed so
I ask in dismay?

The man leading the nation
Is devoid of grace and good sense.
Has no kindness and vindictive as hell.
Separates babies from moms
Brings misery to distraught.

Billions in tax cuts to his rich cronies
And nothing to Puerto Rico
Hurricanes, flood, and lack of power

They brought on themselves
Says Man in Trump Tower.

Destroying the environment
Rewarding polluters
Denying Climate Change
Ignorant anti-science clods
Are courting disaster.

I hope that change will come
Soon and rascals will be out of power.
Men and women
With wisdom and sense
Will again wield power.

– August 20, 2018

Melancholy

You had a moment ever
When discontent wraps your being
When darkness envelopes you
And you seem to lose your moorings.

Then some thing magically
Lifts your mood
And you again can
Deal with the world.

Do you know what
darkened your mood
And what again
Made it lightened?

I envy those who
Always know what
Brings them sorrow
And what makes it depart.

For me, blues often hit
Unawares with no clear thought
And of their own without reason
They depart.

Sometimes of this lemon
I make a lemonade.
I pour my sorrow
In written word.

I think I know what Shelly meant
When he said
Our sweetest songs are those
That tell of saddest thought.

– September 9, 2018

My Resolution for Today

Life is what happens before you die.
No one knows for sure
What happens after death
So focus your attention
On life and living till you are no more.

All strive for happiness in life.
The irony is that when you focus
Too narrowly on yourself
Happiness eludes you.
Sort of like the eyes that
Make you see the whole world
You can't see except in a mirror.

To be happy every day
When you wake up
Resolve to make at least
One person happy today
As Nietzsche presumably said,
According to Ricard, Andre and Jollien.

I resolve to be kinder today
To telemarketers, hucksters,
Jehova's Witnesses,
Morman missionaries,
And door-to-door salespeople.
I will still not buy anything
Material or spiritual from them.
But couch my refusal in kind words.

I will be pleasant
To all beings I encounter.
I will try not to kill
A spider or any other bug

Except for mosquitoes, knowingly.
I don't know anybody except
Some Jain monks who
Are kind to bedbugs and mosquitoes.

I will pray for all
Sentient beings' well-being
Including our dishonorable
Deluded, narcissistic
Commander-in-Chief's
Hoping earnestly
That he does not plunge us
Into greater and greater chaos,
Misery and grief.

– September 18, 2018

Sing A Song

Sing a song when you are feeling blue.
You will feel better, it is tried and true.
Smile and the world smiles with you.
Complain and people turn away from you.

Don't start reciting your woes
When someone asks, "How are you?"
Everyone is busy with their own issues.
How can they solve your problems for you?

Happiness is a choice you can make.
Misery is there for you to forsake.
A smile, a friendly nod or a harmless joke
Act as lubricants in social discourse.

Next time when you think things look bleak
Take a walk and give it another think.
It may not be as bad as you think.
You can still be happy regardless of things.

A sense of humor goes a long way
To alleviate your pain, I dare say.
This too will pass, as they say.
Impermanence is nature's way.

Tread lightly on the path of life.
Take everything in steady stride,
Cultivate kindness it is worth your while.
Compassion makes life worthwhile.

– October 10, 2018

Akshaya Patra of Draupadi

Just the other day, I met a young man named Akshaya. I asked him if he knew the meaning of his name and ended up telling him this story from the Hindu epic, the Mahabharata.

In the days of the Mahabharata, there was a great rishi Durvasa, known for his quick temper. He was urged by the evil Duryodhana to visit his cousins the Pandavas who lived in a forest with their common wife Draupadi.

Durvasa with his entourage of many disciples arrived at the Pandavas' hermitage in the late afternoon. Now Draupadi had been given an inexhaustible vessel (the Akshaya Patra) by Surya, the sun-god. This vessel could feed any number of people until Draupadi ate and the vessel was washed. When Durvasa arrived Draupadi had already eaten and the vessel was cleaned.

Draupadi didn't know what to do. She prayed Krishna who immediately appeared and proclaimed to be starved. Draupadi explained why there was no food but Krishna insisted that she should show him the pot. When Draupadi did, Krishna found a little leaf stuck in the pot and ate it. Immediately Durvasa and his disciples who had gone to a nearby stream to perform their ablutions felt totally satiated. Embarrassed they fled and did not return to The Pandavas.

– October 20, 2018

Unemployment in Hell

Good Lord Vishnu was recumbent
On Ananta, the infinite serpent
In the milky ocean, with Lakshmi
Gently massaging his feet.
Suddenly you could hear
the sweet notes of Vina
Narada, the wandering rishi
Was approaching but surprise!
Yama, the lord of death was in his tow.
The Lord wondered what is going on.
Narada and Yama bowed to the Lord
And Goddess Lakshmi, the bestower of boons.
The good Lord blessed them and inquired
What brought them there.
Yama started his tale of woe.
Blessed Lord, the situation at hell,
My dear abode is very bad indeed
With problems galore.
The Lord said, speak plainly
And not in riddles.
Yama said he has come at the
Counsel of the sage Narada
With high hopes for the Lord's help.
The problem, my Lord is
That the science of healing
Has truly advanced in the land of mortals
So much so that people live far too long.
So few die that there is a steep rise
In unemployment in my dear abode.
I have made some of my attendants who
Supervised torture chambers of hell

Part-time, some I have laid off
And transferred some to Indra's heaven.
Chitragupta, my book-keeper
Who keeps an account of the deeds of
All arriving souls has very little work
For his staff who just sit idly
And nap. So he has started installing
A new computer system just to keep
His employees busy.
But all these solutions are just make-shift.
Only you dear Lord can devise a solution
That will endure.
Narada added that Yama is indeed
Stating facts without exaggeration.
As you know Lord, I am a wanderer
Always on the move to heavens, hell, earth
And the Netherlands, always singing your praise.
I beseech you, Lord, please find a solution
To Yama's problems and save his domain
From despair and destruction.
The good Lord smiled and spoke,
My children, do not fret
I am aware of your problems
And have already taken steps
To ameliorate your woes.
You know Christians have a God
Who actually is just a form of mine
Has created a very powerful demon,
He calls Satan.
His function is to create havoc
And misguide people away from righteousness.
Now you know that the richest country on earth is
The United States of America.

Satan with the help of his agent Putin, the Russian
Made an idiot named Donald Trump, the president
Of the US of A.
Now Trump does not believe in climate change
And gradual deterioration of the environment.
So he will restart burning of coal
Lift the regulations that limit harmful emissions
And destroy the environment.
Whatever the US does, other nations follow
Like a bunch of morons.
So you will see people destroying
The environment with increasing pollution.
The Earth will be warmer, glaciers will melt,
Ocean levels will rise.
Coastal cities will begin to sink.
Epidemics will surge.
People will start dying like flies
And Yama, your hell will
Once again flourish
And your attendants will again be
Happily frying sinners in hot oil.
And all will be well!

– October 30, 2018

Forms of the Formless

Formless is He but all forms are His.
He has no abode but all abodes are His.

He has no name but all names are His.
He does no work but all work is done by Him.

All this riches belongs to Him but He owns nothing.
All the world thinks of him but He is beyond thought.

He is never born but all births are His.
Death never came near Him but all deaths are His.

He never uttered a word but all words are His.
He never wrote a word but all writing is His.

How do we bow at His feet, He has no feet.
How do we bow at His feet, all feet are His.

– November 2, 2018

Nanak Shah Fakir

I have been drawn to Sikh religiosity for many years. Apparently, there is a movie by the above name.

– November 3, 2018

Dadhichi

There are many tales of selflessness in Hindu mythology. The story of Dadhichi is an excellent example of the genre.

In mythological times there was a dragon named Vritra who had trapped and hoarded all the waters of the world and so no rain would fall. There was a terrible draught and people were dying of hunger and thirst. Indra went to Brahma seeking a solution. Brahma said he has to have a weapon strong enough to penetrate the dragon's tough hide. He also told Indra that the illustrious sage Dadhichi, a son of sage Bhrigu had a very strong spine and a weapon made from his spine would certainly kill the dragon.

Seeing little choice, Indra went to Dadhichi and presented his case before him. Dadhichi without a moment's hesitation relinquished his body through the power of yoga and Indra had a weapon called vajra made from his bones. He was able to kill Vritra with the vajra.

The waters were freed and the world rejoiced.

– November 10, 2018

Donald's Prayer and Confession

Glory! Glory! Hallelujah!
Happy days are here again.
America is becoming great again.
Where White is White
And Black is Black.
Where might is right
And that is that.
Where men are masters
And women serve.
Where master race rules

And others get what they deserve.
Isn't that the natural order of things?
Let God grant Donald his wish.
Let all our immigrants be Norwegians
Send all the coloreds where they came from
Be it China, Africa, Mexico or Japan.
May be we can make an exception for Australia
I hear their skin tone is not at all wrong.
I don't know much history or civics
And have no manners to speak of.
But my superb intuition and boorishness
Have served me well in business
And have made me unbelievably strong.
I lie constantly but never admit to be wrong.
I contradict myself every few minutes
But remember I am the president, my friends.
Nobody in the world knows more than me.
I know more about warfare than generals.
I use fake news to defeat democrat fools.
The reason I have to say all this is
Because people are too stupid to see
What is before their eyes plainly.
My friend, master, and mentor
Putin, let all blessings be on thee
My benefactor and teacher
Without you where will I be?

– November 12, 2018

Being Fluid

I can't imagine a life bound
By rigid conventions
By superstitions
And worn out traditions.

I don't want to be button-holed
As a theist, atheist, agnostic
Or some other label.
Being sensible and sensitive
To all ought to suffice.

Consistency is good
But sometimes you realize
You were wrong
Then you have to say so
And move on.

So long as we live in harmony
With our inner nature,
We are joyous and thrive.
Otherwise, we are miserable
And lose our stride.

Being fluid is gracious
Being rigid is graceless.
Bend not break
Flow, not stagnate.

– December 6, 2018

The fiction of Our Lives

Fiction writers we all are
Framing and telling
The story of our lives.
As seen through the mist
Of our biases and conditioning.

A version of events
We freshly construct.
Our sins ignored
Our deeds perfect.

We may be at fault
We sometimes realize.
So we tweak the story
So our fault is minimized.

This is not a conscious act, I think.
Our minds are cunning
In devising new tricks.

We fool ourselves
Each in his own way
Weaving a wondrous
Web of confusion.

This wonderful bewitchment
Keeps this world going.
Otherwise humdrum uniformity
Will be fatal to our being.

This is not good or bad
Pass no value judgement.
Business of the world
Will stop without this bewitchment.

– Dec. 18, 2018

A Meditation on Self-Pity

Self-pity is one of
The worst emotions.
It saps your strength and
Weakens your resolve
It serves no useful purpose.
I wonder why
Did such a thing evolve?
Perhaps to soothe one's
Wounded Ego
To caress wounds
That nobody sees.

Perhaps it is a cocoon
Where you hide
To escape temporarily
The troubles you are in.
Perhaps it is alright if indeed
The stay is temporary.
If prolonged the cocoon
Becomes a prison
Where you live
A barren existence.

For a fulfilling life
You must risk something
Take your knocks
Pull yourself up
With your bootstraps
And don't get mired
In self-pity
Howsoever seductive
It may appear.

– December 26, 2018

Lady Liberty Is All Wrong

The statue of Liberty says,
"Give me your tired, your poor,
Your huddled masses yearning to breathe free,
The wretched refuse of your teeming shore.
Send these, the homeless, tempest-tost to me,
I lift my lamp beside the golden door!"

Donald Trump says No, No, No,
Those tired, those poor, those huddled masses
Consist of rapists, drug pushers,
Murderers and criminals.
We must build a wall on our southern border
To prevent their entry into our beautiful land.

Lady liberty is all wrong.
Let us set her right.
Such trash as she proclaims
From those shit-hole countries
Must not be allowed in our pristine land
Which I believe but can't openly say
Belongs only to whites.

We must keep our country
Safe and our borders secure.
We will keep the government closed
Until Pelosi and Schumer
See the error of their ways.

If not, probably, one hundred percent,
Certainly, perhaps I will declare an emergency
And divert funds approved to help lazy PuertoRicans
And from other worthless undeserving moochers
And build my beautiful wall, you will see.

My people will willingly sacrifice, go hungry
Do garage sales, sell house-hold items
Because they prefer being safe and secure
To mundane things like food, fuel and clothes.

Better to die safe and secure
Protected by my beautiful wall
Than to eat, drink and be merry
But always looking over shoulders
For criminal illegals, need I say more.

I am the president, I am supreme
I am the smartest, the wittiest,
The most stable genius you will ever see.
Smarter than the generals and fake news pundits
Let alone Bush, Obama and sundry democrats.
Trust me, endure me, increase my glory
Watch me, making America great again!

We will send troops to the border
Separate the babies from their mommies
Teargas them, put them in cages,
Mistreat them and if they die
It is the fault of their stupid parents
To bring them here illegally.

– January 11, 2019

Live Till You Die

To die before you are dead
Is not a terribly good idea, my friend.
Death will be here soon enough
There is no need to rush it.
Live as well as you can
While you are still here.
If life is good, enjoy.
Even if it is not
Endure, persevere
Drink it like the poison
Lord Shiva drank
For the benefit of
All sentient beings.
Face whatever comes
With quiet grace.

Die today or live for years
Just live as well as you can
So long as you live.
If death comes
No problem, it was bound to come.
Live without regrets
And die with no regrets.

– January 13, 2019

Pain and Empathy

Debilitating pain makes
You self-centered
And shrinks your perceptions
You are rendered into
An unfeeling stone.

Just as a starving person
Becomes devoid of compassion.
One with immense pain
Comprehends not
Others' pain and suffering.

When extreme pain ceases
And becomes manageable
One can look at the world
With the eyes of compassion
And have empathy with
Fellow sufferers
And offer them hope
And mitigate their pain.

– January 20, 2019

Equanimity

Feelings atrophy
Emotions wither
Memory wanes
Images fade.

We become jaded
Not too joyous
Nor too sad
We have equanimity.

But this equanimity
Is false
It lacks color
Substance, life-blood.

This peace is static
The peace of death
What is called for
Is meaningful action.

We need equanimity
In the middle of action
Inaction within action
The dynamics of calm.

– Feb. 23, 2019

King Shibi

Once upon a time a righteous and virtuous king named Shibi ruled over the kingdom of Ushinara in central India. He was renowned for his generosity and large-heartedness.

Two celestials Indra and Agni set out to test the king.

Indra took the form of a falcon and Agni a pigeon. Falcon chased the pigeon to the court of Shibi where the frightened pigeon took shelter in king's lap. Falcon who was right behind wanted the pigeon who was his prey. King agreed to cut an amount of flesh equal to the pigeon's weight from his own body and give it to the falcon. But no matter how much flesh king placed on the scale, pigeon overweighed it. Finally king placed himself on the scale when it balanced. Indra and Agni revealed themselves and king's body was made whole.

This story is told in the Hindu epic the Mahabharata. It is also told in the Buddhist Shibi Jataka. In there Shibi is a Bodhisattva I.e. Buddha in a previous reincarnation.

– Feb. 27, 2019

One More 'Bodhisattva' Story from the Mahabharata

Once upon a time a pigeon couple lived in a tree in a dense forest. The pigeon wife had gone to forage for the food while the husband was waiting for her. The sun had gone down and there was torrential rain and strong winds. The male pigeon was worried for his wife's safety and calling her. Meanwhile a fowler with his net full go captive birds had taken shelter under the tree. The pigeon wife was one of those birds. She heard the lamentation of her husband and told him where she was. She also told him that this tired and worn out fowler was their guest and as such they should do everything to serve him. The male pigeon flew out and got some twigs and a burning stick. He helped the fowler ignite a fire. So the fowler warmed up and was not shivering from cold any more but he was hungry. The male pigeon without hesitation jumped into the fire so the fowler could have a meal. At this the fowler was struck by deep remorse and he freed all the birds from his net. The pigeon wife realizing what her husband had done also jumped in the fire.

As the fowler was repenting the pigeon couple were given heavenly bodies and taken to heaven in a golden flying chariot. The fowler decided to give up his birding and took to asceticism. He too in time entered heaven.

– March 2, 2019

Come Together

Real leaders bring people together,
Build bridges to enhance
Communication and commerce.
Increase fellow feeling
And nurse old wounds.

Demagogues fire hatred and bigotry
Break asunder the fragile bonds
Incite malice and mischief.
Bring out the worst in people.

They do so much harm to the national fabric
Hard to see why some people
Support such charlatans
Who thrive on lies, deceit and chicanery.

I appeal to the good sense of my fellow citizens
To expose these miscreants and their misdeeds.
Bring them to justice for their crimes
And throw them out of office in the next elections.

Our future as a nation depends on US
Future generations will blame us for not acting
While there was still time
And matters could be salvaged.

Throw the ruffians out
Bring back good sense and compassion
Bring honor back to America
Tell the world we still value decency.

Show the world that
We still stand for human rights
For compassion and goodwill for all.
We still stand for humanity

And we will punish wrong-doers.

We will not let crooks get away
With their crimes.
Our justice system will prevail
And criminals will get their just desserts.

Our people will unite again
And repair our tarnished reputation
And will again be a nation that
Values human rights, decency and integrity.

– March 15, 2019

Living in the Moment

Live in the moment
So say mystics of East and West.
Buddha and Jesus agree
That this is the way to go.

Old age has forced me
To live in the moment
But it is causing me
Problems you bet.

Just the other day
I was going to shave
To my chagrin I found
Tooth paste on my face.

Often I think of doing something
And figure I already did it
So I get scolded
By you know who.

Living in the moment
Is not all that it is
Cracked to be. Good to have
Some previous moments too.

You know people with Alzheimer's
Live in the present moment
And in the moments of many years ago.
Feeling enthused about it is hard to do.

It is entirely possible
I don't understand.
If you do
Please let me know.

– March 23, 2019

Desire

Nothing at all happens without desire.
Vishnu lying on the goat serpent Ananta
In milky ocean sleeps on and on
Until a germ of desire awakens him
And springs from his navel a lotus
With Brahma sitting on it.

Brahma will carry out Vishnu's
Desire for the world to come into being.
He will put desire into
The hearts of all sentient beings
A germ of desire
Will keep the world going.

When desire is sublimated
The great works of art
Architecture, music
And literature are produced.
So are the great victories
And empires.

When desire wanes
Aversion from desire
Creates ascetics and monks
Who crave release from
The alluring net of desire
That snares all.

I think if there indeed is a divine
She must want the world to go on.
Desire is the goddess incarnate
The essence of all gods
Nothing happens without her.

You can't even keep yourself alive
Without satisfying
Your desire for food and drink
A roof over your head
And company of relatives
And friends.

So I worship her and adore her
And trust her to wean me away
From her bosom
When time is ripe
For me to go
To an unknown destiny.

– April 7, 2019

Advice for Troubled Times

Thank heavens for household chores
Be it cleaning, cooking, or washing clothes
Because it gives one respite from
Trump's tantrums,
Horrors of Sean Hannity
And Fox News' distorted reality

Thank God there is laundry to be done
A garden to tend
A robe to mend.
So one can escape temporarily
From Barr's attempts
To bar crooks from going to prison.

Meanwhile we have to try
In whatever small ways
To change this awful reality.
Sign petitions, march in protest
Write letters and most important
Don't forget to vote.

None of this may make things much better
But you have to do what you can
Some detachment makes it easier
To cope with all perverse horrors
And cruel despicable acts of a wan' to-be despot
That in no way make America great.

– April 15, 2019

My Life

This is a wonderful translation of my Hindi poem, "मेरा जीवन" by my esteemed friend Dr. VV Raman.

Dear Laxmi:

I have recast (below) your poem with rhymes, keeping its thrust and spirit. I am sending it to you just for your amusement. Bes1.

Keep up your creative writings!

V.V. Raman

My Life

It's moving along, seventy years and some
Time for reckoning has indeed come.
How much my loss, how much gain?
To whom all have I caused some pain?
Whose sufferings I heard not?
What helping hand I gave not?
Many a mistake have I done:
Some unknowingly. some for fun.
But I have tried at any rate
In every case to integrate.
How I have lived, I don't regret
If to live again a chance I get
I'd do the same, less or more
That I have done before.
In life's evening I'm perplexed thus:
What 's been my own life's purpose?
Will this I ever come to know?
I fear the answer is a definite No.
The remaining years will all be done.
What comes next is known to none.

– Translation by V. V. Raman: 23 April 2019

On Both Sides

On both sides
There are good people
So says the president.
There are good Nazis
There are good commies.
There are good morons
There are good eggheads.
There are good angels
There are good devils.
There are good legals
There are good illegals.
There are good pro-Trumps
There are good anti-Trumps.
There are good citizens
There are good criminals.
There are good wise folks
There are good bozos.
There are good pundits
There are good idiots.
There are good cops
There are good robbers.
There are good law abiding citizens
There are good law breaking crooks.
And all is good in between.
It must be so
Because Lord God
Made them all.

– May 11, 2019

The Story of Nala and Damayanti

The Indian epic Mahabharata has many embedded stories. Story of Nala and Damayanti is one of them. This story is told to Yudhisthira when he is lamenting his sad fate due to his gambling habit. Nala also came to grief due to his gambling.

In the days gone by, a young handsome prince Nala ruled in the kingdom of Nishadha in central India. In the neighboring kingdom go Vidarbha, King Bhima's daughter was well-known for her exceptional beauty. Once Nala caught a swan in his pleasure-garden. The swan spoke to the king, "O valiant prince if you let me go I will go and tell princess Damayanti of your love for her." Prince was overjoyed and a delightful dialog between the king and the princess ensued facilitated by the charming bird.

Nala found out that a svyambara was going to be hand for Damayanti's hand in marriage. Gods Indra, Agni, Yama and Varuna were also on their way to Svamvara. They intercepted Nala on his way and bade him to convey to Damayanti that she should choose one of the gods as her husband. By their divine power, they transported Nala to Damayanti's chambers. As bid by gods Nala pleaded gods'case to Damayanti. Neither could hide their attraction to each other. Damayanti said she will choose Nala with gods' permission.

At the svamvara Damayanti found herself facing five identical Nalas. She prayed to gods who gave her the insight to distinguish Nala from gods. She noticed that gods' eyes did not blink, they did not sweat, their garlands did not fade and their feet didn't quite touch the ground. She garlanded Nala. Nala and Damayanti were married and returned to Nishadha.

Meanwhile evil demons Dwapara and Kali were late in arriving to the svayamvara and on learning that Damayanti was already married to Nala the demons were furious. Dwapara entered the dice and Kali found Nala in a state of ritual impurity and entered into him.

Bewitched by Kali, Nala invited his brother Pushkara for a game of dice. He lost everything and had to leave the kingdom with Damayanti with nothing but a single piece of clothing on their bodies. Nala saw a flock of birds pecking at food on the ground. Wanting to catch them he flung his dhoti on the flock but the birds flew away with his dhoti. Soon Damayanti was tired and they rested under a tree. Damayanti fell asleep. Nala cut half of Damayanti's sari and wrapped it around himself. Hoping that Damayanti will go to her parents' place if he wasn't with her, he left.

When Damayanti woke up and found Nala gone, she frantically tried to find him. All alone in the forest, she went through terrible hardships, and deadly encounters which she only narrowly escaped. She did not want to go her parents' without Nala. In the end, she went to the kingdom of Chedi with a carvan going that way. Queen of Chedi treated her kindly and found a secluded place for her to live. Meanwhile king Bhima, her father had sent his envoys everywhere to find Nala and Damayanti. One of the envoys found Damayanti in Chedi and brought her to her parents.

Wandering in the forest, Nala helped a serpent escape from a curse. Surprisingly the serpent bit him. His bite changed Nala's appearance. The serpent whose name was Karkotaka, told Nana that he did it for Nala's sake, to discomfiture the demon possessing him. He also advised Nala to go to the king Rituparna of Ayodhya. Nala became Rituparna's charioteer. Nala was famous for being an expert charioteer. Of course Rituparna was not aware that his charioteer was Nala.

Damayanti sent out envoys to look for Nala. Envoys were to ask this question, "O gambler, where are you now having left your wife dressed in half a sari?" If any body replied they were to bring the news back to Damayanti. In Ayodhya Nala, who was changed in appearance made the reply that the husband who deserted his wife, bears her no malice and is actually looking for her everywhere.

Damayanti sent the envoy back with a message for Rituparna that

Damayanti is holding a second syamvara at dawn the next day. Now Rituparna knew what a superb driver his disguised driver Nala was and he set out for Vidarbha with Nala driving the chariot. Nala drove fast and furious. On the way they saw a huge tree. The king predicted the number of leaves tree had. Nala stopped the horses and counted the leaves and found the king was right. The king said that he knows this because of his skill in gambling. Then Nala taught king his skill in driving and the king taught him the skill of gambling. At this point the demon Kali left Nala's body, apologized and departed.

As the king reached in time for the purported svyamvara, Damayanti knew that no one but Nala could drive so fast to cover the distance from Ayodhya to Vidarbha.

Rituparna was cordially received by the king Bhima but was perplexed why he had made the trip. Damayanti had not told her father any thing about the matter.

Damayanti sent a learned brahmana to talk to Rituparna's charioteer and enquire about Nala. The brahmana reported back that the charioteer became very agitated and disturbed when asked about Nala. Damayanti sent her son and daughter to meet the charioteer. The charioteer wept bitter tears on seeing his children and ultimately revealed to Damayanti that he indeed was Nala and the reason for his disfiguration. The gods were pleased and restored Nala to his normal form. Thus the couple was united.

After resting for a few days Nala and Damayanti rode to Nishadha. Nala challenged Pushkara for another game of dice and this time Nala won his kingdom back. Nala treated his brother kindly and did not retaliate against him.

Thus Nala and Damayanti ruled over Nishadha again and all was well.

– May 15, 2019

Gratefulness

I am grateful for each moment free pf pain.
I am grateful for each moment of joy.
I am grateful for the moments of lucidity
When all things seem clear.

I am grateful for simple things
That delight the heart
Like the laughter of children
A flower blossoming
Smell of freshly cut grass.

I am grateful for the bounties of life
Like watching children play
Love given and love received
Friends with whom I share
Life's joys and sorrows
Physicians who alleviate my pain.

I am grateful for decency
And kindness of ordinary folks.
Generosity that my fellow citizens
Have for the world's poor and afflicted.

I am grateful for the beauty
Of sunrise and sunsets.
I am grateful for these
And many other things
That the providence
Has bestowed upon us.

– May 30, 2019

Importance of Giving Food and Drink

This rather strange tale is from Valmiki's Ramayana, told by the sage Agastya to Rama. Agastya says:

One day on stepping out of my ashram I saw a dead body and then I saw a heavenly chariot descend from sky. Out of which came out a resplendent divine being who ate the corpse and was about to depart. Not being able to control my curiosity I stopped him and asked for an explanation. The man said he used to be a mighty king on earth and after ruling his kingdom justly for many years he died and ascended to heaven. However he was still plagued by hunger and thirst unlike other devas. He asked Brahmaa the reason for it. Brahmaa said, " You did penance with your body only. Since you did not give any food or drink to any body, you are still subject to hunger and thirst. You can satisfy your hunger only by eating corpses. However, when you meet the sage Agastya you will be freed from this curse."

As a parting gift, the celestial offered a rich ornament to the sage. Agastya offered this ornament to Rama, pleased by his protection of forest-dwelling rishis.

– June 11. 2019

The Origin of the Invocation, 'Svaahaa'

This story is from the Shatpatha Brahmana, dated approximately 900 BCE.

Prajapati (not yet called Brahmaa) was to embark on his work of creation. His son Agni (the Fire) was born from his mouth. As Agni's nature is to devour, he was about to make a meal of Prajapati himself. Prajapati was afraid and started sweating. He was pondering whether he should offer his sweat to his son to eat. A loud voice said, "Offer." Prajapati realized that he himself had spoken, that is sva(himself) Aahaa(Spoke). That is why we say Svaahaa whenever we make an offering to Agni. This invocation is common to both Hinduism and Buddhism.

More than a thousand years later, Puranas depict Svaahaa as the consort of Agni.

Agni and Svaahaa

Reference: Ardor by Roberto Calasso. Published by Farrar, Straus and Giroux, New York.

This work is essentially an exposition of the Shatpatha Brahmana. Calasso had an earlier work called Ka(a name for the prajapati) also based on the Shatpatha Brahmana. Ka was not a very successful work; Ardor is much better.

– June 17, 2019

A Short Note on the Sacred Syllable Om

According to Mandukya Upanishad, human consciousness has four forms:

1. Ordinary Waking State(Jagrata)
2. Dream State (Swapna)
3. Deep Sleep (Sushupti)
4. The Fourth State (Turiya) is conscious deep sleep.

Now the sound OM is analyzed as AUM.

A represents the Waking State.

U represents the Dream State.

M represents the Deep Sleep.

And the following silence represents Brahman, the universal consciousness. (Be still and know God.)

– June 22, 2019

Five Sheaths Enveloping the Self

Five sheaths are first described in the Tattiriya Upanishad (6th century BCE). These are:

1. **Physical Body (Annamaya Kosha)**: Anna is food. Body is made of food. It is not the Self or Atman as the body did not exist before both and will not after death. But Atman is deathless.
2. **Vital Body (Pranamaya Kosha)**; Prana or Chi i.e. the life breath and organs of action, constitute this sheath. This is what that makes the body engage in action. This is not the Self because The Self is aware of the Prana. So You the Self is the knower of the Prana and not the Prana.
3. **Mind (Manomaya Kosha):** This consists of our thoughts, desires, and emotion. Again we are not our minds. We can observe the mind. We are the experiencers of the mind.
4. **Intellect (Vigyanamaya Kosha):** It is our ability to understand, analyze, critique and reason. Again we are aware of our intellect. So we are not our intellect either.
5. **Bliss(Anandamaya Kosha):** When we enjoy something like food, sex, or a work of art, this Is the bliss enjoyed by the Self so it is again not the Self.

So the Self is not identical with the five sheaths. The Self is the consciousness itself, the Brahman or God.

– June 30, 2019

Deportees By Woody Guthrie

The crops are all in and the peaches are rotting
The oranges are filed in their creosote dumps
They're flying 'em back to the Mexico border
To take all their money to wade back again
Goodbye to my Juan, farewell Roselita
Adios mes amigos, Jesus e Maria
You won't have a name when you ride the big airplane
All they will call you will be deportees
My father's own father, he waded that river
They took all the money he made in his life
It's six hundred miles to the Mexico border
And they chased them like rustlers, like outlaws, like thieves
The skyplane caught fire over Los Gatos Canyon
The great ball of fire it shook all our hills
Who are these dear friends who are falling like dry leaves?
Radio said, "They are just deportees"
Is this the best way we can grow our big orchards?
Is this the best way we can raise our good crops?
To fall like dry leaves and rot on out topsoil
And be known by no names except "deportees"
Listen to the song as sung by Woody's son Arlo

This song was written by Woody over seventy years ago but it still seems timely.

– July 1, 2019

An Unusual Creation Story

In the beginning there was only the self in the shape of a person. He saw that he was alone so he was afraid. So we are afraid when we are alone. But then he said what am I afraid of? There is no one else. His fear passed but he felt no joy because he was alone. He desired another for company. He became large and assumed the shape of a man and woman in embrace. Then he caused the two parts to separate and they became a man and his wife. So a man and woman are like two peas in a pod. He united with her and thus the race of humans was created. She thought how could he unite with me after producing me from himself? She hid herself and became a cow. He sought her out and became a bull. He united with her to create all the bovines. Then she became a mare and he a stallion. Then she became a she-donkey and he a male donkey. Then one became a female goat and other a he-goat. In this way the whole creation came into existence.

He knew that he indeed is all this creation as it all came from him. He who knows this becomes himself a creator.

This story is from Brihadaranyak Upanishad (around 700 BCE).

– July 7, 2019

Addendum

It just occurred to me that Plato in his Symposium says that originally a human was actually two humans with four feet, four legs, and a head with two faces. So there were three types of these humans: (Man, Man), (Woman, Woman) and (Man, Woman). Gods were afraid that they are two powerful. So they split them in two. So present humans long and look for their counter-part. So a man is looking for a man or woman and a woman is looking for a woman or man.

A Note on East and West

Abrahamic religions arose basically to answer the primordial human's question: Where did I come from? Who made me? This quest is external.

In contrast the Indic human asks: Who am I? Where does this awareness of self(Atman) come from? This quest is internal. Both Indic religions and philosophies arise from this internal quest and that is why they are intrinsically inseparable.

Western philosophy, on the other hand, derives from Greek sources which are essentially secular. Where as religion comes from semitic sources. Thus religion and philosophy are not inter-mixed as they are in India.

Indic religions(Hinduism, Buddhism, Jainism and Sikhism) are all introverted. You look within to find answers. God not just dwells within you: It is you. That's why Upanishads say: तत् त्वम् असि (Thou art that). You are what you are seeking. Buddhism denies Atman but still remains rooted in it, paradoxically.

Western people conquer the external world, subjugate nature and make great discoveries. Whereas eastern people dwelling on the internal search devise yoga, dhyana, and tantra.

Agreed that this description is not rigid. They made scientific discoveries in East too and western humans contemplated the mysteries of psyche.

– July 10, 2019

Uddalaka and Shvetaketu

Shvetaketu, son of Rishi Uddalaka came back home after studying Vedas for twelve years with a guru. He seemed very proud of his learning. Uddalaka said, "You are very proud of your learning but did you acquire the wisdom by which unbearable can be heard, the unperceivable can be perceived and the unknowable can be known." Shvetaketu said, "No father. My teachers did not teach me that. Please teach me, father."

Uddalaka: Please bring me a fruit of the fig tree over there.

Shvetaketu brought the fruit. Uddalaka asked him to break the fruit.

Uddalaka: What do you see , son?

Shvetaketu: A bunch of seeds, all very small, father.

Uddalaka: Now break a seed, what do you see?

Shvetaketu: Nothing father.

Uddalaka: That nothing is the subtle essence from which a whole fig tree grows. The subtle essence of everything is the Self from which everything arises. And that Self is you, Shvetaketu. Thou art that.

> **PS:** The dialog between father and son is quite long. I have just taken one little part of it. It is from Chhandogya Upanishad (6th or 7th century BCE).

– July 11, 2019

Two Inseparable Birds

In Hindu upanishads and other scriptures, one finds two kinds of statements about the self (Atman). In one the self employs sense organs and organs of action to experience the world and is subject to pleasure and pain. In another self is beyond all perceptions and is the embodiment of Sat, chit. And Ananda I.e. reality, consciousness and bliss. It had me totally confused until I read and pondered on a saying in Mundaka Upaanishad. It says:

> "Two birds, inseparable companions dwell upon one and the same tree. One of them eats the sweet fruit, the other looks on without eating. Being seated on the same tree, the Jiva immersed in ignorance and deluded, grieves on account of helplessness. But other, the Brahman, simply witnesses the acts of Jiva."
>
> – (Translation by Swami Shivananda)

I have taken the liberty to paraphrase part of above translations. Simply put, there are two aspects of us: Jivatma is the self that partakes of the worldly pleasure and pain and is deluded by Maya, the world-illusion.

The other aspect is Parmatma, the supreme self dwelling in the hearts of all, witnesses all but does not enjoy or suffer. She(he) is just pure reality, consciousness and bliss.

Easily said than done is to identify with our true witnessing nature which is real, conscious and blissful.

– July 14, 2019

Uddalaka and Shvetaketu 2

Uddalaka asked his son Shvetaketu to put a lump of salt in a glass of water and bring it to him next morning. Shvetaketu did that. Uddalaka asked, "Where is the lump of salt that you put in here?" Shvetaketu groped for the lump but couldn't find it.

Uddalaka asked his son to take a sip from a corner and asked how it tastes.

"It tastes salty, Sir." Shvetaketu said.

Uddalaka asked his son to taste the water from the center, from the other corner and so on. Shvetaketu found it salty everywhere.

Uddalaka said, "Salt is everywhere but we don't see it. Similarly Atman (the Self) is everywhere but we don't see it. Atman is the subtle essence of everything. It is the Self of everything in the world. And that essence is you, Shvetaketu. Thou art that (तत् त्वम् असि)।"

Metaphysics of Pain

Torn between hope and despair
Strung between heaven and hell
Like a modern day Trishanku
A sufferer doesn't know which way to turn.

Driven mad by debilitating pain
But even a slight relief
Revives resilience and
Brings hope and uplifting of mood

There is no pleasure without pain
But perhaps the converse is true as well.
Pain brings pleasure when
It lessens or if by sheer luck disappears.

When you rejoice you write a poem
Thanking the powers that be
With pain also you write poetry
When it is not crippling and is subsiding.

Hindus say Atman is forever blissful
No pain can touch it.
Buddhists say there is no Atman
So no one is there to feel the pain.

So they both seem to say
That the pain is illusory
What confounds the suffering person
Is the reality of suffering.

Hindus will say
The you that pain is killing
Is not real you.
Buddhist will say
Neither you nor pain are not real.

PS: Trishanku is a figure in Hindu mythology who wanted to go to heaven and to rule. His guru Vishwamitra was strong enough to propel him towards heaven. Indra, the current ruler of heaven stopped his progress so he is stuck between heaven and earth.

– July 14, 2019

Aging Is Bitter Sweet

Aging is bitter sweet
As so many other things.
On one hand you are glad to be alive
Able to enjoy sunrise and sunset
Enjoy the great play of Nature
See your grand-children grow
And your children thriving
In their chosen professions.
Also able to do what you want
With no particular schedule.
Taking each day as it comes
And try to make best of it.

On the other hand
Myriad pains and ailments
Begin to plague you.
Many of your loved ones,
Friends and acquaintances
Depart from the scene.
Some departures burn
A hole in your heart.
Grief lingers.
Even happy moments
Become tinged with sorrow.

– August 13, 2019

Unwelcome Companion

You pesky friend
You have overstayed your welcome
You are not welcome now
If you ever were.

O Companion, I beseech you to leave me alone.
Your constant company I can not endure.
Enough is enough
Now be gone.

You nag me, torture me
Want always to have your way.
You have such a hold on me
I suffer but you do not sway.

What I refer to is
This miserable pain
This miserable neuralgia
On my head.

I do not love you.
I do not crave you.
Paradoxically I seem
To cooperate with you.

When you are coming on
I flinch, push or pull
To facilitate your arrival
Even as I know I will suffer.

You have tortured me
Pestered me, abused me
Impaled me on an invisible cross
Enough I say, your time must be up.

– September 9, 2019

Lute of Life

Notes of the lute of life
Are still sweet but tinged with sadness.
It's sound is subdued
And notes are not bold as before.

I am not complaining
As change is nature's eternal law.
A raging fire eventually burns out.
A fruit ripens and eventually drops.

It is a time to recon
What is lost and what is found.
What moments of life
I should keep in memory
And which to discard.

Things I want to forget
I can't.
Those I want to remember
I forget.

Some time one feels that
To live long is not altogether a blessing.
Painful to see loved ones
Departing before you.

– September 10, 2019

Life Unbound

Dharma books say be steadfast
Treat happiness and sadness as same.
I often question this wisdom.
Is it human not to feel sorrow
When a loved one passes?
Is it human not to be joyous
When your child is born?

Perhaps I understand
The teachings imperfectly
And putting undue emphasis
On detachment.

But I think it is wise
To live without any philosophies
Take life as it comes.
Laugh when life makes you laugh
And cry when it makes you cry.

To be wise means
Not to seek wisdom
Neither to seek happiness nor sorrow.
Whatever comes, comes.

Now wait it seems like
I have propounded a philosophy.
I beg your pardon
Just ignore the whole thing
And live your life.

– September 20, 2019

My Faith or Lack of It

I don't know why I am loath to belong to any group.
When I see a religious group full of piety and earnestness
Bordering on arrogance my mind turns away in dismay.

A Hindu by birth and temperament
But not beholden to rituals and ancient superstitions.
I often find myself standing alone
Among true believers and people of faith.
Does it mean I am an anomaly?

I am a watcher and not a joiner.
I don't want fame and riches neither do I want acclaim.
I like to write for friends and family
People who have some affinity for my way of thinking.

I am afraid of being button-holed
Into a position with no wiggle room.
Clinging too tightly is not my way.
Messianic zeal scares me I am wary of too much certainty
I like periods of solitude when I am alone but not lonely.

I like to reflect on things and share my thoughts
But not driven to more active participation.
I feel guilty sometimes but not motivated enough
To make a drastic change.

I take refuge in the Wisdom of the poet
John Milton who famously said:
They also serve who only stand and wait.
I also like the wisdom of Zen
Where Roshis advise pupils
Not to stink too much of Zen.

– October 3, 2019

Hope

Why do we cling to hope
When nothing really warrants it?
I think, It's because
Hope creates its own dynamic
Which brings comfort
To one who is desperate.

Hope is a salve
That helps a wounded soul heal.
Hope sees people
Through horrendous times.

Hope, despair and equanimity
Are the three states of human condition.
Equanimity seems the best
But sometimes I wonder
If it's human
Never to rejoice and never to despair.

Hope is what all people of God
Cater, be it a pujari, mulla, priest,
Monk, brahmin or abbot.
A promise of heaven, nirvana
A better rebirth, salvation or moksha.

I call them all
The merchants of hope.
Hope springs eternal
As Alexander Pope famously said.

– October 10, 2019

Shame

Shame is a multifaceted word.
It's meaning often decided by the context.
Some people are without shame in any context
Like the present occupant of the White House.
But most people have a modicum of decency and
Can feel ashamed of their misdeeds.

Sometimes shame is just embarrassment
Such as in a party when everyone is wearing a suit
But you showed up in
Jeans and your old army jacket.

Some time an entire group pf people
Lose any sense of shame
For example most
Republicans in the Nation's congress with
Lindsay Graham, the most shameless of them all.

Sometimes shame leads to a lack of spine
Or may be it is the other way round.
I have to ask a life scientist
If reptiles can feel shame.

Some people are parasites
Living on the earnings of others
Shamelessly without
Any sense of gratitude
And without guilt.

It can be dangerous to shame
A powerful person
Who can seek revenge and create havoc.
Draupadi embarrassed Duryodhana
When an optical illusion made him

Enter a pond and getting wet
And the results are well-known.

A person who is made to feel ashamed
Can become so depressed and despondent
So as to cause herself injury
And may even take her life.

The most famous reptile of all
The Devil in the form of a snake
Was a conniver and deceitful
But did he feel any shame afterwards?

Of course the shame that Adam and Eve
Felt on being naked, the knowledge
That was revealed to them after they
Ate from the tree of knowledge
At the snake's urging
Led to this whole shebang we call humanity.

I have always loved the account in
The book of genesis where
God makes clothes for Adam and Eve
Before exiling them.
Was god ashamed of expelling them
So as a recompense he dressed them?
Not only that he asked them
To be fruitful and multiply.
And as a result here we are.

– October 25, 2019

Our Lives

Our lives are made of
A little love, a little hate.
A little honey, a little vinegar.
A little despair, a little hope.
A little pleasure, a little pain.
A little sorrow, a little bliss.
A little conviction, a little disbelief.
A little concentration, a little distraction.
A little honesty, a little deceit.
A little cruelty, a little compassion.
A little clarity, a little confusion.
A little courage, a little fear.
A little foolhardiness, a little prudence.
A little desire, a little aversion.

They say to be enlightened
Means to look beyond dualities..
I think life is made up of dualities.
I can't imagine life without dualities
What is an unconditioned life I can't imagine.
Conditioning begins even before we are born.
None is born as a tabula rasa
Our genes, and our environment
Make us who we are and how we think.
So I think friends
Best we can hope for
Is to have more love than hate.
More hope than despair.
More courage than fear
More compassion than cruelty
More clarity and less confusion.

– November 1, 2019

Anonymity

I want anonymity but
Not a complete anonymity.
Some recognition is welcome
If it is without much fuss
And without requiring a speech
And other annoyances.

Wallace Stevens, a great poet
And Insurance executive
Infuriated his visitors by
Talking only about insurance.

A little flirtation with
Name and fame is alright
But more than that
Is bad for your sanity and health.

So if I have no name or face
Recognition and hear
Some one praising my work
It is gratifying
But a criticism would
Truly be a bummer.

Little unobtrusive praise
Does wonders to your
Creative spirit
Just as undesired criticism
Dulls and kills poetry of your heart.

Of course if there is
No poetry in your heart
Your heart can't sing
And neither would your voice or pen.

– November 6, 2019

Winter of Our Discontent

Why do we hurt most
Those we love most?
Why our sharpest barbs are aimed
Towards we cherish most?
Why is the emotional world
So topsy turvy?

Why are we thirsty
When our cup is full?
We are satiated
But remain hungry.
Why do our lives seem empty
Even when blessed with plenty?

These are the questions
I would like to ask
But the sages and wise ones
Are not on the scene
Or else I don't know
How to find them.

Our hearts are timid
We can't feel love.
Our brains have taken over
And that spells trouble.

What leading light
Will lead us out of
This winter of
Our discontent?

– November 18, 2019

Wine, Women, and Song

(Written from the perspective of a male. No offense intended to other genders)

When we are young
We want wine, women and song.
As we age we give up wine
Because it no longer agrees with us
And doesn't give pleasure it used to.
As we age further
Women become less attentive.
And to us they seem less attractive.
Then they ignore us
And we don't implore them.
But song, my friend
Doesn't abandon you
Unless you abandon it.
Song is the music of your soul
If you nurture it, it nurtures you.
Song here stands for
Music, theatre, poetry
And myriad other things
That appeal to your heart and mind.
Heart more than the mind.
Go where your heart takes you
And you can't go wrong.
You may not have fame and fortune
But you will be happy.
Your heart will sing a song
And you might as well sing along.

– November 22, 2019

Musings on Life and Death

Time is running out
And I wonder still
What this all means.
I meditated for years
Hoping that like Buddha
I too will figure out What is what
But no such luck Came my way.
I wonder what I Should
Have done and should
Do in remaining time
So life will unfold its mysteries
And the grand plan be revealed.
Or else, I will die Without knowing
If there is some deeper
Meaning of existence.
Does one continue in some way after death?
No one seems to know.
Are scientists right
In assuming that death is final?
I am not alone in
Wondering about such questions
But I don't think an answer
Can be expected.
Some times believers are lucky
To have found comfort in their faith.
But a modern man
Is cursed by his skepticism
And must take comfort
In that very skepticism
And be content in that very discontentment.

– December 4, 2019

In Defense of Boredom

Boredom has a bad name
But it actually is quite useful.
In this age of entertainment
And information overload
One is hardly ever bored.
But imagine if you turn
These mindless actions off
And be properly bored
You will be creative in getting rid of boredom.
You might write a poem, write a computer program
Compose a song, tend your garden, dance or sing.

I think boredom indeed
Is the womb from where
All creative endeavors ensue.
It is the source of all thoughts
And is pregnant with meaning.
So next time you are bored
Don't turn that TV on
Don't play silly video games
Or eat because there is nothing better to do.
Let boredom goad you
To reflect, to meditate
Or just be with yourself.

Children play when bored
And so do gods and other celestials.
Lord Vishnu after dissolution of universe
Sleeps for an eon.
On waking up he is bored
So he engages in Lila,
The divine play of creation.

– December 7, 2019

A Guilty Pleasure

If you are sick but not too sick
Sick enough so you are
Not expected to do anything
There is a guilty pleasure in it.

Now you can be justifiably lazy
And read a cozy mystery or thriller
You wanted to read for some time.
Spouse's job jar can wait.

You can shave or not
Take a shower or not
Take trash out or not
Pay bills or not.
So even sickness
If not long has a saving grace

All these things can wait a bit
So you can relish your sickness
You want to get better
But wouldn't mind
Being sick just a tad bit longer.

Just like an introvert
Who is inwardly happy
That plans got canceled
You enjoy your sickness
For whatever it's worth.

You can eat junk food
How can you cook
You are sick?
Perhaps some chips
And salsa you bought last week.

– December 18, 2019

Pain

Are there any life forms that don't feel pain?
I hear that even amoebas act to prevent danger
Perhaps because they too are afraid of pain.
Famous physicist Bose demonstrated that
Even plants feel pleasure and pain.

Pain can color how you view the world.
It can ruin your life if you let it.
You have to remind yourself
That you are not the pain you feel.

Pain does have some positives to offer.
It conditions you to empathize with pain of others.
In stead of self-pity it can make you feel
Genuine compassion for all sentient beings.

I am not saying that you should
Create pain for yourself.
But if you have it, you can
Use it for your spiritual practice.
If life gives you lemons
You must make lemonade.

– January 24, 2020

Pleasure

Absence of pain is pleasurable
But you can have pleasure
Even in presence of pain.
Say you are hurting
And you take a bite of a luscious fruit
Now that is pleasure
Isn't it?
Neither pleasure nor pain
Define us.
We are not identical
With our pleasures and pains.

We can take delight
In everything we do.
Even lowly home chores
Can be enjoyable if
Done with joy.
Peeling potatoes
Doing laundry
Washing dishes
Reading a book
Listening to music
I am happy.
Activity distracts you from the pain
And makes you suffer less.

Some have said
That pleasure rather ecstasy of divine love
Is comparable to sexual bliss.
But whereas sexual bliss
Doesn't last long
Divine bliss is for ever.
That's why, I think,

The older folks
Are drawn to spiritual pursuits.
Thus spirituality is sublimation of sexuality.
No surprise here, Dr. Freud would agree.
Art, music, poetry, and other fine arts
Are all sublimation of sexuality.

Tulsidas, the great Hindi poet
Became so after being rebuffed by his wife.
Coming back to our theme
Tulsi's Ramayana has been
A source of great pleasure
To generations of Hindi speakers.

Hope dear reader that reading
This poem has given you
Some pleasure as
Writing this has given me.

– Ground Hog Day, 2020

Open Those Windows

Open those windows, let fresh air in.
Open the shades let sunshine in.
Let the stale air out of the house.
Sweep the floor, let dust and dirt out.

Open the windows of your mind
Let new ideas in.
Vanish the darkness of your mind
Let the light of knowledge in.
Let old destructive habits die a natural death.
Clear the cobwebs of your heart and mind
And let the rotten stale air out.

Your eyes not used to light
May be dazzled momentarily
But let them get used to it.
Let fresh notes enter your ears.
Visit places you have never been to.

Worry not about afterlife
Take care of life here and now.
Don't inflict harm on any one
Help others if you can.
This world is full of good and bad
Engage your innate wisdom to sort it out.
Spend your life in peace and contentment.
If death come as it does invariably
Welcome it as a door to new experiences.

– February 12, 2020

Forbidden Fruit

Why do we long for what we can't have?
Allure of forbidden fruit feeds our delusion,
Clouds our vision, diminishes clarity
And in the end makes us unfulfilled and unhappy.

If perchance we manage to get
What we thought we wanted
We are soon disillusioned
To discover that what we wanted
Was no panacea for our ills.

This is because true happiness
Springs from within.
No matter where we go
If we are unhappy
That unhappiness stays with us
There is no getting away from ourselves.

What we ought to do is to meditate
And examine our mind
To discover our maladies
And then act to remove the irritants
If possible or if that can't be done
Train our minds to live with it.

– March 7, 2020

Diamond Sale

You standing there like a question mark
How can I say, "No?"
How can I bear to see tears
In those proud and defiant eyes?

You win this contest hands down
Dear, I lay down my arms.

But hurry those diamond rings
Are on sale now.
Buy one get one free.

– March 14, 2020

In Memoriam

This post celebrates the life of beloved brother-in-law (Older brother pf my wife) Komal Chandra Agrawal (1943-2020) who passed away suddenly on March 18.

In Memoriam

Grief feels like a pit in your stomach
A churning of your inside
Like a hole in your heart
A deep void that refuses to be filled.
A wound that would not heal
Perhaps in time it would
But for now life seems dreary.
Like nothing will bring back
The joy of living.
In time it will be ok
As they say life goes on.
So I will keep faith and go on.
The forced isolation of
The corona virus
Makes life even harder.
My dear Bhai Saab
I dearly miss you and
Your kindness, great sense of humor
And your great passion for
Making life better for common folks
Of your motherland India.

– March 21, 2020

Anatomy of Grief

At first it is utter disbelief and denial
Then the reality sinks in.
And leads to anger
As to how this could be.
Anger subsides
Giving way to despair
Despair ends eventually
But the mood remains
Heavy and somber.
You feel empty
Morose and sad.
There is not much joy to be felt.
You feel guilty if you laugh.
Eventually grief abates
And life reasserts itself.
Living must keep on living.
There is no other way.
That's how it has been
Since the beginning of time
And so it will remain.

– March 28, 2020

Times That Try Men's Souls

These are the times that try men's souls
So said Thomas Paine in seventeen seventy-six
For the perilous times facing the continental army.
Their enemy was British army and King George, the third.
We Americans measured up to the task and won.

The horrific times due to deadly corona virus
Are now trying men's and women's souls.
This time the enemy is intangible and invisible.
But is far more deadly than any army.
Can we measure up to this seemingly invincible foe?

Our leader is inept and corrupt
Incapable of meeting the challenge.
But we are Americans
With our 'Can do' approach
We can meet any challenge.

So we will practice social distancing
Remaining physically apart
We will stand together
And, "We shall overcome"
As Martin Luther King Junior proclaimed
Over half a century ago.

– April 5, 2020

Our Dual Curses

Our world is cursed by two entities.
Corona virus and Donald Trump.
One is subtle and invisible.
Other is very much visible
And thinks that all that happens is about him.

Corona is the biggest tragedy
Faced by world in my life time.
It is very hard on little kids
Who only imperfectly understand what's happening.

Trump bickers and clashes with scientists.
He wasted precious two weeks
In which a solid working mechanism
Would have been created
To fight the vicious pandemic.

He understands nothing
But claims whatever he
Has done is for the best.
Probably by his blundering
Inaction and foolishness
He is partly to be blamed for the horrible toll
The pandemic has taken.

I sincerely hope and fervently wish
That he is not reelected.
He already thinks he is
The emperor of these states.
God knows what he would do
If he is going to be taking the oath
On January twenty
Two thousand twenty-one.

– April 14, 2020

Behold Mighty Trump

Behold mighty Trump
Who can order hurricanes to change course
The second coming of Lord Jesus Christ
Most stable genius of all
Who can bend science to its will
Who in his great unmatched wisdom
Promised to destroy Turkey
If it misbehaved in Syria.

Who can fire scientists who didn't see the Truth in time.
Who knows more about warfare than any general
Who is a better mangler of English language
Than the great bard himself.
Who by his own admission is so great looking and smart.
The uncrowned emperor of these United States
Perhaps the spirit of King George, the Third
Resides in you.
Perhaps it has come to reclaim his lost colony.
Perhaps then it can be made safe from the Chinese
And bequeathed to Czar Putin of the great Russian nation.

Behold Lord Trump
Mightier than the mightiest
Great scholar of Latin
Who figured out what, "Quid Pro Quo"
Means all by himself.
Who knows history well
Including the fact
That Lincoln was a republican.
Who knows that Kansas City
Ought to be in Kansas.
Who thinks Andrew Jackson
Could have the Civil War worked out.

Lord Trump who has gone to great lengths
To Make America Great Again
By refusing to accept any responsibility for any thing
Pulling out of all treaties.
He has facilitated the death
Of frail old seniors in nursing homes
By his mishandling of the disaster.
Who suggested that people inject disinfectant
To kill corona virus and suggested it was said in jest
Who else but Trump would find the pandemic humorous.

We pay homage to Thee mighty Trump
Please deliver us to Evil.
Deliver us from the clutches of Globalism
And deliver us to tribalism.
Make the white Nation rise again
Making minced meat of all other nations.

– April 24, 2020

Strange and Crazy Times

What a strange and crazy time to be alive!
You can't get hair cut, have your nails clipped.
Forget about a massage and chiropractor
Your doctor would prefer to see you on only Zoom.

Kids are stuck at home
Going crazy and driving parents crazy.
Millions are unemployed.
So many poor kids going hungry.
Corona has caused horrible devastation
And untold misery.

When Trump became the president
I thought that was the weirdest thing
I had seen happen.
But the pandemic has replaced
Or supplanted Trump as national
Or rather international virus.

Trump is worse than ever.
Every day you hear a new assault
On the rule of law,
On decency and ethical behavior.
Our reputation is sullied around the world
I hope not beyond repair.

Trump is just the latest wondrous gift
GOP has given us!
Starting with Joseph McCarthy
In the fifties followed by Tricky Dick
In sixties and seventies
And then such luminaries as
Dan Quayle, Sara Palin,
Sean Hannity And Rush Limbaugh.

I almost Forgot the loonies at the Fox News
And to top them all the
Vilest and the craziest villain of all
(Dis) honorable Donald J. Trump.

I thought the cartoon below
From the Mad magazine
Said it all.
But nowadays neither Trump
Nor Putin say anything about Each other.
Perhaps the romance
If that's what it was has cooled.

Now Trump is mad at China.
I don't know why can't Chinese
With their mastery of corruption
And Trump's lack of ethics
Can't offer him something he can't refuse.

I think Trump has a point
When he claims to be chosen by God.
Have you noticed that all Talk of his tax returns and
Myriad Cases against him are not heard
Any more as Corona Virus has
Taken up all the media coverage.
If that's not God protecting
Teflon Don
Who is?

– May 6, 2020

Giving Way to Anger

Have you noticed how small things
Sometimes barrel out of proportion
And create a crisis?
Both the parties speak in anger
And say things which they regret later.

Giving way to anger
And act instinctively without thought
Is epitome of mindlessness
And lack of compassion.

Not only that but you don't
Get your point across either
Because you have put the other party
On defensive which solidifies
Their resistance to the point
You were making.

These days of pandemic
Are grating on nerves.
Kids are antsy and anxious.
It's easy to get mad
At trifles during duress.

So friends stay six feet apart
But take care of each other.
A little compassion
And understanding
Goes a long way
To build a bridge
Over troubled waters.

– May 11, 2020

Justice in America

If you are looking for justice
You will not find it in Trump's America.
A black man is murdered by a cop
While three other cops simply watch
Complicit in murder.
The whole nation watches with them
In horror and disgust.
White supremacists perhaps watch it with glee.
The nation burns in its wake
While the president tweets in hateful terms
With not an ounce of sympathy or empathy
For victims of racial hatred.
As a friend said recently
Even a clod of earth has more empathy
In comparison to the leader of free world.
A pandemic rages unabated
Hate is in the air
Its vicious flames are aided and abetted
By the leader who should be putting them down.
People await horrors still to come
Such as US military deployed to battle
Against its own citizens by an imbecile
Who happens to be our commander-in-chief.

– June 2, 2020

Pain vs. Suffering

Chronic pain frames your existence.
It limits your actions to remain within the frame.
You would like to override the boundaries
And widen the frame.
Often it doesn't work.
Just when you think you have succeeded
Pain flares up and tells you not so quick buddy.
You ask it to get lost.
Some times you succeed
But often you fail.
Buddhists draw a distinction
Between suffering and pain.
You will have pain for sure
But suffering is your choice.
But often the difference
Between pain and suffering eludes me.
I find writing cathartic
Whether any one reads it or not.
I don't know why
But it ameliorates my pain.
A Buddhist teacher suggested
That you should be friends with your pain
It is your longtime companion.
I find I am not able to do it
This companion is not welcome
I want it to leave and never come back.

– June 9, 2020

Strange and Scary Time

Such a strange and scary time to be alive
Like of which I haven't seen in my life.
A blazing pandemic and tepid federal action
'It will just disappear' says POTUS
Justifying his inaction.

Putin paying bounty to kill American soldiers
One hundred thousand dollars a piece.
Not a single word of recrimination from our
Commander-in-chief.
Despite this despicable act by Putin
To rejoin G-seven he wants to send an invite.
When rebuffed by the allies he cancels the meet.

Is refusing to take any action
Against a nation that pays bandits
To kill our soldiers an act of treason?
Do pandits know
What says the constitution?

Racial injustice and strife continues.
Killings of minorities by racist cops continue.
One hundred and fifty-five years after abolition
Of slavery, systemic racism endures
Much like thousands of years old
Evil caste system in India.

Every day reveals new horrors.
One wanton act after another.
Vindictiveness and lawlessness
Often prevail over kindness and good sense.
Justice department of Mr. Barr has gone awol.

I urge my fellow citizens
On this July fourth to pledge to vote
In November to defeat morass, idiocy
And lack of propriety and ethics
And to restore decency and rule of law
To the governance of our great nation.

– July 2, 2020

Hopes and Aspirations

When pain soars high
Spirit dives low.
Then nothing seems
To bring pleasure.

The remedy is
To start doing something.
Any thing will do.
Do the laundry
Do the dishes
Pay bills
Read a book.

Soon the pain seems lighter
Melancholy abates a bit
And you are prepared
To wage the battle again.

Meeting friends and family
Is also great
But is hard in these
Days of pandemic.

Zoom is a boon
In these trying circumstances
In keeping one sane
And soothe nerves.

Some day soon
The pandemic would end
Though the pain
Is not likely to go away.
But it will be mitigated some
If the emperor of lies

Ceases to live in the White House.

I am keenly waiting
For the day when
Life returns to normal.
When every day doesn't
Bring a new outrage.
When we stop resembling
A banana republic.
When rule of law is restored
And the current occupant
Gets his just desserts.

The world heaves a sigh of relief
Environment becomes a priority again
Treaties are honored
Corruption at high places lessens
Race relations improve
And real reforms
Take place in the way
Police treats black and brown folks.

That will folks indeed
Be a brighter day
When these hopes and
Aspirations come true.

– July 11, 2020

Search

I don't know what is making me restless
Something vague and unfinished
Ill-defined, indefinite
Yet somewhat disturbing.

Hard to get at but always nagging
Often at the end of a day
I have the feeling
That there is something amiss.

I keep on searching
Through the recesses of my mind
To reveal what it is I am looking for.
But largely in vain.

It is like the feeling
That there is something in your eyes
That you can't get rid of
No matter how hard you try.

I have to keep searching
Though I may never find
This mystery that so far has eluded me.

I only half wish for this mystery to be solved.
We need mystery, awe and wonder
To prevent life from becoming boring insipid and dull.

Some may accuse me of Grandiloquence
But I seriously think that some illusion
Some mystique, sme romance
Is necessary for survival of spirit.
Otherwise dull plodding everyday existence
May swallow us whole.

– July 21, 2020

Fragility of Life

Life changes in a moment
And sometimes there is
Nothing you can do
But watch helplessly
As events unwind.

There is nothing as fragile
As human ego
A single careless word
Can set a war in motion.

So tread lightly friend
As you travel through life
As walking on an egg shell
So you don't bruise any one's
Pride, ego or dignity.

Keep mum if you can't
Utter a kind word.
Speak truth but not a bitter one
If it can be helped.

Remember not to speak in anger
As you for sure will regret it
Once the embers of anger cool
But then it may be too late.

– August 5, 2020

Pandemic

Pandemic has killed
Thousands and thousands of folks.
Right wingers still claim it's a hoax.
People who are
The greatest purveyors of fake news
Call the factual news fake news.

The greatest patron and creator of fake news
Is our commander-in-chief
Who is neither fit to be a commander nor a chief.
It is such a topsy-turvy world my folks
Perversion of facts is the new normal
For Trump and his toadies of course.

Pandemic has taken its toll on all
Not just those who became sick.
People confined at homes with little to do
Kids going crazy and making parents go nuts
Tempers flaring, arguments blaring
We can't even have a good night's rest.

People keep dying
And Trump irresponsibly claims
He is not responsible and takes no blame.
He made states responsible
For the tests, PPE, providers and workers.
States competing against each other and FEMA
All due to Trump's incompetence.

Pandemic is tearing families apart
Some anti-mask, some pro-mask
And some simply confused
With no clear views.
With no leadership at the top

With clear guidelines and scientific reports.
CDC muzzled not to provide daily updates.

With luck pandemic may run out sooner than later
And Trump may move from White House to Jail House.
He can petition to be placed there with
His buddies like Cohen and Flynn.

– August 13, 2020

Uncertainty

Mind is clouded with uncertainty.
Don't know how to deal with this calamity.
Social distancing is the right thing to do
But people want to touch and hug
Kiss, make love in spite of pandemic adversity.

Nobody knows when things
Will return to normal
And will it be a new normal?
We don't know what the future holds.

Children's education is another question mark.
Online education doesn't meet the mark.

Children learn from teachers
Fellow students and school environment.
Buses, gyms, cafeterias
Bus drivers, custodians and school functions
Also play a role in education.

With millions out of job
What will happen to the economy?
Stocks keep surging but millions keep hurting.
You see they own no stocks.

Rome burned while Nero played fiddle.
Trump denies all responsibility
For the mismanagement of pandemic.
Does nothing to address
The racial injustice and police brutality.
The Nation is burning
But Trump is busy playing golf.

– August 25, 2020

Stranger

If you can't see him in daylight
Look for him in dark by starlight.
If open eyes don't see him
See him with eyes closed.
If awake you don't see him
See him in your dreams.
You don't find him in busy streets
Look for him in silent woods.
You always saw him from afar
But now see him up close.
For centuries you saw no sign of him
But suddenly you see him.
You cried unconsolably
When you couldn't find him.
You thought he was far away
But he was always at your door.
You thought he was a stranger
But he turned out to be most familiar.

– August 30, 2020

Loser

Who is actually a loser, do you know?
Our Commander-in-chief says
All soldiers, veterans and martyrs are losers
Because they received no material gains
And any body who doesn't is a loser.

So according to this definition
Jesus, Buddha, Gandhi and Mandela
Were all losers because they
Made no money from their activities.

Whereas Donald is not a loser
Because everything he says or does
Is for his personal gain
Or for his business.
If it is not in national interest
He as well as Melania do not care.

A non-loser has only one value to go by
In life and that is to make money.
If that goes against the nation or people
That's OK because who deserves it more
Some loser or a bonafide Trumper?

God save a nation that's ruled by
A non-loser like Bolsonaro and Trump!
Please give us losers
Who will work towards people's gain
And will not further divide
An already divided and troubled nation.

– September 7, 2020

Interesting Time

We are living in an interesting time
As the Chinese proverb would say.
There is danger and uncertainty every where.
Covid-19 prevents us from even Shaking
Hands with friends and family.

Children are the worst sufferers
Their education is adversely affected
They may end up a year behind
In academics when all this is over.

On the top of it our president
Is revealed to be a fraud, crook
And a con-man to the boot.
He says no ballots and no transfer of power
But a continuation of power.

So he has no intention to leave
Even if he loses the election.
Our nation is facing a crucial test.
As some body on the news said
It is not an election between Trump and Biden
But an election between Trump and democracy.

Every day there are harrowing revelations
Of greed, corruption and narcissism at the top.
Over two hundred thousand of our fellow
Citizens are dead and certainly there will be more.

If federal government had acted responsibly
How many lives would have been saved?
I have heard some experts say
That it would have been over thirty-six thousand.

If I were a believer I would pray

But as it is I can only hope
And fervently wish
That Trump would soon be gone
And face charges for his many crimes.
And corona will soon only be a memory
Never to be repeated.

– September 27, 2020

Drop the Load and Be Happy

For something that does not exist
Self seems pretty heavy.
It asserts itself at every chance
And throws its weight around.

Self-importance is to carry
A lot of dead weight and be weary.
That's why Buddha preached
To drop the load and lighten up.

Have you noticed that
Happiest moments of life
Are when you let go of your self
And just be here and now and enjoy.

Self insists that you must always be right.
Must always have the last word.
Win at any cost.

The cost of this my friend is very high.
It deprives one of happiness
And brings untold miseries.

So I say my friend
Drop the self, lighten up
And then drop the dropping
As the Zen masters say.

Wise say that there is a lot of hurt in life
Both physical and mental
But suffering is a choice you make.

Drop the load and be happy
As Buddhas of all ages have preached
Since times immemorial.

– October 26, 2020

What Happens after You Die

What Happens after You Die

As the greater part of my life is over
I begin to wonder
What happens after you die.
Many scenarios are provided
In world religions and literature.

Egyptian book of the dead
Says afterlife is wonderful.
You get everything you desire
But you have to chart your way carefully
If the book is in your grave
You have all the instruction you need.

Tibetan book of the dead
Guides you through the afterlife.
If you are worthy you get nirvana
The ultimate release from samsara
Otherwise it guides to get the best
Possible rebirth you are fit for.

Multiple Hindu scriptures
Say you get moksha, the liberation
If you have exhausted all your karma.
Otherwise you may spend time
In heaven and/or hell.
Eventually you are born again
In the world of mortals
As a being depending on your karma.
Sikhs and Jains have
Somewhat similar beliefs but details differ.

Abrahamic religions believe

In an eternal heaven or hell.
Catholics throw in a purgatory
For those who are essentially good
But have not accepted Jesus.
After they are purged of their sins
They are admitted to heaven
Dante has described all this delightfully
In his Divine Comedy.

None of this I find convincing.
So I am resigned to the fact
That I will never know
What happens if any thing
After you die.

– October 31, 2020

Meaning of "Hanuman"

'Hanu' in Sanskrit means chin. So Hanuman means one who has a chin. Hanuman is a monkey but monkeys don't have a chin!

The story goes that even as a baby Hanuman was very powerful. Once baby Hanuman saw a sight of rising sun which he mistook for a ripe sweet fruit. Hanuman reached out for the fruit and got very close to sun. Indra sensing a catastrophe struck Hanuman's lower jaw with his Vajra. Hanuman's lower jaw became dented, giving him a chin I.e. a Hanu. So he became Hanuman.

Force of Vajra knocked Hanuman senseless. Indra revived him and granted him several boons as did Agni, the fire-god, Vayu, the wind-god, Varuna, the god of waters, Shiva and Brahma.

Hanuman is presumably a son of wind-god Vayu. As a child he was very fond of pranks. He annoyed a rishi by his mischiefs. Rishi cursed him that he will forget all his powers. That's how he ended up as a meek follower of Sugriva who was hiding from his powerful brother Bali. When Hanuman and other Vanaras are sent by Sugriva to search for Seeta. Hanuman is reminded of his great powers by Jambvan and he flies over the sea to Lanka, the kingdom of Ravana. As everyone knows Hanuman finds Seeta and conveys Rama's news to her, promising that Rama would soon invade Lanka, kill Ravana and take Seeta home.

– November 21, 2020

Images supplied by my friend David Farnsworth:

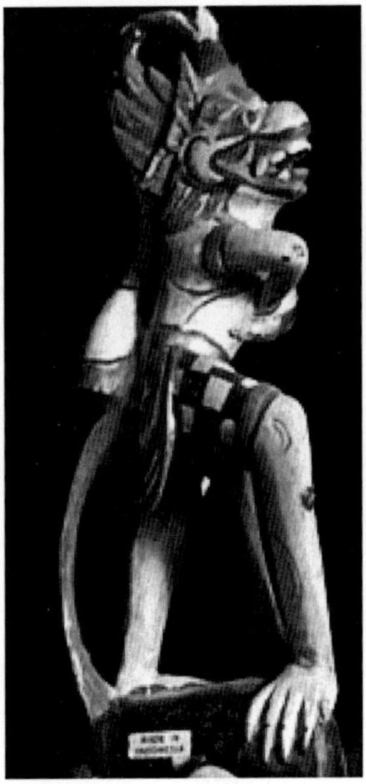

From Bitter to Better

It is just as important to know what
You failed to do as what you did.
Not noticing your grand kids' achievements
Not noticing your wife's new hairdo
Not acknowledging work she has done
Are all serious offenses.
You may not even be aware of your thoughtlessness
But it does not excuse your insensitivity.
Preoccupation with your business or your job
Is not an excuse for poor behavior.
Stop making excuses
Apologize for past mistakes
And promise to do better in future.
I guarantee that
It will change your life
From bitter to better
And a whole lot sweeter.

– November 29, 2020

In Defense of Kaikeyi

As every Hindu knows that King Dasharatha exiled his eldest son Rama due to machinations of evil queen Kaikeyi. But perhaps the matter is not that simple.

Dasharatha wanted to enthrone Rama not as king but as yuvaraja i.e. the crown prince. But why? Generally the oldest son was automatically the yuvaraja so why was this ceremony necessary?

In Valmiki Ramayana, Dasharatha sends for Rama to give him the news and Rama departs to give the news to his mother and wife. The king sends for Rama again. When Rama comes, the king talks of many evil omens so he wants to enthrone Rama yuvaraja immediately before his fickle mind changes. He also wants to do it before Bharata comes back from the king's father-in-law's that is Kaikeyi's father's place. He says that Bharata is a good boy but who knows how would he react.

So what is the king afraid of? Now we know that Kaikeyi used to accompany the king in battle and had once saved his life. Perhaps the king promised to anoint Bharata as yuvraja and now he was about to renege on that promise. It is also interesting that the king did not send the news of this auspicious occasion to the king of Kaikaya Desh, the place of Kaikeyi's kins.

We will perhaps never know the whole truth but there are hints in the scripture telling that there is more here than meets the eye.

– December 3, 2020

See Things as They Are

Ever wonder how little it takes
To tip our mental balance.
If somebody says something
Which we think slights us
We lose our equanimity.
If we do not get the praise
We think we deserve
We are hurt even if we don't show it.
Yet we feel upset when we are
Blamed for something
Which indeed is our fault.
Instead of owning it up
We try to find an excuse
Or shift the blame to someone else.
Our minds are fickle
Flitting constantly from one thing to another.
We are not happy with what we have
Because our neighbors
Got something better.
If we could truly observe us from outside
We would stop this madness.
But we delude ourselves
And needlessly suffer
From the pangs of jealousy and desire.
If only we could detach ourselves
From our insatiable ego
We will be truly happy.

– December 9, 2020

"To See a World..."

(Fragments from "Auguries of Innocence"

To see a World in a Grain of Sand
And a Heaven in a Wild Flower,
Hold Infinity in the palm of your hand
And Eternity in an hour.

A Robin Redbreast in a Cage
Puts all Heaven in a Rage.
A dove house fill'd with doves and pigeons
Shudders Hell thro' all its regions.
A Dog starv'd at his Master's Gate
Predicts the ruin of the State.
A Horse misus'd upon the Road
Calls to Heaven for Human blood.
Each outcry of the hunted Hare
A fiber from the Brain does tear.

He who shall train the Horse to War
Shall never pass the Polar Bar.
The Beggar's Dog and Widow's Cat,
Feed them and thou wilt grow fat.
The Gnat that sings his Summer song
Poison gets from Slander's tongue.
The poison of the Snake and Newt
Is the sweat of Envy's Foot.

A truth that's told with bad intent
Beats all the Lies you can invent.
It is right it should be so;
Man was made for Joy and Woe;
And when this we rightly know
Thro' the World we safely go.

Every Night and every Morn

Some to Misery are Born.
Every Morn and every Night
Some are Born to sweet delight,
Some are Born to Endless Night.

– Dec. 17, 2020

To See a World

William Blake

A Note on an Upanishadic Verse

I have been fascinated by the following verse from the Ishavasyopanishad:

> हिरण्यमय पात्रेण सत्यस्यापिहितम मुखम
> तत् त्वम पूषन अपावृणु सत्यधर्माय दृश्टये

> The face of truth is covered with a golden disc. Unveil it, O Pushan, so that I who love the truth may see it.
>
> – Translation by Dr. S. Radhakrishnan in his 'The Principle Upanishads.'

Pushan is the divinity who controls the sun.

The straightforward interpretation is that the rishi who composed it, is looking at the shining golden orb of the sun and wants to identify the being who is behind the orb.

Now, normally we think that the truth is obscured by darkness. In stark contrast to this, in here the truth is obscured by a bright light and the rishi wants to identify who or what is obscured by it.

I think there are parallels to it elsewhere. When Krishna shows Arjuna his Vishwarupa, he grants Arjuna divine vision but even then Arjuna is bewildered and terrified. The effulgence this cosmic form is as if hundreds of thousands of suns arose in sky simultaneously. Arjuna pleads with Krishna to resume his normal form.

In the Old Testament, Moses sees the burning bush I.e. a bush that is burning without being consumed. He is instructed by Yahweh to take his sandals off when approaching the bush and then an angel of God delivers the plate with the ten commandments engraved on it.

– December 24, 2020

Indic Philosophies in a Nutshell

Hinduism

Predominant philosophy in modern Hinduism is the non-dual Vedanta which is a systemized version of Upanishadic thought. The self of an individual is called self or Atman and the self of the universe is called Brahman. The great Upanishadic wisdom is:

Atman = Brahman

Atman due to ignorance or Maya is born again and again until it realizes the great equality.

Buddhism

There is no independent self or Atman. Well, then how does rebirth come about? The best analogy that I found in a work by Ananda Coomaraswamy is to imagine a series of billiard balls in close contact. If a ball is moved against a stationary ball, the first ball will stop dead but the stationary ball will move on due to the momentum imparted by the first ball. That is in essence the Buddhist concept of rebirth.

Jainism

Each sentient being has a self or Atman but there is no universal self or Brahman. The transmigration of souls is similar to that of Hinduism.

Sikhism

The basic philosophy of Sikhism is similar to Upanishadic thought but with a strong tinge of devotion or Bhakti.

This is a barebone description admittedly with gaping holes.

Perhaps a poem may clarify(or, further confuse) the matter. Here we go:

Self or No-Self

Self or self if you may
Has been wreaking a havoc
In Indic philosophies
For very very long.
Hindus maintain that
The self of the universe
Is the same as the self
Of an individual and
That's the knowledge
That sets us free.
Mahavira in some six hundred
Years before Jesus
Threw a monkey-wrench in this philosophy
By claiming that all sentient beings
Have selves but the universal self
Is nowhere to be found.
Buddha exacerbated the situation to the extreme
By claiming that there is no such thing as self
Neither individual's nor universe's
Sometime soon after Mahavira.
No one has settled the matter for good
To everyone's satisfaction
Nor it is likely to be settled ever.
So make whatever you make of it
But leave my self or my no-self
Alone please, if you will.

– December 28, 2020

Who, What, and, Why?

We come into this world with no agenda.
As children, we are, aware, and blissful.
In other words, we are sat-chịt-ananda.
But as society tries to mould us
We lose this awareness and bliss
And become anxious and start asking
Questions such as, "Who am I?'
"Why am I here?"
"What is the meaning of all this?"
"What is the point of living and dying?"

None of these questions has an answer.
But they give rise to civilization, culture
Art, philosophy and religion.
Oh, I forgot to list the most important
Item on the list namely desire, love, sex and lust.
The all-encompassing word for this is the Sanskrit, "Kama."
The Kama actually is the source of all creation,
Mischief, mayhem, pleasure and pain.
Religions come partly to discipline
The primitive impulses of Kama.
Krishna, Buddha, Moses, Mahavira
Jesus and Mohammad
Provide the ethics, laws and morality
Needed for a functioning society.

The modern man recognizes that
No one actually has answered
The basic questions satisfactorily.
Modern man does not have strong faith
That sustains the religious and provides
Meaning to their existence.
He recognizes that basically

He himself has to provide meaning to his existence.
No one else can do it for him.
One can find clues to the mystery
Or glimpses of truth in great art
Music, poetry and literature
But one has to build his own
Psychic world by his own effort.

– January 2, 2021

PS: My apologies for using 'man' and 'his' instead of more awkward-sounding 'human' and 'his/her.'

I Long for the Days

I long for the days when only
Actors and robbers wore masks
When you could greet people on the streets
With a visible smile and shake hands
Instead of joining elbows and
Moving away for social distancing.

I long for the days when
Few knew what a pandemic meant.
When a virus meant common cold
And at worse a flue.

I long for the days when
You were not afraid of
Catching a deadly disease
Every time you went out in public.

I long for the days when
You don't have to wash
Your hands and disinfect
Everything and every surface ad nauseam.

To make matters worse
There is racial, political
And social strife
With tribalism ripping the land.

I long for the days when
You could go to a show
Visit a museum, go to a beach
Have a picnic in a park
Without the fear of a pesky pest.

– January 17, 2021

The Woman

Kali, the terrible black goddess
Dancing in cremation grounds
Is no other but your honey-lipped lover.

She is Radha of Krishna
And Laila of Majnu.
Juliet of Romeo and Seeta of Rama.

She is the night of the full moon
And also the night with no moon.

She is the one who grants all your wishes
And also the one who dashes
All your hopes and desires.

She is the mother who nourished you
And also the enchantress
Who seduces and enthrals you.

Dancing in theatre with abandon is she
Poison girl and villainous whore is she.

Dancing on Shiva's lifeless body is she
Entering her lord's funeral pyre is she.

– January 21, 2021

PS: This is a translation of a Hindi poem I wrote in 1994.

Dear Don

Dear Don
Since you are gone
I miss your antics
For their entertainment value.

But your innumerable lies
Your flair for firing people
Your show of raw power
Your vindictiveness
Your unspeakable cruelty
Towards immigrants, particularly children
None of these is a laughing matter.

I would much rather have
Sleepy Joe as you called him at the helm
Than an ethically-challenged blow-hard like you
With no capability to think
To organize and mobilize
For many problems facing the nation
Not the least of them
The blazing pandemic.
You should have some sleepless nights
Thinking how many thousands
Of lives have been lost
Because of your incompetent handling
Of the pandemic.
But I doubt that you do.
It is not in you to admit
That you made a mistake.

So it is good that you are gone.
I just hope that you never surface again
In a public role.

You have done terrific damage
To our prestige in the world
And our democratic institutions.
Lastly, you engineered an insurrection
Which is an act of treason, you must know.

With all the crimes you have committed
I can't even wish you a happy retirement.
I hope you get to live in another
Type of government house pretty soon.

– Feb. 6, 2021

Riddle of the Universe

This universe of ours is a riddle
Impossible to solve or even comprehend.
Neither science nor religion
Is able to grasp its essence.
Perhaps it is just as well
Because the universe without mystery
Without a sense of wonder
Would be such a dull thing.
I don't have much faith
In a bearded man in the sky
Charting our destiny
But I do appreciate what a marvel
This universe is.
Each leaf, each tree,
Each animate or inanimate object
Is so wondrously intricate and delightful.
To watch the night sky is thrilling
So is the perennial show of light and shade.
I take delight in
The sunrise and sunset
The mountains, lakes and rivers
Wilderness and civilization.
I think it is lovely to be alive at this moment
And take all this in.

– February 28, 2021

Conflicted

The body is decrepit with numerous ailments
But desires and hunger of all colors and hue persist unabated.
The desire to be desired is problematic indeed.
So is the desire to be acclaimed.
There is a spiritual hunger
Dissatisfaction with beliefs and creeds.
Can arts and literature fill this need?

On one hand, I don't want fame and acclaim
On the other hand, I don't want anonymity either.
I need friends who can discuss matters deeply
Without committing to any fixed thoughts or attachments.
This is where my attraction to Buddhism comes in.
Because it warns against mental rigidity
In favor of maintaining fluidity.

On one hand, I don't like rituals
On the other hand, I don't like the emptiness and
Banality of Life without rituals.
How is one to strike a balance
Between these conflicting modalities
I don't know but I keep seeking.
Time is running out though as I age.
There are more funerals than weddings I have to go too.
Actually, the Virus has solved this problem for now.
I can go to neither funerals nor weddings.

I feel so conflicted that at times I fall into inaction.
I am like Arjuna but without a Krishna to advise and guide me.
Even if a wise Krishna type is available
I don't know if I have enough humility
To follow his/her sage advice.

– March 17, 2021

Self-Knowledge

The rarest kind of knowledge is self-knowledge.
Do you always know how you're going to react to a situation?
Me, not really except when I am in a situation
Where I have been before.

Analyzing your mind is one of the basic goals of Buddhism.
This reminds me of the aversion
I have against belonging to a group
Especially a religious or spiritual group.

I am some times asked
If I am on a spiritual path.
My inevitable answer is I am on no path
And my path is really no-path.

My predilection is to admire, enjoy or be aghast
At the beauty or cruelty
Of the awesome majesty and heartlessness
Of the Universe without theorizing
About its reason or aim.

Even Buddhism which I generally like
I do not belong to
Because I don't want to be
A card-carrying member of anything.
And in that, I am being true to myself
Or perhaps I should say to my no-self.

The irony is that Buddha would approve
Otherwise, he wouldn't have said
Be a lamp unto thyself
Or be called Tathagata
The one who 'Thus Came.'

– March 20, 2021

Human Condition

Illusion, delusion, wisdom, confusion,
Hope, faith, aversion, affection.
Greed, creed, deed and devotion.
All these serve as binders to the human condition.

What separates humans from beasts
Is our awareness that we will die
Or, perhaps this is our arrogance
To put us above the rest of creation.

We are all stuck in this quagmire
Which is what this samsara is.
Freedom is an illusion or perhaps a delusion.
Presumably, some have escaped this entangled mess
We call them Buddhas.

Sometimes I doubt even if that is true.
But we have to have this trust to persist.
Ah but do you see that this is also a binder
To the above-described human condition?

– March 31, 2021

A Sort of an Easter Story

This happened:

Sometime in the mid-nineteen nineties.

I was still teaching at RIT. Our new president was doing strategic planning. For this purpose, he had recruited representatives from each department to survey their colleagues to gather their ideas. So my department representative came to interview me.

I quoted or rather paraphrased from The Sermon on the Mount:

"Which of you by taking thought can add one cubit unto his stature.

And why take ye thought for raiment? Consider the lilies of the field, how they grow: they toil not, neither do they spin;

And yet I say unto you, that even Solomon in all his glory was not arrayed like one of these."

King James Bible, New Testament Matthew 6: 27-29

So this was my input to the strategic planning. Meaning to cool it essentially.

The department rep. reported this faithfully to my department head, a very good friend of mine, but withheld my name. No matter how hard my friend thought it didn't occur to him that I might be the culprit. He thought the person must be one of our colleagues who was something of a Christian evangelist. It thrilled me to no end.

– April 4, 2021 (Easter Sunday)

Pandemic

Pandemic has skewed our lives so much
It is amazing. We have to stay six feet apart
So later, we can be together again.
A neighbor lost his wife to Alzheimer's
The poor fellow couldn't even bid her good-bye
Due to covid restrictions.

People's nerves are frayed
With the frequent loss of temper.
An increase in spousal abuse
And mistreatment of older people
Have been noted
Perhaps due to added stress on the caregivers.

Without the theatre, the movies, concerts
Arts and music,
Life seems primitive and brutish.
Misery and loneliness
Affect public morale and dampen the spirit.

How things would be past pandemic
Is anyone's guess.
At least for now, the fear of this dreaded virus
Keeps us away from parties or picnics
Barbecues or sporting events.
At least we can visit a library
That's a distinct blessing.

I am glad for the existence of the zoom
Enabling some contact and communication.
I guess we should count our blessings
And wait till this vicious storm blows over.

– April 13, 2021

Development of the Ideas of Transmigration of Soul in Ancient India

It may come as a surprise to some that the Vedas have no mention of the idea of karma and the doctrine of rebirth. Actually, the word karma is there but it is used in the sense of ritual karma I.e. karma-Kanda. This includes yajnas, homas, maintenance of ritual home-fire etc.

Karma as ethical action and as a determining factor of the afterlife I.e. mukti, heaven, hell, rebirth is totally missing from the Vedas.

Only in Upanishads, this new way of thinking is introduced. That would be approximately somewhere between 900 BC (time of Brahmanas) and 600 BC. By the time of Buddha (roughly sixth century BC) the idea of transmigration was well-established and a part and parcel of all Indic religions (Vedism, Jainism, and Buddhism).

I think it is safe to assume that the doctrine of karma and rebirth and its ethical basis came to the forefront pretty much at the same both in Hinduism and Buddhism. I imagine that in the same family some were Hindus and others Buddhists. This seems similar to China where the division amongst Taoists, Buddhists and Confucianists was not very clear cut. Just as image worship was developed first in Mahayana Buddhism and then passed on to Hinduism.

For whatever reason, the transmigration idea first becomes known to Kshyatrias and they transmit it to Brahmanas. Actually, a Kshatriya tells a Brahmana that it is for the lack of this knowledge that all the kings so far have been Kshatriyas.

How the idea might have come about is discussed in great detail in:

Imagining Karma by Gananath Obeyeskere

During the early Vedic period, it was assumed that people who die go to Pitraloka, the land of fathers. The question arose why the land of fathers does not get overcrowded. The idea of rebirth provided an answer to this question.

Upanishads talk of the two paths that the soul of a dead person can take. One that leads to Brahman (or, Devas) and the other that leads to rebirth. Gita says that those who die during the day in the light and waxing moon and during the sixth month period after winter solstice go to Brahman. Those who die during smoke at night and waning moon and the six month period after summer solstice are reborn. Bhishma, the patriarch of the Kuru clan, had the boon to be able to choose the time of his death, waited on his bed of arrows to die until after the winter solstice.

I think that this doctrine must have a spiritual meaning that I don't know. It seems too strange otherwise.

– April 15, 2021

Ego

I am upset when things don't go my way.
My ego is bruised, my pride is hurt.
Why is our ego so fragile and brittle
Not able to absorb even minor blows?

Ego is a problem
Very hard to overcome.
It bruises easily
Like a ripe peach
Falling from its tree.

Ego sucks out joy from life.
Creates misery and a bad temper.
But it is tenacious
And hard to let go.

Ego interferes with the natural flow of life
And for this reason, should be cast aside.
As long ego runs the show
No lasting joy can be had.

When Buddhism denies self
I think they are also denying ego.
Our ego even though
Philosophically non-existent
Is so bloated, it weighs us down
Increasing our sorrows and miseries.

– April 23, 2021

A Short Note about self and Self

Sometimes more things change more they remain the same. A case in point is "the self" in Hinduism and Buddhism.

Hinduism talks about Atman (the self of an individual) and Brahman (the universal self) and the great insight of the Upanishads is:

Atman = Brahman

Sometimes It is also expressed by:

self = Self

This is expressed in the great Upanishadic mahavakya:

तत् त्वम् असि

Thou Art That

This means you are what you seek. It is not your ego that is meant but your essential self.

Now Buddha denied the self of Upanishads both Atman and Brahman. Brahman essentially was replaced by something called Buddha nature which everyone has. Ishwar, the God with attributes that Hindus worshipped was replaced by the Shakya muni Buddha himself.

In Zen formulation of Buddhism, they talk of the little mind and the big mind and the great realization is:

The Little Mind = The Big Mind

Isn't it similar to Atman = Brahman?

It is not to say that many new ways of looking at things didn't come with Buddhism. Just to give one example, unlike Abrahamic religions there is no satan like figure in Hinduism but there is Mara, the tempter in Buddhism, somewhat similar to satan.

– May 2, 2021

Dual/Non-Dual

It is natural to think in terms of dualities in life. We have duality pairs everywhere. There is birth/death, light/dark, good/evil and countless more. So early philosophers and theologians thought in terms of duality. So ancient Persians imagined Ahura Majda, The God of pure light, all good and Angre Manu, the representative of evil. This was passed on to the ancient Hebrews and thereon to all Abrahamic religions.

Meanwhile, there was another current of thought was emerging in India, leading to the non-dual type of theologies. The Upanishads develop the ideas of the self(Atman) and the universal self(Brahman) and the realization that Atman = Brahman. So non-dual Vedanta reduces all reality to Brahman. So there is only one self and is the only thing that is real. This reality is called Sacchidananda = Sat + Chit + Ananda. Sat means real, Chit means conscious and Ananda is bliss. So Brahman is Real, conscious and Blissful.

Buddha realized that the essence of all is Shunyata, the emptiness. This emptiness is not a thing to be visualized but it is not nothing. It is nothing in the sense of 'not a thing.' This emptiness is pregnant with all the potentialities of all things that come to be. So it is like a field, sometimes referred to as the Buddha field.

Thus in a mathematical formulation, we might say that in Advaita Vedanta, the reality is reduced to one and in Buddhism, it is whittled down to zero.

So in the early history of Buddhism, Vedantins were Astikas(Those who believed in 'Asti' meaning 'Is,' and Buddhists were Nastikas(Those who believed in 'Nasti' I.e. 'Not Is.'

If memory serves me right, the well-known Buddhist scholar Nagarjuna, says in his book on the Madhyamika philosophy that his theory can be developed by assuming a Being and just as well assuming No-Being. However, he is inclined towards No-Being.

To summarize,

Abrahamic Religions: God/ Devil

Vedanta: God but no Devil (Somehow God mangos to perform the functions of both)

Buddhism: No God/ No Devil

But there is Nirvana vs. Samsara. But in the final analysis, esp. in Mahayana Buddhism, Nirvana = Samsara.

So either it is all clear or I have muddied the waters even more than before.

– May 7, 2021

Yoga, Vedanta and Tantra

In yoga, we control our natural tendencies. We suppress our desires and engage in activities that are prescribed for us without any desire for the fruits of our actions. So yoga is the path of restraint and denial. Once we overcome our nature (Maya) and take refuge in the self which is the same as the universal self we attain liberation.

Tantra on the other hand is not the path of denial. As Rajneesh pointed out it is a path of indulgence but with awareness. We are all Shiva/Shakti. Shakti or Maya is what makes the world possible. Shiva in his perfect state does not recognize his own nature so by his Shakti, he contracts himself I.e. becomes less aware of his absolute nature. He can do this because he has the freedom (swatantrya) to do so. In this contracted state he enjoys the world and strives to go back to his absolute status. As Shiva is not different from his Shakti(which has made the phenomenal world possible), he can enjoy this world with awareness and pursues self-realization I.e. his true nature. In other words, he can have his cake and eat it too. When he realizes his absolute nature, he realizes that he never really lost it. It was there all along.

Agamas(Tantra Scriptures) have described five powers of Shiva: Creation, Maintenance, Destruction, Concealment and Revealing.

Shiva conceals or contracts himself through the agency of his Shakti because he wants to experience the world and recognize himself in it. Then to complete the cycle he goes back to being Shiva again.

At the level of the sadhaka (practitioner), disappearance (tirohan) and reappearance (grace) of Shiva.

In the non-dual Vedanta of Shankara, the question of what is real is paramount. Real here means what is everlasting. It is concluded that only Brahman is real. The phenomenal world is unreal but Brahman residing in the human heart viz. Atman is real. The liberation is to recognize this. So the path as in Yoga is that of the rejection of Maya, the phenomenal world. Bondage is caused by Maya and liberation is to know that Brahman is the only reality. So cling only to the real and stop identifying with Maya. So this is also an austere path of renunciation and suppression of desires.

Tantra on the other hand accuses Vedanta of creating a false duality. Shiva (Brahman) and his Shakti (Maya) are not separate. Shiva is Shakti and Shakti is Shiva. Both are real. So, see the divine in everything and everywhere, reject nothing. Indulge but with awareness. You are Shiva and you are free to contract (nimesha) or expand (unmesha) at your volition (iccha shakti).

There are also Buddhist and Jain Tantras. In the seventh and eighth century, many great Buddhist teachers visited Tibet from India and introduced Buddhist Tantra. The most famous of these teachers is Padma Sambhava. This form of Tantra came to be known as Vajrayana. Vajrayana in the US after the exile of the fourteenth Dalai Lama to India, quite a lot of teachers have been lecturing and some have established their own centres. I may point out that Vajrayana has roughly the same spirit as the Hindu Tantra.

– May 13, 2021

Spanda

Spanda is a key concept in Kashmir Shaivism. It literally means vibration in the divine consciousness which is Shiva. Shiva wants to contract himself to enjoy the world which is actually his Shakti, he does it by spanda, often termed vibrationless vibration.

Something stirs in Shiva which is manifested as the primordial sound, called Nada. This nada gets concentrated into a point(Bindu). This Bindu is the energy of Shiva which includes all potentialities of becoming. This Bindu, the seed of everything, now expands into the phenomenal universe. Shiva is not different from this universe which is spread forth from him. It is said this universe mirrors Shiva but the image is not outside Shiva which is pure consciousness. There can be nothing outside this consciousness. Shiva in an eternal embrace with Shakti is a very apt image of this non-dual apparent duality.

Spanda in an individual can be felt by yogic techniques. It can be thought of as a divine creative impulse.

It is interesting to note that the word Brahman comes from a root which means to expand. So brahman literally expanded into this universe. Upanishad say, “sarvam khalu idam brahma.” All this is just Brahman.

– May 19, 2021

A Little Ditty

How much little things matter
Has been made clearer to me
In the aftermath of surgery
On my right hand.
First I had a dressing covering
My hand and much of my forearm.
After a couple of weeks
The dressing was replaced by a cast.
After another couple of weeks
The cast was removed
And replaced by a brace.
After using the brace for a couple of weeks
My spirit rebelled and
Yesterday I put aside the brace
And was able to clip nails of my left hand
With my right hand
The same one I had surgery on.
Friends that seemed like
A crowning achievement
Like a glorious miracle.
Today I went for physical therapy
Without my brace on
And was duly chastised for this lapse.
I hope friends you will forgive
My lapse in using my right hand
To write this little ditty
For your info and pleasure.

– August 10, 2021

Approval

Have you ever thought
That much of our happiness depends
On how others view us.
We all want to be liked, loved, appreciated
Admired, respected, applauded
Lauded, venerated and idolized.
When we perceive it happening
We feel deserving and content.

We want others to admire
Our wit and wisdom
Our accomplishments, our humbleness
And our sophistication in the affairs of the world.

Even a baby looks for parents' approval.
Teenagers rebel against parents and teachers
But want approval from their peers.
A student thrives on teacher's approval
And in this day age, a teacher's pay raise
Depends on pupils' approval.

In Gita, Lord Krishna says,
Those whose wisdom has matured
Are satisfied and happy within themselves.
They don't need anyone's approval to be happy.

Now look around you
And see if anyone fits the bill.
I for one have never found anyone
So blessed and fulfilled
That they want nothing
And expect nothing from anyone.

Our swamis desire obedience

And reverence from their devotees.
Our leaders thrive in public adulation
And wither without it.

Our actors, artists, authors, poets
Performers and professors
Priests, preachers, pandits
Acharyas, mullahs, and pastors
All crave applause, adulation and veneration.

I pretend to be a poet
So I need your admiring comments
Please don't be stingy
It costs you nothing
But proves my point that
There are hardly any exceptions
To the rule that we all need
Others' approval to be satisfied and happy.

– August 21, 2021

Aging

As we age, we witness
Our bodies deteriorating
Our faculties diminishing
Our memory worsening
Our desires diminishing
Our spirit flagging
Vitality declining but folks proclaim
These are your golden years.

I have to admit that
If you have worked all your life
You would have sufficient money
To 'enjoy' life that is if you are still
Capable of enjoyment.

Aging makes you witness
The dissolution of
Your body and mind.
It dims hope and illusion.
Without hope there is dissolution.
Without illusion and dreams
Life is dreary and romance impossible.
So we often fall prey to despair.

Age brings wisdom, they say
But the sad truth is that
Nobody wants to heed it
In this age of moral confusion.

In the end, we turn to
Philosophy or religion for consolation
Hope that the former is not just confusion
And the latter delusion.

– August 30, 2021

Kabir and Krishna

Life is full of pleasure and pain.
You can't have just pleasure or just pain.
Dualities can't ever exist alone.

Everywhere there are flowers and thorns.
Everywhere there is pleasure and pain.
Without going overboard, enjoy your pleasures
When in pain, remember its transient nature.

Staying still or walking the road
Surrounded by beauty if you just behold
The wind, the sky, the sun, the moon
People, plants, deserts and dunes.
Mountains, valleys and prairies plain
Hills, rivers, valleys and all terrains.
Clouds, fog, mist, rainbows and rain. Enjoy it all while it lasts.

Do what you can without any expectation
To relieve the miseries of the world.
Hold nothing and covet nothing.
Departing you will lose everything.

Kabir says: Standing in the marketplace
I pray for everyone's welfare.
No friends and no enemies, I have.

Live like a lotus leaf, Krishna said,
Which has water as its abode
But low and behold, wonder of wonders
Leaf by water is never wetted.

– September 5, 2021

For those who know Hindi: Kabir's saying in the penultimate stanza is:

कबिरा खड़ा बजार में, सबकी माँगै खैर।
ना काहू सो दोस्ती, ना काहू सों बैर॥

Advice for Men Only

If you love your woman
Don't behave as if you are smarter than her.
Don't talk about things in which you are smart
Instead, talk about things in which she is smart.
I say even play stupid deliberately.
Because women like to point
Out how dumb you have been
Or you have no sense of style or fashion
Or how wrong you are in this and that.
It gives a woman satisfaction and happiness
To admonish her man now and again.
Most wives consider their husbands to be idiots.
Just go along with this fact or fiction.
Let her have her little pleasure
It does you no harm.
Perhaps she will reward you
In the bedroom as a result
Or cook your favorite meal
Or go to theater with you
For a play, concert or movie.
She may even learn
To watch football with you.
Possibilities are endless
All you have to do play
A little dumber than what you are.
You were dumb when you married her
And over the years you have become dumber still.
Use your dumbness to your advantage
And all will be well.

– September 24, 2021

Old-Age and Happiness

Old age is no fun but it can be lively.
You can think of the days when you were happy
Even though you had no money.
Then money came with all its trappings
Job, house, cars, maids
And you married your darling honey.

You enjoyed that life to the hilt
But the good life took a toll
And heart trouble bought you down a peg.
You took measures to improve your health
But as all things body declines with age.

You started to get old.
Fires of passion began to cool
And the spectre of decrepitude and fear of death
Began haunting you every now and then.
Now you are old and some but not all your fears
Turned out to be true.

You still have reasonable health
And you are not desperately holding on to wealth.
You can laugh and enjoy your friends and folks
And grand-children if you have any.
All you have will be taken away someday
So why not give it away today.
Be compassionate but remain detached
Till your day under the sun is ended.

Laughing at yourself is a very good medicine
When your soul is troubled and weary.
Wallow not in self-pity
And find satisfaction in some activity.

It seems paradoxical but true
That self-importance brings misery.
You are just a speck of dust
In this vast and mysterious universe
Do your part until you depart
Just know that this is not the end of the story.

– October 6, 2021

I Long for the Days

I long for the days
When lies were not called alternate facts.
When everyone agreed as to what was news
And what was a commentary on news?

I long for the days
When Donald Trump was just a hack
And not a political force in right-wing politics.

I long for the days when
Even villains had some decency.
Nixon resigned when facing certain impeachment.

Now we had a con man impeached twice
But still shamelessly hung on to power
And not willing to concede
Even now that he lost.

I long for the days when you lost an election
You conceded and didn't conspire
To lead an insurrection to topple
A lawfully elected government.

What baffles me is
Why about a third of the voters
Are so much taken by a dishonest
Conman to support all his
Fantasies and part with their hard-earned
Money to this good-for-nothing dolt.

This man has done an incalculable harm
To our democratic institutions, Judiciary and environment.
He has tarnished our reputation in International circles
And betrayed our long-cherished ideals.

– October 23, 2021

Oh, What a Thrill That Would Be!

When I read that the Andromeda galaxy
Is two and a half million light-years away from us
It made me think that when you look at it
Through a powerful telescope
You are seeing what it was like
Two and a half million light-years ago.
It boggles my mind just to think of such enormities.

But it made me wonder if somehow
We could see our own past
Here on earth from many millions of thousands of years ago,
What a treat that would be to our eyes and ears!

We could see dinosaurs roaming the earth,
We could see and hear woolly mammoth trumpet,
We could see the evolution of species
Through our own eyes.
Imagine what a thrill that would be!

We could see how we survived the last ice age
A mere ten thousand years ago.
We could the cosmic form
Krishna showed to Arjuna in the middle of the battlefield,
We could see the exodus of Jews from Egypt.
We could see Jesus delivering the sermon on the mount.
We could watch Buddha delivering his fire sermon.
We could see Plato and his academy
And watch Aristotle teach Alexander.

We could watch the encounter between king Puru and Alexander
Alexander asked defeated King Puru
How he should treat him.
Puru's majestic reply was, as a king should treat another king.
We could see how wily Chanakya and Chandragupta

Took over the kingdom of Magadha
From powerful Nanda kings.

We could watch King Ashoka recoil from violence
And receive Buddha dharma.
We could see the hands that carved Kailash Mandir
Out of a single rock at Ellora
And hands that painted caves of Ajanta.
We could see the magnificent sun temple
Of Konarka being created.
We could see the monk Xuan Zang
Make a journey to the west
Teach at Nalanda and carry
Sacred Buddhist scriptures back to China.

We could see Akbar and Birbal jesting with each other.
We could witness the sculptors of Chola kings
Make beautiful Nataraja images.

This and much more we would experience
If indeed such a thing were made possible
By the skill and ingenuity
Of modern human scientists and engineers.
Oh, what a thrill that would be!

– October 24, 2021

Strife and Progress

Have you ever thought
That all progress in the world
Is rooted In chaos, conflict, disorder,
Confusion, enchantment, Delusion,
Desire, power-lust, murder and plunder?

In Judeo-Christian tradition,
Satan connives with Eve to persuade Adam
To eat the forbidden apple.
In a direct breach of God's command.

Adam and Eve are exiled from Eden
And creation ensues.
Their sons Cane and Abel quarrel
Abel is killed by Caine
And Caine's progeny inhabits the earth.

That makes all of us descendants
Of a murderous villain.
Shouldn't this be called the Original Sin
Instead of the disobedience of Adam and Eve
To a tyrannical Jehova, a jealous God?

Struggle, strife, war and disorder
Bring forth, art, literature and poetry.
What would Homer write about
Without the Trojan war
And the murderous return of Odysseus?

Without the awful feud between
Waring cousins Kauravas and Pandavas
Vyasa couldn't have written The great epic
The Mahabharata and there would be
No propounding of the Gita, the Song of the Lord

To a despondent Arjuna on the battlefield.

Some of the most significant literature
Has been produced in the wake of
Two terrible world wars.
Korean and Vietnam wars have also given rise
To myriad novels, movies, TV shows and plays.

I think this uncomfortable fact
Must be reckoned with
That wars and destruction in their wake
Often bring progress, jobs,
Prosperity, literature and arts.

– November 2, 2021

Masked Beauty or Beauty Masked

I ask if there will come a time
When only bank-robbers will wear a mask
When we will be able to shake hands
Without fear of getting infected.

Will there be a time when this
Pandemic will be a distant memory
And normal human discourse will resume
And people will not be running scared?

Will a time come when
Our schools, colleges and universities
Would be functioning like before
And our churches, temples, mosques
And synagogues conduct
Proper worship and prayers again?

If this does not happen
I have a ridiculous vision
Of white might happen.

If evolutionary forces reckon
That those wearing masks
Survive longer than those who don't.
A mutation may produce children
Born with a mask
Sort of like kangaroo babies
Born in a pouch.

Such a child will be naturally protected
By this biological mask
From the pesky coronavirus
And the whole world
Will propagate this ugliness.

Perhaps in time people will
Compare these masks
And standards of mask beauty
Will be established.

Perhaps there will be unisex
Mask beauty contests.
People will not only accept
These biological masks
But will also be conditioned
To think of them as beautiful.

– November 30, 2021

A Clear and Present Danger

Do you know that there is another pandemic out there
Which makes the corona pandemic
Pale in significance?

Worse still no one has come up with a vaccine
For this strange illness
That is sweeping across the nation
And perhaps the world.

The folks who suffer from it consider themselves totally normal
And go about their business
Not only risking their lives
But also the lives of others.

Perhaps you guessed what I am talking about.
It is a disease highly prevalent
But not yet recognized
By the medical profession.

I am, of course, talking about
Mass idiocy which has taken
The nation by storm and is threatening not only
Our well-being but our very way of life.

These folks are against vaccine, masks, social distancing
And other life-saving measures.
They misconstrue that
These measures impinge on their liberty.

These right-wing ideologues
Are also poisoning the public discourse
And endangering democracy.
Can you, dear reader, figure out
A way out of this clear and present danger?

– December 17, 2021

Passion vs. Compassion

A full life is a passionate life, be it a passion for fine arts
Sciences or mathematics or politics, social service
Or anything you feel deeply about.

With passion you also need compassion
For who are left behind or were never in the game
For their own fault or for no fault of theirs.
Compassion that reaches out to friend and foe alike
Because we all have our problems
We are trying to resolve and make sense of our lives.

For some like the holy lamas of Tibet
Compassion itself is a passion
That is to say that they are passionately compassionate.

Even though it is impossible to live
Without some violence to other sentient beings
We ought to minimize it as much as possible.
All sentient beings are subject to pain and suffering
Just like us so we all are fellow sufferers.

It takes very little to smile at someone
Or say hello to a passer-by
Any act of kindness or sympathy
Helps both the receiver and the giver.

My new year's vow is to be a little gentler, a bit kinder
Be happier and more cheerful
Smile more and share happiness.

I think for a balanced and happy life
Both passion and compassion
Are required, perhaps compassion
A bit more than passion.

– December 28, 2021

The Safer Shores

It is an understatement to say
That we are living in strange times.
People are upset, disturbed, bored
And many are downright unhappy.

Corona like the many-headed
Monstrous snake hydra of
The Greek mythology
Has spread its fangs far and wide.

It is affecting travel, supply chain
International and domestic commerce
People's livelihood, freedom
And right to remain safe.

So far the only effective tool
Has been the vaccine and the mask
But many misguided souls
Threaten our safety and well-being
By refusing to wear a mask
And getting vaccinated.

These misfits presumably believe
In alternate facts
Popularized by the wrong-headed
Kelly Ann Conway.
But alternate facts are just lies
Believed by morons and misfits.

An ancient Chinese curse says
May you live in interesting times.
Interesting for historians may be
But decidedly deadly for common folks.

Many if not the most of us

Wouldn't mind trading interesting times
As they indeed are
For a more prosaic and dull but safer existence.

I pray to all divine beings, bodhisattvas
Saints, living and dead wise persons
To bestow their blessings on us
And let our boats cross to the safer shores.

– February 13, 2022

Lack of Vision

If there is a scriptor for life
He must be asleep on the job.
Life seems to go where it will
Without a clear purposed intent.

Belief systems have fallen away not by design
But by gradual loss of faith.
One is alone in this vast cosmos
Trying to find a way.

Freedom is a good thing
But useless without a sense of purpose.
At times, there seems to be no clear reason
To choose one thing over the other.

Life is neither good nor bad.
It is what you make of it.
A purpose or focus is helpful
But not mandatory.

Covid has destroyed much of
Social life and simple pleasures.
Fresh thinking is needed
To bring back the zest in life.

The world is in a terrible place
With Putin's unnecessary war
Bringing doom and destruction
To both Russia and Ukraine.

We all have to pull ourselves with our bootstraps.
There are no gods to help and no demons to hurt.
It is for each of us to make a stand
With forbearance and dignity.

– March 17, 2022

Modern Maladies

They say happiness is a choice we make.
After all, nobody gets up in the morning
And tells himself that he is going to be unhappy today.

Then why it is that invariably we succeed
In making ourselves unhappy
Over something trivial
Or over nothing at all.
Sometimes sadness swoops over us
Coming from nowhere
And makes us miserable.

We often feel that we have lost our moorings.
It is true that for many moderns
Religion or spirituality does not satisfy the soul anymore.
You can see how empty
Are the traditional places of worship.

On the other hand, you can see
How crowded the evangelistic churches are.
Obviously, they are providing people
Something they want or need.
But I don't think these institutions
Will work for secular humanistic
Modern humans.

One religion that seems to have made
Some inroads in the modern American psyche
Is Buddhism, sometimes called
The favourite eastern religion of the West.
The two popular Buddhist sects
Are Zen and Tibetan
Both varieties of the Mahayana Buddhism.

Of the two Zen is sterner and less voluble.
Tibetan Buddhism is wordy, lofty
And full of great platitudes.
People pick them according to
Their own predilections.

One path that should be better known
Is Kashmir Shaivism.
Its great proponent was Abhinavgupta
Author of the great five-volume tome
Called Tantraloka.

This path is not ascetic like Buddhism
But sees all things as sacred
And infused with the divine.
It exhorts the followers
To enjoy the world and its bounties
But with awareness of the ever-present
Divine power.

– April 22, 2022

Ominous Clouds

The news is so horrific
It is hard to wrap your head around it.
Images of children mercilessly slaughtered
Teachers horrified, and some also killed
Dance before the eyes.
Poor parents drowning in grief
Their darlings are never coming home.
They didn't know that when their children
Left home this morning
They will never see them again.

A callous youth of eighteen
Carries out this act of terror
Prompted by what I can't imagine.
The killing of blacks in Buffalo
Just a few days ago
Was prompted by hateful philosophy
Of white supremacists
But what prompted this kid in Texas
To engage in these horrendous murders
Of little kids, I can't fathom.

It was almost fifty-six years ago
When I first set foot on the American land.
Just a couple of months before I arrived
There was a mass murder at the University of Texas.
Fifteen people were gunned down by this crazy kid
From a campus tower.
We have to wonder why this outrage continues
Year after year, only in the United States of America.
The merchants of death keep selling their AK forty-sevens
And AR fifteens indiscriminately
Without any background checks and no scrutiny.
Politicians in cahoots with the gun lobby
Prevent any legislation
That could prevent these senseless tragedies.

These events weigh heavily on us
Leading to a deep soul-searching
Isn't there anything that we can do
To lift these ominous clouds
And restore sanity?

– May 26, 2022

Our Moods

How much of our lives
Do we really control?
You may wake up in the morning
And anticipate a terrific day ahead.
But the news comes of a dear friend passing.
There is nothing that can be done
But your mood turns sombre.
If it doesn't you would feel guilty
Of being insensitive to the memory of your friend.

Sometimes I think that
Moods are like clouds
Occluding our true being.
Clouds pass as clouds do
And our true nature shines through.

Do you realize that often
We don't even know how we are
Going to react to something
Unless we fall back on the memory
Of something similar that happened in the past.

Much of the practice of the psychologists
And the psychiatrists consist in part
Of these learned human behaviors
And basing their treatments on these observations.

Tribal witch doctors do much of the same thing
In their cultural settings in
Time-honored shamanic practices.
Such practices can be found all over the world.
I have seen examples in India in my ancestral village.
These treatments appeared to be
Just as effective as the modern treatments

Albeit a whole lot cheaper.

Sometimes we may control events
Howsoever imperfectly
And at other events control us
And sometimes overwhelm us.
You are enjoying your day
But then you hear that a loved one is sick
And you are filled with anxiety.

Have you noticed that at times
You are sad and depressed
For no tangible reason.
Maybe it is bad weather
That is fouling your mood.
But you can't tell for sure
Because sometimes the weather is terrific
But you may still feel bad
Perhaps because you are not able to go out
But maybe not, you can't say.

The fact of the matter is
That there are too many variables
Controlling our mood
To say much with absolute certainty.
I sometimes just wait a bit
For uneasiness to ease
Which it invariably does.

At other times, I just get busy
Maybe cleaning my office
Rearranging my books
Cooking dinner, doing dishes
Or, read a trashy thriller.

Great literature is good
When your mood is normal

But reading Dostoevsky
When your mood is already sombre
Is a very bad idea indeed.

When my mood is like that
I read fantasies like the Hobbit
Or, Castenada or Murakami
To revive my sagging spirit.

Meeting a good friend
Is also a sight for sore eyes
And a balm to the spirit.
So friend, when we meet next time
It will put me in a good mood
Even if it is initially not so.
So let us meet soon
And help both of us feel good.

– May 28, 2022

Old Age

I know that all is impermanent.
There is nothing you can grasp and hold onto.
But still, my heart aches when I see
A formerly confident and proud person
But today old and decrepit
Doesn't even seem like a shadow of what he or she was.

I recently attended a retirees lunch-one
It was good to see old friends and colleagues
But it felt bitter-sweet.
I am saddened to see old age and disease
Having ravished bodies of many.
Nothing any on can do; change is the law of nature.
Time which in Hindi is called Kala
Also means death appropriately
Keeps marching on unhindered and unabated.

It is satisfying to see that many including me can still
Walk and talk and in spite of all their afflictions
Can still function and enjoy life to some degree.
But for how long is anyone's guess.

I have only one wish that I die
Before I become a burden to
My loved ones.
I hate to exercise but I do
So as to ward off disability
And other horrors of old age.

I will at this sobering note
Wishing you all good health
And a long and joyous life.

– June 23. 2022

Nine Gems

The idea of nine gems is extremely popular in India since ancient times. Early on these were real physical gems:

1. Pearl (मोती)
2. Ruby (लाल)
3. Topaz (पुखराज)
4. Diamond (हीरा)
5. Emerald (पन्ना या मरकत)
6. Lapis Lazuli (लाजवर्द)
7. Coral (मूँगा)
8. Sapphire (नीलम)
9. Zirconia (गोमेद या अमेरिकन हीरा)

Later on, this concept was transferred to royal courts and kings and rulers started certain of their courtiers gems which were nine in number.

The first king to do so, as far as we know, was the king Vikramaditya, presumably of Ujjain. In 57 BCE, a calendar called Vikrama was started in his name. His nine jewels based on the legends were:

1. Dhanavantari, a physician
2. Kshapanaka
3. Amar Sinha, compiler of the famous Amar Kosha, a Sanskrit thesaurus giving synonyms for a number of words.
4. Sanku
5. Vetal Bhatta (There has to be a relation between him and Vetal of Vetal pachisi)
6. Ghata-Karpara
7. Kalidas, the foremost Sanskrit poet. Often called the Shakespeare

of Sanskrit literature. Ironically he lived approximately sixteen centuries before Shakespeare.

8. Varahamihira, a famous astronomer and mathematician.
9. Yararuchi.

Akbar, the Moghul emperor from 1556 to 1605, also had nine gems in his court:

1. Abul Fazal
2. Faizi (Abul Fazal's brother)
3. Abdurrahim Khankhana, a military commander, a generous philanthropist and a popular poet.
4. Mulla Do-Piaza
5. Raja Todarmal (Headed Akbar's Revenue Department)
6. Tansen, the foremost classical musician of the time
7. Raja Birbal, a constant companion of the emperor. Well-known for his wit and common sense.
8. Raja Mansingh of Amber. He famously tried to make peace with Akbar and Maharana Pratap of Mewar.
9. Fakir Aziao-Din (Not much is known about him.)

– August 20, 2022

Pain, Pain Go Away

You and I have a long history together
But you are not a friend
At least I have never thought of you as one.
You have been a constant source of suffering
And untold misery.
How can I think of you as a friend?

In past when you were not quite
As painful now
I thought of some positive things
That I could attribute to you.
Because to alleviate the misery
I met with many experts
Psychologists, healers, energy medics
And myriad others.
Nobody could heal my malady
But I valued the association
With the people I met.

Now with you becoming
Much more severe with no tangible
Relief in sight, I can't think of you
In such positive light.

You indeed are an awful demon
With myriad fangs and talons
To torture me and make my
Life an absolute hell.
Why don't you just leave me alone
And just fade away.
No one will mourn you
I assure you.
You serve no useful purpose

To me or anyone else.
You are a scourge indeed.

I have been advised that
Due to my long association with you
I should extend a hand of friendship to you.
But I can't bring myself to do that
You have all but ruined my life.
I have no reason to befriend you
And all the reason to detest you.

So you miserable pain in my head literally
Go away and stay away
Don't even think of coming back another day.
I don't like you so why do you persist
In staying with me.
Go away and find peace in oblivion
Which you so richly deserve.

– September 10, 2022

Shakuntala

One of the most charming stories told in the Mahabharata is that of Shakuntala and Dushyanta.

Once upon a time, the royal sage Vishvamitra was undergoing a severe tapasya(penance). As usual Indra, the king of heaven was scared that Vishvamitra was after his throne. So he sent a heavenly nymph Menaka to distract and seduce Vishwamitra. This she succeeded in doing and in due time a lovely baby daughter was born to her. Now heavenly nymphs don't care to take care of babies so she abandoned her baby and flew to heaven. Nearby some birds called 'Shakun' were nesting. The birds covered the baby with their feathers. The baby was discovered by a forest-dwelling Rishi Kanva. He brought the baby to his ashram and named her Shakuntala, the one protected by Shakun birds.

Shakuntala grew up to be a very beautiful maiden. One day while Rishi Kanva was gone to pick flowers for his daily puja, Shakuntala had a royal visitor, King Dushyanta of Hastinapur. He had lost his way while chasing a deer. He fell in love with Shakuntala and her with him. Overcome with desire for one another, they performed a Gandharva Vivaha(an accepted form of wedding for the royal personage) and made love. Rishi Kanva accepted Shakuntala's choice. In due course, Shakuntala delivered a handsome baby boy. The boy was named Bharata.

When Bharata was three years old, Shakuntala took him to meet his father but King Dushyanta refused to recognize her due to fear of public scandal. Then a voice from the heavens came like thunder instructing the king to accept Shakuntala and her son.

In due course, Bharata became an illustrious king and some say that the ancient name Bhaarata for India comes from this king's name.

Kalidasa, the second-century poet and dramatist wrote his most famous play, Abhijnan Shaakuntalam (The Recognition of Shakuntala) based on the Mahabharata story. But he added a twist to the story. In this account, Dushyanta gave Shakuntala a ring that she should bring when visiting him. Now once Shakuntala was daydreaming about her love, while a Rishi named Durvaasaa, known for his fierce temper visited Rishi Kanva's ashram. Shakuntala failed to welcome the Rishi. Durvaasaa cursed her that the person she was dreaming about would not recognize her. Now, when Shakuntala was going to visit her love, she inadvertently dropped the ring in a stream and indeed Dushyanta failed to recognize her. She had to leave and raise her son by herself. Now it just so happened that a fish swallowed the ring. The fish was caught by a fisherman who found the ring with the royal insignia in its stomach. Recognizing the royal seal, the fisherman took the ring to the king. On seeing the ring, the king remembered Shakuntala and was full of remorse about his harsh treatment of Shakuntala and her son. He sent his royal entourage to bring Shakuntala and Bharata to him and all was well.

– November 27, 2022

A Folk-Tale about Kalidasa

Once upon a time, there lived in the city of Ujjain, a wise princess who had vowed to marry only a man who defeated her in a religious debate (Shastratha in Sanskrit). Many ambitious princes bit dust in debate with princess Vidfyottama. Some vanquished princes sought revenge. Providence helped them when they found a young man trying to chop off a branch of a tree on which he was sitting. They got him off the tree and told him that he will get to marry the princess if he did as they told him to. This man was Kalidasa.

The princes and their Brahmana advisors instructed him not to speak at all when they took him to see the princess. At the king's court, they declared Kalidasa had taken a vow of silence and so he will speak only in signs. Debate started. The princess raised one finger to indicate that there is only one God. Kalidasa thought she wants to poke him in an eye. Kalidasa raised two fingers to indicate he would get her in both eyes. Pandits accompanying Kalidasa explained that even though God is one, he is manifested in two forms: Paramatma (the supreme God who is absolutely free) and Jivatma (a creature who is limited and bound by his karma.)

The princess raised her hand highlighting the five senses. Kalidasa thought she wants to slap him so he raised a fist. Pandits explained that it means that one should keep the five senses under control.

There were some questions and answers in the same vein and Vidyottama consented to marry Kalidasa. So they wed and started living together. One night she heard a camel bleat and was afraid. Kalidasa said it was just a camel. A camel is called an Ushtra (उष्ट्र) in Sanskrit but Kalidasa pronounced it Utra (उट्र). The princess was livid at the deception and pushed Kalidasa out a window into a well. It just so happened that the well was dry and inside it, there was a statue of the Goddess Kali (the back one). In being thrown out of the window, Kalidasa cut part of her tongue which fell on the Kali idol. Kali thought Kalidasa was offering his tongue to her as a sacrifice. Devi blessed him to instantly acquire all knowledge and blessed him with proficiency in the language.

This story also explains the name Kalidasa, a servant of Kali.

– December 6, 2022

Trishanku

Once upon a time in ancient India, there was a king named Satyavrata. He was a great warrior and a great king. He became very much enamoured of his great glory and he thought he was deserving of going to Indra's heaven with his physical body. He asked Rishi Vashistha to help him ascend to heaven with his physical body. Vashishtha tried to convince him that it was against all rules. The king was not convinced and asked Vashishtha's sons for help. The sons took it as an insult to their father and cursed him to become ugly and unattractive. He was wandering around in a forest distraught and heartbroken. He chanced to run into Rishi Vishwamitra, a great rival of Vashishtha.

Vishwamitra decided to help the king in this endeavour. He tried to make the king ascend to heaven but Indra, the king of heaven stopped his progress. Vishwamitra was enraged and started creating an alternate universe with a new Indra. Indra was alarmed and explained to Vishwamitra that no corporal bodies were allowed in heaven. Vishwamitra finally understood this but still wanted to stand by the promise he gave to the king.

Vishwamitra making the king ascend to heaven and Indra kicking him with face down towards the earth. A compromise was reached with Vishwamitra allowed him to keep the heavenly constellations and creatures that he had created. For example, Vishwamitra created Water Buffaloes and coconut. The king was allowed to stay in a luxurious palace between heaven and earth created by Vishwamitra.

The name Trishanku(three sins) refers to the three sins he had committed. As a prince, he was temporarily exiled by his father for some misdeeds. The second sin was that he killed the milch cow of Vashishtha and the third was that he consumed the unsanctified meat of his kill.

In common parlance when one is compared to Trishanku, it is meant that this person is in limbo, not able to go up or down, just hanging upside down in midair.

– December 17, 2022

Harishchandra

Harishchandra, son of Trishanku, was even more illustrious than his father. He is known for his devotion to truth. He is celebrated even today in folk arts and popular theatre. I remember watching a performance of "Satya-Harishchandra" by a travelling theatre group in my village over sixty years ago. Gandhi ji was profoundly moved by a performance of Harishchandra's story when he was a young boy.

Aspects of Harishchandra's story are similar to the story of Job in the Old Testament. Job is a righteous and upright man, devoted to God. Satan claims this is all due to God having provided Job with everything. God allows Satan to test Job with no holds barred except that Satan will not deprive Job of his life. The job comes through all the trials that Satan puts him through. Job remains steadfast in his devotion to God.

Once upon a time, Narada(a wandering sage and musician), Indra(the king of heaven), Sages Vishwamitra and Vashishtha were having a discussion about whether there was a righteous and truthful king on earth. Vashishtha said yes indeed King Harishchandra was truly noble, righteous and a lover of truth. Vishwamitra was assigned the task go testing the king.

Once when the king had gone on a hunt, he inadvertently offended Vishwamitra by intruding on him while he was performing a holy sacrifice. Vishwamitra was livid with rage. The king tried to placate him by offering him whatever he wanted. He demanded the king's whole kingdom. The king was allowed to leave with his son and wife with only the clothes they wore.

Harishchandra goes to the holy city of Kashi with his wife and son. He finds employment with a Chandala who was to collect a fee from anyone who came to cremate a body on the cremation ground. His son fell ill and died. Vishwamitra appeared and he demanded Dakshina, a customary tribute after a sacrifice. The king is willing to sell himself to the Chandala to procure money to pay for his son's cremation and to pay Vishwamitra.

Before the king is able to do that, Indra appears. Vishwamitra and Indra are satisfied with the king's virtuous conduct. His son is revived by Indra. Vishwamitra returns his kingdom. The king and his family return to Ayodhya, his capital and all is well.

– January 23, 2023

The Descent of Ganga

What do you think when you take a look at the magnificent collection of stars called The Milky Way? Ancient Indians saw it as a heavenly river of stars and called it the Akash Ganga.

How does The Akash Ganga relate to the Ganga, the holiest river of India? The Hindu myth relates how the heavenly Ganga was brought to the earth.

King Sagara of Ayodhya was an ancestor of lord Rama. Sagara had two queens. One queen gave birth to an enormous gourd which was cut apart into 60,000 pieces and each piece was placed in a jar of milk. In due time this queen had 60,000 warrior sons. The second queen had just one son who was not very well-behaved. King Sagara was performing a horse sacrifice. The horse was let loose and 60,000 princes were following it. In the subterranean, a Rishi named Kapila was busy in tapas and the horse was grazing peacefully near the rishi. Sagara's sons thought that Rishi had stolen the horse. They spoke to Kapila rudely. The Rishi gave them a fierce look, reducing the princes to heaps of ash. King Sagara sent his other son to look for the lost sons but to no avail. About three generations passed with attempts to salvage 60,000 princes and send them to their proper places in heaven.

King Bhagiratha, the great-grandson of Sagara was persistent and after a great tapas, found that if the great Ganga were to come down and wash down the ashes of dead princes, they will get their proper release. Bhagiratha prayed to the creator God Brahma who advised him to pray to the heavenly Ganga to come down and to lord Shiva to receive Ganga on his matted forehead so the earth can sustain the fierce current.

Thus Bhagiratha was able to bring the divine Ganga to earth where all beings could enjoy her blessings.

Even now when somebody makes an extraordinary effort to achieve a goal we call this effort the Bhagiratha effort.

Here is a 1910 painting of the descent of Ganga by Raja Ravi Varma:

– February 8, 2023

Prequel to Harishchandra Story

King Harishchandra and his wife Shaibya (Taramati in some sources) were very happy except for the fact that they had no children. They prayed To Varuna, the deity of open skies who later became the lord of all waters. Varuna granted their wish but on one condition. If the first child was a male they had to sacrifice him to Varuna. The first child was indeed a byname Rohitashva (meaning a red horse). The king kept postponing the sacrifice but eventually tried to acquire a human substitute for his son.

They found a dirt-poor Brahman with three sons. The oldest son was very dear to his father and the youngest to her mother. The middle son Shunahshepa (literally meaning the tail of a horse) was the most disposable so he was to the sacrificial grounds. Varuna was happy too as he preferred a Brahman over a Kshatriya for sacrifice.

Nobody wanted to perform the sacrifice until the Shunahshepa's father the wretch that he was willing to snuff the light out of his own son. Shunahshepa started praying to Agni, the bearer of all sacrifices to the gods. Agni advised him to pray to Varuna and Indra. Shunahshepa prayed very eloquently And the gods relented and prevented the sacrifice. Shunahshepa became a famous Rishi and contributed many verses to Rigveda, the oldest book of the Hindus.

Some scholars have opined that this might have been a step in turning away from the human sacrifice that was performed sometime in Vedic times.

– February 27, 2023

Vritra, the Dragon

In the hoary mythological past, Vritra, the handless, footless dragon held all the waters of the world making it desolate and causing untold miseries to living creatures. Indra, the king of gods and the wielder of thunderbolt struck the dragon and killed him. The whole world rejoiced.

Then problems arose. Vritra was a Brahmin and killing a Brahmin was considered a heinous sin. Brahma-hatya, the demon incarnation of Brahminicide started chasing and harassing the king of gods. Indra went hiding in a lotus stalk. Jupiter, the preceptor of gods sought out the illustrious human king Nahusha and requested him to rule in place of Indra.

Nahusha obliged and moved to svarga, the abode of Indra. There he met Shachi, Indra's wife who was beautiful beyond words. Nahusha wanted to make love to her. She asked for time and sought the advice of Jupiter. Jupiter advised her to ask Nahusha to come to her palace in a palanquin carried by the seven sages. Nahusha obliged and spoke rudely to sages to hurry. Agastya, one of the seven sages cursed him angrily and made him fall from svarga.

The Vritra's story is told in Rigveda around 1500 BCE. Here Indra is glorified after killing Vritra. A thousand years later, Indra has become a minor deity in India. Vritra is supposed to be a powerful virtuous king. Indra is jealous and thinks Vritra is after his throne. So he kills Vritra causing an uproar. He is redeemed only with the help of Lord Vishnu. He performs a horse sacrifice per advice of Vishnu to atone for his misdeed.

– March 14, 2023

Here and now

If you are old it is not a choice.
You don't remember the past.
There is no future.
There only is here and now.

As Zen Buddhists say eat when hungry
Sleep when tired above all don't wobble.

Be steady and steadfast
Play your hand as well as you can.
All is impermanent.
Misery results when we fail
To accept the inevitability of change.

Ancient wisdom from India says
All this is Lila, the play of the divine
And you and all sentient beings are part of this play.

So don't worry, rejoice.
Remember everything passes including you.
So let go of everything.
There is nothing to grasp
And nothing to hold on to.

Let all be happy.
Let all be well.
Let no sorrow touch
Any sentient being.

As in an ancient Hindu prayer
We pray the divine
To lead us from darkness to light
From death to life immortal.
And let peace reign supreme.

– March 25, 2023

Yaksha Prashna

Once upon a time while Pandava brothers were in exile, they took an errand to help a Brahmana. Pandavas got lost in the forest and they were all terribly thirsty. Yudhisthira sent his brothers in search of water. There was a lake not too far away. Nakula, Sahadeva, Bhima and Arjuna all went one by one but no-one came back. The lake was guarded by an Yaksha. Each Pandava was asked by the yaksha to answer before drinking the water. But each one ignored the yaksha's request, drank the water and fell unconscious.

Finally Yudhisthira himself came and decided to answer the yaksha before drinking water. The yaksha asks a total of thirty-three questions. I will mention just few:

Q: What does not close its eyes while asleep?

A: Fish

Q; What does not move after birth?

A: An egg.

Q; What if renounced makes one agreeable?

A: Pride

Q: What if renounced leads to no regret?

A: Anger.

Q: What is the most surprising thing about humans?
A: Everyday, numerous living entities are dying but those who remain believe that they will somehow live for ever.

Q: What is the highest dharma in the world?

A: Refrain from injuring others.

Q: Who is the friend of an exile?

A: A companion.

Q: Who is a man's best friend?

A: Wife.

At the end of the dialog, the yaksha reveals that he is Yudhisthira's father, the god Dharma and he has come to visit his son. Then Yaksha asks Yudhisthira to revive one of his brothers. Yudhisthira choses Nakula. The Yaksha questions his choice. Why did he not chose the great bowman Arjuna or tremendously powerful Bhima. Yudhisthira says he wants each of his mothers have a surviving son. As Nakula is a son of Madri, he is his choice.

Yaksha is well pleased by Yudhisthira and revives all his brothers.

– April 16, 2023

Ruru- Pramadvara, A Love Story

Once upon a time, a heavenly damsel (apsara) Menaka gave birth to a daughter and promptly abandoned her near the hermitage of a well-known Rishi, named Sthulkesha (literally one with thick hair). Rishi brought her up lovingly and she developed into a lovely young lady. She was named Pramadvara.

There was a great sage, a scion of the Bhrigu dynasty, named Ruru, who saw Pramadvara and was smitten by her. He let his friends inform Sthulkesha of his attraction to Pramadvara. Sthulkeshaa was glad to permit Ruru to wed Priyamdvara.

Ruru and Pramadvara were a very happy couple but their happiness would not last. One day, Pramadvara was bitten by a snake and died. Ruru was inconsolable, taking her body to a sacred grove and wailing. An envoy of gods came to console him but Ruru wanted his wife to live again. The envoy said that was not possible. Her life is over. After much haggling, the envoy asked Ruru to contribute half his remaining life span to his wife. And so it was.

This story is from the Indian epic, The Mahabharata which has many lovely stories like Nala-Damayanti and Satyavan-Savitri. The story of Ruru and Priyamdvara is less well-known but deserves to be better known.

– April 17, 2023

Tilottama

Once upon a time, brothers Sunda and Upasunda ruled over the earth. Brothers wanted to live forever and lord over all the creation. They engaged in arduous tapas to please the creator god Brahmaa. Brahmaa said he can't grant immortality. What the brothers got from Brahmaa is that they can't be killed by anybody but themselves.

The brothers terrorized the Devas and drove them out of heaven. They went to Brahmaa and asked them to restrain the demos Sunda and Upasunda. Brahmaa then created a lovely damsel using all the magic and mystery of Devas.

The demon brothers heard about Tilottama and went to see her in the hermitage of the rishi where she lived. They quarrelled over her. Both wanted her as a wife. So they wrestled to death.

Tilottama went to Indra's heaven and became one of the heavenly apsaras in Indra's realm.

– May 1, 2023

Yudhisthira's Accent to Heaven

Thirty-six years after the Mahabharata War, a fraternal war broke out among the Yadavas leading to the total destruction of their clan and the death of Shri Krishna. When Pandavas heard about it they were heartbroken. They visited Dwaraka, the abode of Krishna. Then they handed over the kingdom to Yuyutsu, the sole brother of Duryodhana to fight alongside Pandavas with the understanding that Abhimanyu's son Pariksit to take over the domain when he comes of age.

Pandavas, followed by Draupadi and a dog who had been following Yudhisthira. One by one Draupadi, Nakula, Sahadeva, Arjuna and Bhima all succumbed to snow and ice, leaving only Yudhisthira and the dog. Indra sent his envoy to bring Yudhisthira to heaven. Because of his steadfast behaviour, Yudhisthira was allowed to heaven with his physical body.

On his way, he saw Duryodhana and his brothers enjoying themselves in heaven. Yudhisthira was none too happy to see this. But the envoy advised him not to entertain such thoughts. Kasuravas fought bravely, followed Kshatra Dharma and were so entitled to enjoy themselves in Indra's heaven. Yudhisthira wanted to find out about his brothers and Draupadi. So the envoy took him to a place that was filthy and miserable. Gradually he recognized his brothers and wife. As he watched them, a gentle breeze blew and the environment became somewhat cheery. As Yudhisthira was asked to leave, his brothers and wife became miserable again beseeching Yudhisthira to stay. Yudhisthira relented and refused to leave.

At that moment Indra himself appeared and told Yudhisthira that this was an illusion. He had to go through this to expiate the one sin he had committed during the war, leading to the killing of Dronacharya. His brothers and Draupadi were already in heaven. Leave the dog behind as there is no provision for dogs in heaven. Yudhisthira said he was not going to leave the dog behind. As the dog was faithful to him, he would be faithful to the dog.

The God Dharma spoke to his son Yudhisthira, praising his truthfulness, steadfastness and devotion to duty. It was revealed that the dog was none but the God Dharma himself.

– May 18, 2023

The Story of Rishi Mandavya

This is a story from the Indian epic, The Mahabharata, a virtual treasure trove of history, myth, folklore and much more.

Mandavya was a well-known holy man, usually doing tapasya that is meditating on the supreme Brahman. One day while the rishi was absorbed in Tapasya, some robbers who had stolen from the king's treasury came by his ashram and hid the stolen goods in the ashram without Mandavya noticing anything. Thieves ran away followed by the king's lawmen in hot pursuit. They questioned Mandavya who gave no answer. The lawmen found the loot in the ashram and figured Mandavya was responsible somehow. They put Mandavya on a cross.

When the king got to know what had happened, he hurried and had Mandavya taken off the cross and profusely apologized. Mandavya accepted his apology but was deeply disturbed as to what sin made him suffer.

By his yogic powers, he summoned Lord Dharma and asked him to explain what sin of his almost crucified him. Dharma explained that as a child of age ten, he had impaled small insects with a needle. Mandavya said that this punishment was disproportionate to his offence as he was only a small child then.

Mandavya ruled that from now on an offence carried out by a person of less than age fourteen will not be punishable so harshly.

The Mahabharata is about three thousand years old and tells even older stories. This was perhaps one of the earliest instances when it was argued that the offence carried out by a minor should not be punished in the same way as the offence carried by an adult.

– May 18, 2023

A Bodhisattva Like Story from The Mahabharata

After the Mahabharata War, Yudhisthira held a horse sacrifice. The great archer Arjuna followed the sacrificial horse and invited the princes from the kingdoms the horse visited to the festivities. If the horse was captured by any state officials, Arjuna had to defeat them and extend and ask them to attend the festivities at the Hastinapura.

The Yajna was held on a grand scale with dances, processions and feasting lasting for days. At the time, a huge mongoose with half his body golden appeared and rolled on the banana leaves that Brahmans had eaten from. He loudly proclaimed that he was just coming from a meagre feast that a Brahmana couple where rolling on the leftover food had turned half his body golden. He expected the other half of his body to turn golden. But it appears that Yudhisthira's big feast did not merit as much as the poor Brahmana couple's feast.

Now coming back to the Brahmana couple's feast. After starving for a time, they found some foodstuff and were going to eat but a guest appeared who was hungry. The father gave his share of food to the guest but he was still hungry so the wife gave him her share of food too. The guest was still hungry, so the couple's son also gave his share. Now the guest was full but the family was left starving. Then the guest revealed that he was the Lord Dharma himself and he had come to test their generosity and steadfastness. The family had earned their place in Indra's heaven.

Thus the story teaches that you don't have to elaborate feasts to earn merit. Generosity and good deeds trump elaborate feasts and rituals.

– May 31, 2023

Fog

Sometimes I feel like I am in a fog
With vision unclear
And no clear sense of direction.
When fog lifts
It is like I am out of a well
And out in the open air again.

Sometimes it's hard to put
Things into perspective
When you are in the middle
Of a turmoil mental or physical
Because you need a temporal distance
And emotional detachment
To judge matters objectively.

An old Vedic prayer says:
Lead us from darkness to light.
I pray or wish:
Lead me away from the mental fog
That hits from time to time
To a clear vision and lucidity.

– June 6, 2023

Vishnu

INDIAN ART, primarily religious, finds its major expression in architecture and sculpture. This panel in a seventh-century temple at Deogarh shows the god Vishnu reclining on the World Serpent. Above him, on a lotus, Brahma.

This is one of my favourite images. Vishnu recumbent on Ananta (Also called Sesha Naga).

Ice Cream

If you are suffering from existential angst
Looking for the meaning of life
Mired in doubt and floundering
In this uncertain and unpredictable universe
Listen to me and don't laugh
Just try it out before you balk.
An antidote for this malady
Has been found, tried and tested
You will want to know
What it is, wouldn't you my friend?

It is incredibly simple
I wish I had known it earlier.
Have I built enough suspense
To awaken your curiosity?
It is ICE CREAM
End of all sorrows
Panacea for everything
You suffer from.
Be it vanilla, chocolate,
Or, my favourite strawberry.
In a dish or cone
Or how so ever you like.

There is no substitute for
A luscious dish of ice cream
Sweat, delicious ice cream.
Drown your sorrows and enjoy.
Life will feel sweet again
I tell you, you will not regret it.

– June 25, 2023

Lost Thoughts

Last night as I was trying to sleep
I had so many ideas about what to write.
But when I woke up this morning
I couldn't recall anything.
All those ideas vanished
Like a donkey's horns
As if they never existed.

So dear readers
Here is my sorry poem for the day.
The moral of the story is the old adage
Strike the iron while it is hot.
I should have gotten off my arse
And written out my thoughts
Before they disappeared into oblivion
Never to be heard or seen again.

Well, that's how life is.
No point in complaining.
I will just wait for the next inspiration
To strike and turn it into the written word.

– July 4, 2023

Worth of a Donkey

A donkey is one of the most maligned animals and quite undeservedly and without any fault of its own. It is a very studious animal. In India and perhaps in many under-developed countries, a potter and washerman can't function without the help of this poor animal. It works day and night without complaining. All for a bit of fodder and water. They tie its hind legs so it can't even kick its offender with a swift kick. Even a mule who is a half horse and half donkey, carries heavy loads to help the ungrateful humans.

In return for all its service, what does the society give him: beatings and verbal abuse. A foolish human is called a donkey. Even in a developed country like the US, when someone does something really stupid is called an ass. Even though no one has ever observed a donkey engaging in a silly activity. In India and I think in the middle east when they want to embarrass and insult someone, they color his face black, make him ride a donkey facing backwards and parade him through the city streets.

Even God is against the poor donkey. God has incarnated himself as a boar, turtle, fish and lion but never as a donkey.

All these thoughts arose after seeing this image:

In Hyderabad, they conducted a wedding ceremony for a male and a female donkey. Apparently, Indra, the god of thunder and rain is pleased by this act and sends rain to scorched earth. In my childhood, when someone got smallpox, they fed roasted chickpeas to a donkey. The belief was that smallpox was brought on by the goddess Shitala who rides a donkey. Goddess is pleased by this act of charity to her vehicle and alleviates the miseries of pox. In the Christian bible, Jesus arrives in Jerusalem riding a donkey. In Hindi, there is a saying that people will even honor a donkey if it serves their purpose.

– July 4. 2023

A Brahmin and a Chaste House-Wife

This is another interesting story from the Mahabharata. Once a Brahmin named Kaushika, well-versed in the Vedas acquired a certain amount of spiritual power due to his sadhana. He was annoyed by a heron pooping on him unceremoniously. The Brahmin glared at the heron and the poor bird dropped dead. Brahmin was so pleased with his power as he went begging for food.

He went to beg for alms from a household. The lady of the house asked him to wait as she went inside to get him alms. But meanwhile, her husband came home hungry and tired. The woman attended to her husband before serving the Brahmin. The Brahmin was none too pleased and opined that she should have served him first but the woman begged to differ. She said she knew all about the heron and she was not about to fall dead due to Kaushik's angry stare. She said her first duty was to her husband and then any guest. She told him that he should go to this butcher in Mithila for an elaboration.

The brahmin Kaushika somewhat deflated went to meet the butcher. The butcher met the Brahmin and asked him to wait while he took care of his old parents. When he finally was ready to talk to Kaushika, the latter expressed shock at his 'despicable profession.' The butcher explained that slaughtering animals and selling their meat was his family profession and he did it without shirking his other responsibilities. What followed is a great discourse on Dharma and its subtle ways.

– July 9, 2023

A Review of "In the Time of Our History" by Susanne Pari

It is the story of two sisters Mitra and Anahita. The dead sister carries a lot of weight in the story but the dead usually do, pun intended.

Mitra is older and rebellious. Their father Yusef Wants, as most fathers from his background would, his daughters to marry, raise their families and be good housewives and mothers. Ana complies, gets married and has kids. Older sister Mitra is rebellious and does not want to get married and has her tubes tied. No Iranian man would marry a sterile woman.

Ana and her two children Nina and Niku die in a car accident. Mitra who lives in San Francisco is visiting the east coast to participate in the death anniversary of her sister.

Yusef and his wife Shireen migrated to the US some forty years ago. Mitra and Ana are born in the US four years apart. Ana, while still a child. is molested by a cousin named Kareem and rescued by Mitra or so she thinks but the molestation continues for years and only ceases when Ana gets married.

Ana is an artist and designs silver jewellery. Aden whose wife owns a jewellery shop, helps Ana. Even though Ana is happily married and has two kids. Her husband is a good traditional husband but not an artist type. Ana falls for Aden who really loves her and they are artist soul mates.

Yusef who is an accomplished builder is very modern in some ways but very traditional in matters of women. Shireen is tired of Yusef's overbearing ways and leaves New Jersey for San Francisco to be with her daughter. It is not clear whether she is going to seek divorce from Yusef.

Mitra reveals all that happened to Ana to Yusef in a letter. Yusef has been taking care of his brother Jafar who is an invalid. He also has

Jafar's son Kareem working for him. Yusef sells the property where Jafar and Kareem live and tells them to move out to a place he has arranged. He scolds Kareem for what he did with Ana and tells father and son to get out of his life.

I enjoyed reading the book. Many of the cultural things and Persian words are familiar to me. Farsi as well as Sanskrit, the ancient language of India are Indo-Iranian languages. All north Indian languages are derived from Sanskrit, my mother tongue being one of them.

The characters especially women are vividly drawn and sound very real. The situations depicted are quite realistic.

– July 12, 2023

The Story of Rishi Dadhichi

Once upon a time in the hoary past, lived a great sage named Dadhichi. He was a great devotee of Lord Shiva and well-versed in Vedic lore. He was gentle and kind to all living beings and at the same incredibly strong.

This was also the time of the serpent dragon Vritra who had hoarded all the waters within his coils and made the rest of the world barren and dry. All the creatures and even Devas were suffering from hunger and thirst. Indra was worried about the welfare of all living beings. On the advice of the creator god Brahma, Indra approached Lord Vishnu. Vishnu said that Vritra is incredibly powerful and can't be killed easily. There is only one way to kill him. Approach Rishi Dadhichi in all humility and ask him if he would be willing to give up his life for the benefit of all living beings. After he dies you can use his spine to fashion an instrument that will kill Vritra.

Indra approached Dadhichi who without a moment's hesitation agreed. He went into a yogic trance and self-immolated. Indra fashioned an instrument called Vajra from his spine and killed Vritra and waters were released for the benefit of all sentient beings.

Vritra was a Brahmin and Brahminicide is one of the greatest sins. How Indra coped with this sinful action is a story to be told another time.

– July 20, 2023

Vritra, Indra and Nahusha

After killing Vritra and freeing the waters to flow, Indra was pursued by Brahminicide personified as a terrible woman warrior as Vritra was a Brahmin. Indra fled to the lake Mansarovar and hid in a lotus stalk. As Indra is responsible for the well-being of humans and Devas, chaos ensued. There was a mortal king named Nahusha well-known for his valour and virtue, who was installed on the throne of Svarga. Nahusha thought he was entitled to be husband to Shachi, Indra's wife. Shachi asked Nahusha for some time and went to see Brihaspati, the guru of Devas. Brihaspati told her to be patient for a while as Nahusha's fall was imminent. Nahusha in his arrogance had seven venerable rishis carry his palanquin and abused one of them for being too slow. The rishi was furious and cursed Nahusha to fall to earth and become a snake-dragon. Indra was brought back. He performed an Ashvamedha rite to get rid of the sin of killing a Brahmin and all was well again.

How Nahusha was finally liberated from his curse is a story to be told another time.

– August 1. 2023

Clipped Wings

A bird with wings clipped wings
Is still a bird but only in name.
It remembers what flight was like
But only memories and nothing more.

It is sad but everyone thinks
It's happy as it does not need to strive.
No need to dive and explore
Family brings food and provides all
That it needs.

But its life is empty and dull.
For happiness and fulfilment
Are generated by effort and accomplishments.
Without these life is but an empty shell.

Better to struggle, fight, and strive
Better to face danger
And let the adrenaline flow.
Life feels real, visceral
And worthwhile only
When challenges are squarely
Faced and overcome.

– August 5, 2023

Redemption of King Nahusha

Nahusha fell to earth and transformed into a ferocious boa as he was cursed by sage Agastya. The sage graciously allowed him to retain his memory and indicated that eventually, his curse would end.

One day Nahusha, the terrible reptile was looking for food. It was the last hour of sunlight and he was desperate. Meanwhile, Bhima, the Pandava, had gone hunting and entered Nahusha's cave. Nahusha pounced and wrapped Bhima in his coil. Introductions were made and Nahusha realized he was an ancestor of Bhima but nevertheless said he would eat Bhima.

Meanwhile, Yudhishthira was worried for Bhima and went looking. He found Bhima circled by Nahusha's coils. Bhima related what had happened. Nahusha offered a deal to Yudhishthira that if he answers his questions, he will set Bhima free. A dharma dialogue follows. Nahusha asked who is a Brahmin. Yudhishthira said that a person's conduct determines whether or not he is a Brahmin and not his birth. Many other issues are discussed. In the end, Nahusha is satisfied and lets Bhima go. Nahusha was told by Rishi Agastya that he would be freed by Yudhishthira, so it happened. Nahusha shed his boa body, assuming a celestial body ascended to heaven.

– August 14, 2023

A Tale about Rishi Agastya

There is a very interesting story about Agastaya Muni in the Aranya Kanda of Valmiki Ramayana. The story is told by Rama to Lakshmana and Sita as they are about to visit the Muni.

Once there were two Rakshasha brothers Ilvila and Vatapi. They were both greatly accomplished in Maya which means magic amongst other things. Ilvila speaking the refined language Sanskrita will lure an unsuspecting Brahmin to a Shraddha for this departed father. Vatapi who transformed himself into a goat was then butchered and the guest was fed. After the feast, Ilvila will call Vatapi to come out and he will come out tearing the entrails of the poor Brahmin. The brothers killed hundreds of Brahmins this way.

The brothers were great masters of Maya and even the Devas could not defeat them in battle. The matter was brought to Agastya Muni's attention. He accepted Ilvila's invitation and ate the sacrificial goat Vatapi. After the meal, Ilvila asked Vatapi to get out as usual. The Muni said Vatapi has been fully digested by me and isn't coming out. At this, Ilvila was greatly upset and took his demon form and tried to attack Agastya but an angry glance of the Rishi burned him and turned him to ashes.

– August 19, 2023

From the Womb of Maya

A Buddha is born only from Maya's womb.
A shiny diamond is chemically just coal.
The solid hard rocks of mountain
Are the birthplace of shiny rapid rapid-flowing rivers.
Only a worldly man can abandon the world
And become a sanyasi.
Only a determined sinner like Ratnakar
Seeks redemption and becomes Valmiki,
Who is moved by the killing of a pair
Of kraunch birds engaged amorously
And utters what may be
The world's first poetic expression.
Narayan is deemed great
For granting moksha to Ajamil, a great sinner
Who had the sense to name his son Narayan
Whom he called at the moment of his death
Thus fooling the great Narayan himself
To send his parshads to fetch him.
Vishnu responded to the prayers
Of an elephant to save him from a murderous croc.
But the crock is as necessary
As the elephant in this cosmic play.
And see how the bright flash of lightning
Emanates from the dark ominous clouds.

– August 16, 2023

PS: Buddha's birth mother was named Mahamaya (literally the great cosmic illusion or magic). She died soon after. Buddha was brought up by his aunt Prajapati who was also married to his father.

The concept of Maya curiously does not appear in Buddhism. Even though it is a central concept in Shankara's Vedanta. Shankara is often called a crypto-Buddhist (प्रच्छन्न बौद्ध) for adapting Buddhist ideas into Hinduism.

The verse recited by Valmiki referred above is:

मा निषाद प्रतिष्ठां त्वमगमः शाश्वतीः समाः ।
यत्क्रौञ्चमिथुनादेकमवधीः काममोहितम् ॥'

mā niṣāda pratiṣṭhā tvamagamaḥ śāśvatīḥ samāḥ
yat krauñcamithunādekam avadhīḥ kāmamohitam[16]

You will find no rest for the long years of Eternity
For you killed a bird in love and unsuspecting[17]

– September 4. 2023

Rishi Utanka

Once upon a time, there was a well-known teacher Rishi Veda. Utanka was his most senior student. Once Rishi Veda had to go on a trip. He left Utanka in charge of the ashram and Gurukul in his absence. Veda's wife had the most fertile period of her monthly cycle. She asked Uanka to service her in Veda's absence. Utanka refused thus angering his guru's wife. Guru Veda was pleased by Attack's discretion.

When Uttank's education was finished and it was time for him to leave, He asked Veda what he would like as Guru Dakshina. Veda asked Uttanka to ask his Guru Mata I.e. Veda's wife. Guru Mata who was less than pleased with Utanka wanted The earrings of King Pausya's wife. Pause's wife gladly gave Utanka the earrings but warned him to be careful as Takshaka, the king of snakes also wanted these earrings. On his way back Utanka stopped by a body of water to wash. He put the earrings on the ground. Takshaka who had followed him ran off with the earrings to the underground realm of snakes. Utanka with the help of Indra, the king of heaven located Takshaka in the subterranean Naga Loka. Indra produced flames that started burning Takshaka who in desperation gave the earrings back to Utanka.

Utanka became a famous Rishi in his own right and he was instrumental in King Janmejaya's Naga Yajna (Snake Sacrifice) in which snakes were lured by the magical mantras to the sacrificial flames. Another Rishi named Astika was able to stop Janmejaya from carrying out the sacrifice. Janmejaya had a grievance against Takshaka too as Takshaka had bitten Parikshita, Janamejaya's father causing his death.

– September 24. 2023

Some Favorite Writers and Their Books

This post is about the readings that I have been doing just for enjoyment. I hope you will like my suggestions. Here we go.

The Lord of the Ring Series By J.R.R. Tolkien

- The Hobbit
- The Fellowship of the Ring
- The Two Towers
- The Return of the King

It is a superb mythological epic with grand storytelling and a superb storyline. They also have made movies based on the books and I like those too.

The Carlos Castenada Books

Castenada started out as an anthropologist. He started seeing a Yaqui Indian shaman Don Juan Matus in connection with his research but soon he was completely taken in by Don Juan's world and his teachings. His books include:

- The Teachings of Don Juan: A Yaqui Way of Knowledge
- A Separate Reality
- Journey to Ixtlan
- Tales of Power
- The Second Ring of Power
- The Eagle's Gift
- The Fire from Within
- The Power of Silence
- The Art of Dreaming

There have been controversies about his work but I find his books magical and whether it is all fiction or fantasy does not really matter, at least not to me. Find out for yourself. Incidentally, I found the first book in the series not as interesting as the rest of the series.

Books by Harry Kemelman

The protagonist in these books is rabbi David Small in a small mythical town near Boston. I found his application of Talmudic logic in solving crimes fascinating. The books have titles like

- The Day Rabbi Left Town
- Friday the Rabbi Slept Late
- Saturday the Rabbi Went Hungry

And many more. These books are smartly written and you will learn a lot about Judaism as a bonus,

Books by Tony Hillerman

The setting is the vast Navajo reservation bordering New Mexico and Arizona. The chief protagonist is Lieutenant Joe Leaphorn who is a Navajo himself. Hillerman started his series of books in 1970 and wrote a total of 37 books before he died in 1998. I find the Navajo idea of living in harmony and beauty with nature and our fellow creatures human and non-human much more than our cut-throat culture.

Some titles are:

- The Blessing Way
- The Shape Shifter
- The Dark Wind

After he died, his daughter Anne Hillerman continued writing books with the same characters as his father and her books are equally as good. Some titles are:

- A Spider Woman's daughter
- Rock with Wings
- The Way of the Bear

Books by Tom Robbins

If you have not read anything by Tom Robbins, you don't know what you are missing. He is utterly crazy and yet makes sense. Some titles are:

- Skinny Legs and All
- Jitterbug Perfume
- Another Roadside Attraction

And many more.

Sadhguru Jaggi Vasudeva

I will stop with a spiritual note. Sadhguru is a guru with a wicked sense of humour and uncommon common sense. He has written a book

- Death, an Inside Story.

He says it is a book for all those who shall die. He also has a book called, "Inner Engineering." You can watch his videos on YouTube.

This is it for today.

– October 16, 2023

Marital Mores in the Mahabharata

There is a story in the Mahabharata, which sheds light on how the idea of marital faithfulness may have come about.

Once Rishi Uddalaka, his wife and their son Shvetaketu were conversing when a Brahmana took Uddalaka's wife by hand. Shvetaketu was perturbed by it. His father said that women, like cattle, were free to mate with whomever they wished except when it was their fertile period when they could only sleep with their husbands. This guaranteed the continuation of their lineage.

Shvetaketu was none too pleased with this state of affairs. In time shvetaketu became a very influential Rishi in his own right and was able to change the cultural norms which now dictated that men and women weren't allowed to have sex outside the marriage.

– October 29, 2023

Call to Action

What kind of foreign policy
Can we expect from a person who calls Hamas, humus
And pronounces Nepal as nipple?
No more informed than an eight-year-old,
Rex Tillerson called him a f—ing moron quite rightly.
He knows nothing and reads nothing.
Prefers to remain an ignoramus.
He led an insurrection against the legally elected government of
The United States of America.
An act of treason for which he remains unpunished.
More than seven people lost their lives
On that fateful day of January 6, 2021.
He is clearly responsible for those lives lost.
Our friends on the right want to repeat the grave mistake of 2016
And entrust our country to the criminals
Of MAGA who will most likely
Install this crook as our commander-in-chief
Who will take the country down the tube
And will try to install himself as a dictator
And kill democracy if he gets his way.
Be forewarned and defeat MAGA.
Nip it in the bud before it has a chance to do more mischief.
Take them to the court, fight them locally
And globally till they are utterly defeated.
My fellow Americans, this is a time
For bold action and sitting on a fence it is not a choice.
Support Biden who is not that great
But infinitely superior to the orange menace
Who will come to power and complete
His agenda of ruining the country.

– November 8, 2023

Brihannala

In this day and age of people choosing their gender identities: he/him/his; she/her/hers; they/them/their, it is interesting to talk about the great mythological warrior Arjuna. He was a true hero, a macho man and the greatest archer of his time.

When Pandavas and their common wife Draupadi were exiled after their gambling loss to the evil-minded Duryodhana for twelve years and an extra year of being incognito, Arjuna spent five years in Indra's heaven accumulating weapons and favours for the on-coming war with their Kaurava cousins. While in heaven, Urvashi, one of the heavenly dancers wanted Arjuna to make love to her. But Arjuna said he thought of her as his mother as she was a playmate of Indra who was like his father. Urvashi cursed him to become an eunuch. Indra intervened to have the curse last for only one year in which Pandavas were supposed to remain incognito.

For the incognito year, all five Pandavas and Draupadi took pseudonyms and jobs in the kingdom of Matsyas where King Virata ruled. Arjuna took a trans-gender persona and named himself Brihannala, which means one with a long reed. Perhaps the pun is intended. So Brihannala becomes a dance teacher to Virata's daughter Uttaraa.

When at the end of the year, their identities are revealed, Virata wants Arjuna to marry his daughter, Arjuna refuses because as her dance guru, he treated her as his daughter but he accepted her as a wife to his son Abhimanyu.

In the great Mahabharata war, almost everybody perished. There is a long story about how Parikshita, Abhimanyu's son survived and became the king of Hastinapur after the Pandavas departed. King Parikshita was cursed by a Rishi to be killed by Takshaka, a king of snakes. After Parikshita, his son Janmejaya wanted to avenge his father's death. He started a Naga-yagya (literally a snake sacrifice).

Snakes were called by Mantras and mesmerized to jump into sacrificial fire. A rishi named Astika stopped this wholesale slaughter of the Nagas(snakes). The Yagya concluded with the telling of the Mahabharata story to all posterity.

And what a marvellous tale it is! The Mahabharata is 100.000 verses long, the longest epic poem in the world. The Mahabharata claims that whatever is worthy of being told is here and what is not here is not found anywhere.

– December 2, 2023

New Year Wishes for 2024

Much of our life we spend in a fog
With no clear vision of who we are.
Our path unclear and steps unsteady.
Every once in a while the fog clears
And we get a glimpse of our true nature
Which as scriptures say is
The good, the true and the beautiful.
I am translating, "Satyam, Shivam, Sundaram" from
Sanskrit, the language of gods.

What I wish for all of us to have this clear vision
More often if not always.

I finish with this timeless prayer of Hindus
Of whom I am one.
Lead us to real from unreal
From darkness to light and
From death to immortality.
In Sanskrit, "Asato ma sadgamay,
Tamaso ma jyotirgamay,
Mrityorma amritam gamay,"
Om Shantihi, Shantihi, Shantihi."
Peace now and always.

Wishing all to be happy, and healthy.
I pray for the well-being of all.
Let no one ever come to grief.
I have translated the Sanskrit prayer,
"Sarve bhavantu sukhinah,
Sarve Santo niramayah,
Sarve bhadrani pashyantu,
Ma kashchit duhkha bhagbhavet,"

– January 4, 2024

Narada-Vishnu Dialog

After a long time Muni Narada traveled to Baikuntha
The abode of Lord Vishnu lying on the serpent Sesha
In the comic ocean.
The lord welcomed Narada and asked him what
News he has brought from the land of mortals.
Narada said, "Dear Lord, mortals want to know
Why you wait so long to bring people up here
Until they are old and decrepit with bad joints and poor health.
Why not bring them while they are still healthy and fit.
The Lord replied, Narada, mortals are critical of him when
People with good health die. They say why did the Lord
Make a healthy person die. Why not wait till the person is old and decrepit.
So there you are. Now I wait until the person is in such misery that
The person cries and says, Dear Lord please take me up, I had enough.
And so I comply with their wish.

You know Narada, humans are the crest of my creation
But a human is very obstinate.
This is her best quality and also the worst.
That makes her ambitious and obstinacy helps her to achieve this goal.
But he also misuses this quality to opress the poor
So it becomes necessary to end his earthly existence.

Narada, ris matter is very difficult and complex.
We will talk in detail about this matter some other time.
Right now, the food is ready and Lakshmi
Has invited you share a meal with us.
So please join us and partake of food with us.

– January 4, 2024

Some Rambling Thoughts

On August 15, 1947, India was divided into two countries India and Pakistan. Most prominent leader in India was Mohandas Gandhi and Mohammad Ali Jinnah in Pakistan. Gandhi was a devout Hindu and Jinnah was a thoroughly modern secular man. Jinnah despised Gandhi's religiosity and mocked it. He promised a secular Pakistan and Gandhi a secular India. But look what happened. India more or less remained democratic, had regular elections largely free and fair. There never has been a military take-over in India. But what happened in Pakistan. Jinnah died in 1948. His successor Liaquat Ali Khan was assassinated. So was Gandhi also in 1948. After that except for a few brief years of democratic rule now and then Pakistan has largely been run by the military. Even the democratic rulers had to rule under the thumb of military.

So a religious minded Gandhi had a thoroughly secular minded Jawaharlal Nehru lead India but Pakistan was declared an Islamic republic in 1956 by Major General Iskander Mirza who became the first elected president of Pakistan. So by default all non-muslims became second class citizens. Pakistanis claim to revere Jinnah but all his principles of secularity and equality of all citizens have been thrown out the window.

But since 2014 there is another twist in the situation. Mr. Modi came to power with his Hindutva agenda. Even though he claims to follow the constitution of India, the country has become distressingly xenophobic against Muslims. Even though he has done many commendable things for India and Indians but he has never addressed the extreme hatred and bias against Muslims in Hindutva-dominated current mind set of many Indians.

Unfortunately the venerable old Congress party has a totally inept leader Mr. Rahul Gandhi. Congress party is completely in doldrums and can't offer an alternative to Mr. Modi. So most probably Mr. Modi will win the 1924 elections and the miserable state of affairs will continue.

So Mr. Jinnah's fears of marginalizing Muslims seem to have come true. I deplore this state of affairs but unable to conceive of an antidote to this disease called Hindutva.

– January 7, 2024

A Note about Vegetarianism

I want to share an observation about vegetarianism.

Perhaps India houses maximum number of vegetarians of any nation. Also the percentage of vegetarians is higher in India than any other nation.

But how did it come about? Our beloved heroes in the epics Ramayana and Mahabharata were not vegetarians. It is conjectured that vegetarianism grew in India as a Buddhist influence. As Hinduism reformed to compete against Buddhism. Adi Shankara, often called a crypto-Buddhist led the movement and Buddhism almost completely disappeared from India but vegetarianism flourished.

Buddhism spread far and wide to China, Korea, Japan and South-East Asia. But none of these lands are vegetarian. Even venerable Dalai Lama is not vegetarian. I remember reading a funny incident. Once Dalai Lama was traveling by airplane, he told his seat-mate that only very strict Buddhists are vegetarian. Now, who could be a more strict vegetarian than Dalai Lama, the leader of many Mahayana Buddhists as Pope is the leader of Catholic Christians.

I also recall dimly another incident in which Dalai Lama was to be feted by Zen Buddhists in NY city. Now Zen Buddhists are strict vegetarians. Dalai Lama was staying in Waldorf-Astoria and his people discouraged Zen Buddhists from serving only the vegetarian food. I don't remember how this situation was resolved.

– January 8, 2024

Wars and Epics

Dear readers, have you ever wondered
Why some of the great literary works
Are inspired by wars and strife.
Be it Ramayana or Mahabharata in India
Or Iliad and Odyssey in Greece
Many literary works written
In the wake of the World Wars one and two
American civil war and bloody partition of India
Flowering of literature after Korean and Vietnam wars
Just to name a few?
Now, I am for prosperity and peace just like most people
Except for some mis-guided idiots.
I am simply making an observation.
I have often wondered why is this?
Does peace and prosperity dull our sensibilities?
Is conflict needed to bring us out of stupor?
I remember reading somewhere
That the Creator God Brahma of Hindus
Created conflict in the hearts of creatures
Because he thought it was essential
For their continued survival.
I have no answers so I pose these questions
To you who would read these lines.

– January 22, 2024

Our Enemies

Comparison and self-importance are
Some of the main sources of our grief.
We know that but are unable to disengage from them.
We have to have an upper hand in every argument.
We have to show that we know better than the opponent.
Results are conflict and discord.

We have to learn restraint and seek harmony
Reduce our egotism and be humble.
We know that pride does not help
It hinders us and the opponent from achieving harmony.
No one likes to feel inferior.
So there is no point in pointing out errors in a way
That puts the other party on defensive.

We should try to overlook errors
Or be gentle and kind if we must correct a crucial mistake.
Few years for which we share this earth with fellow creatures
We should try to live with compassion and understanding
As we don't know when the end will come and it will be
Too late to mend the fences.
I will end this with the ancient Hindu prayer for peace.
Om Shantihi, Shantihi, Shantihi.

– Feb 5, 2024

Redemption

Redemption from our errors is a common theme
In great and some not so great persons' lives.

Buddha left his wife and child to seek enlightenment
But he came back as an enlightened being
And his family was so impressed by him
That his father, his son and later his step-mother
All joined his sangha.

Gandhi mistreated his wife but he confessed it in
His autobiography and freely admitted his error.
He also admitted to other errors in his autobiography
Which he called, "My Experiments with Truth."

Nowadays, it has become common to criticize and malign Gandhi in India.
These misguided souls (I am tempted to call them miscreants)
Totally ignore Gandhi's tremendous service to the nation and mankind.
They talk derisively of a truly great man.
And resent having to call him Mahatma
A title that was bestowed on him by Tagore,
The celebrated Bengali poet.
Some clueless folks think it is a university degree.
Some think Nathuram Godse, the killer of Mahatma
Should be called Mahatma
For doing a great service to Hindus by killing Gandhi.

I think some heedless people
With very little knowledge of history or religion
Sprout venom against Nehru and Gandhi.
Even half-wits have freedom of speech in a democracy.

Of course, some so-called great men never admitted
Their mistakes and never sought redemption.
Henry, the eighth who had
two of his wives beheaded on charges of adultery.
While it is not clear whether his wives were guilty
But he surely was guilty of adultery and murder.

Some of modern history's greatest monsters
Never sought redemption.
Be they Hitler, Stalin, Mao, Pol Pot
Or that great hero of West, Winston Churchill
Who by diverting food to the British Army
From Bengali populace, created an artificial famine in Bengal
Killing over two million people.
When told about it his response was, "Has Gandhi died?"
In his callous, racist, imperialist, mind
Lives of brown Bengalis could be sacrificed
To save the lives of their white masters.
Did his opposition to Hitler redeemed him, I can't say?

– Feb 10, 2024

Brahman (ब्रह्मन्)

Brahman (ब्रह्मन्) comes from the root brah(ब्रह) which means to expand or to become bigger. The same root gives us brahad(ब्रहद्) as in Brahadaranfyka Upanishad (ब्रहदारण्यक उपनिषद). Upanishads also say, "All this is verily Brahman (सर्वं खल्विदम्ब्र ह्म). If you put these ideas together then we can say at some point sort of a spiritual big bang occurs and from a single point Brahman expands into this all. Brahman is pure consciousness and all the creation is also pure consciousness. It is not as in Abrahamic religions God creates all creatures but God(Brahman) Is all creatures. Brahman, as a Sanskrit noun is genderless i.e. it is neither male or female.

Shiva-Sutras say: Consciousness is self (चैतन्यात्मा). Thus Brahman is the universal consciousness and atman (self) is the lndividual or localized consciousness. One of the great sentences (महावाक्य) of the upanishads is:

Atman = Brahman.

Perhaps we can express it as:

self = Self.

Just as air in an empty cup is not different from the air outside, individual self(आत्मन्)is not different from the universal consciousness(ब्रह्मन्).

But now the question arises: How does this variegated creation of the physical (earth, planets, soil system etc.) with the plants and animals come into being? One answer provided is that all this already exists within Brahman, the universal consciousness. Perhaps this what this picture depicts:

Vishnu lying on the snake in primordial ocean, dreaming of the universe, he is ready to make manifest. Creation has already begun as we have Brahma and Lakshmi have already made appearance.

– Feb 17, 2024

More on Brahman

This picture on the ceiling of the Sistine Chapel by Michelangelo demonstrates the Christian view of the divine with Man (Adam). Adam's finger almost reaches God's finger but bot quite. The creator and creation remain separate. They can never be equal. Strict duality is maintained.

Hindu view is quite different and I emphasize different, not better or worse. I will quote philosopher John Fuller:

Christopher John Fuller (2004), The Camphor Flame: Popular Hinduism and Society in India, Princeton University Press, ISBN 978-0691120485, pp. 30-31, **Quote:**

> "Crucial in Hindu polytheism is the relationship between the deities and humanity. Unlike Jewish, Christian and Islamic monotheism, predicated on the otherness of God and either his total separation from man and his singular incarnation, Hinduism postulates no absolute distinction between deities and human beings. The idea that all deities are truly one is, moreover, easily extended to proclaim that all human beings are in reality also forms of one supreme deity - Brahman, the Absolute of philosophical Hinduism. In practice, this abstract monist doctrine rarely belongs to an

ordinary Hindu's statements, but examples of permeability between the divine and human can be easily found in popular Hinduism in many unremarkable contexts".

Nineteenth century Hindu saint Shri Ramakrishna made hugely important statements on this issue. I will quote a few:

> "Many are the names of God, and infinite the forms that lead us to know Him. In whatsoever name or form you desire to call Him, in that very form and name you will see Him."
>
> – Shri RamaKrisna

> All religions are true. God can be reached by different religions. Many rivers flow by many ways but they fall into the sea. They all are one. – Ramakrishna

> Have love for everyone, no one is other than you.
>
> – Ramakrishna

The ordinary man says in his ignorance,

> "My religion is the sole religion, my religion is the best." But when his heart is illuminated by the true knowledge, he knows that beyond all the battles of sects and of sectaries presides the one, indivisible, eternal and omnipresent Benediction. – Ramakrishna

Hindu view is that the whole creation is divine. Man is more advanced in this matter than other creatures. Once he drops his ego(easy to say) he/she becomes one with the absolute.

Mystics of all religions have taken this view and some have paid for it with their lives

> Neither this body am I, nor soul, Nor these fleeting images passing by, Nor concepts and thoughts, mental images, Nor yet sentiments and the psyche's labyrinth. Who then am I? A consciousness without origin, Not born in time, nor begotten here below. I am that which was, is and ever shall be, A jewel in the crown of the Divine Self, A star in the firmament of the luminous One. – Persian Poet Rumi

Hussain bin Mansoor [sic] Al-Hallaj was condemned to hang by the neck for shouting in ecstasy Anā al-Ḥaqq, Anā al-Ḥaqq (I am the Truth, I am the Truth). The orthodox understood this to mean that he was claiming to be God himself, whereas he had proclaimed, in his sublime spiritual ecstasy, simply a total annihilation of himself. Mansoor Al-Hallaj climbed the gallows with his head held high, not the least daunted by his imminent death. Nor could his shouts be drowned in the tumult of abuses which were hurled at him; they rose loud and clear and high Anā al-Ḥaqq, Anā al-Ḥaqq until his soul departed to the fountainhead[citation needed] of his life on high.

The other point I was making is just etymological. Brahman comes from the root Brah which means to expand so the absolute consciousness has expanded to become it all. Rumi said even rocks are conscious. It is just their consciousness level is very low.

I hope this helps.

– Feb 18, 2024

God and Man

Once upon a time, long long ago
God and Men were not so far apart.
Men were offsprings of God
And as a good parent God took care of them.

But then men multiplied and became numerous.
They became conceited and insolent
And began to defy God.

They became greedy and corrupt
Moving away from the ideals of humanity that God had set.
They became burdened with
Selfishness, anger, conceit and greed.

They had become very troublesome to God,
Complaining about mere trifles.
They even wanted God to become a party to their evil deeds.

So God reluctantly decided not to live too close to humans
And moved to high places like
Mt. Olympus or Mt. Kailash in the Himalayas.
But crafty and industrious humans reached there as well.
Now, listen carefully friends, what I have to tell you.
Humans have reached the Moon, the Mars
And other planets are also coming within their reach.
God is climbing higher and higher to avoid humans.

Man has begun to doubt even the existence of God.
God is breathing a sigh of relief.
God has decided to leave humans to their designs
And solve their problems on their own.

If humans do that, God will be grateful
And bless them with his weary heart.

– Feb 28, 2024

Man-God Dialog

I was always afraid
That it would happen
And then it did.
God met Man
And a debate ensued.

God said everything and everyone
In this world is created by someone.
There is absolutely no doubt
That I created you.

Man replied, if that is so
Somebody created you
And somebody created your creator
And add on infinitum.

Solution to this problem, O Lord
Is that you are a product
Of my imagination.
Without me, there will be
No churches, synagogues, mosques
Or temples to worship you.
And if I don't go there, these places will be empty.
Moreover I built them in the first place.

If you don't take offense, my Lord
Nobody will recognize you without me.
There will be no rituals, puja, worship,
Adoration, homa or yajna for you without me.

God said, Man you are full of talk, talk, talk.
You win but you are forgetting
That it is time for your
Daily worship of me.

Without worship your life
Would be devoid of any meaning.
If you abandon me you will be
Helpless like a babe in the woods.
You will invariably turn to me for solace
And will take refuge in me.

Maybe, I am just your imagination.
But you trust and rely on me
For your existence and subsistence.
You are nothing without me.
Now go and perform your worship
No harm will come to you.

– March 1, 2024

Bheeshma on His Death-Bed of Arrows

Hello Friends,

I am starting a new project of taking mythological pictures from the internet and posting them with brief explanatory captions. This is the first such picture in the series.

This picture is that of the great octogenarian warrior Bheeshma lying on a bed of arrows after falling in the Mahabharata battle. He fought on the side of unrighteous Kauravas against the righteous Pandavas for reasons too complicated to go into here. Such was his valor and honor that both sides stopped fighting for a while. On seeing Krishna, his pain was alleviated but he was thirsty. Arjuna fired an arrow into the ground, thus creating a stream which could quench his thirst.

– March 12, 2024

This picture is that of the great octogenarian warrior Bheeshma lying on a bed of arrows after falling in the Mahabharata battle. He fought on the side of unrighteous Kauravas against the righteous Pandavas for reasons too complicated to go into here. Such was his glory that both sides stopped fighting for a while. On seeing Krishna, his pain was alleviated but he was thirsty. Arjuna fired an arrow into the ground, thus creating a stream which could quench his thirst.

Kali's Eternal Dance on the Body of Shiva

Kali is the feminine form of Kala which means time. Kali, the black time that devours everything. Shiva lying prostate as a corpse (shava in Sanskrit) represents the absolute consciousness lying inert until Kali (the nature, Maya or Adi-Shakti I.e. the primeval power) starts her dance on him. Shiva who was lying as a Shava becomes energized by Kali's dance and the process of creation begins. The first a in shava is replaced by an 'I' Shava becomes Shiva and the cyclic dance of creation, perpetuation and destruction ensues. The severed head represents the destroyed ego.

– March 13, 2024

Bodhisatva, Padmapani

"Padmapani is another name for Avalokiteshvara, the bodhisattva ("buddha-to-be") of infinite mercy. The meditational quality of Padmapani is emphasized by the fullness of his lips, the slender waist and nose, the sinuous elongated eyebrows, and the almond-shaped eyes, and he is depicted holding a lotus flower. Although the divinity is extremely idealized, the realistic approach is conspicuous. One can infer that the crown and jewels are of secular inspiration, and it is an early example of the wearing of a crown signifying divinity."

– From britanica.com

Avalokiteshwara

Avalokiteshwara is perhaps the best known bodhisattva in the Mahayana tradition of Buddhism. In the Mahayana tradition a bodhisatva is a person who after many virtuous incarnations is ready to achieve Nirvana, the ultimate spiritual attainment but postpones it to relieve the suffering of all sentient beings and lead them to the ultimate release from pain and suffering.

Literally Avalokiteshwara means the Lord looking down (at the suffering humanity) with the eyes of compassion. In China he is known as Guan Yin, a female bodhisattva, In Japan he is known as Kannon. One can think of Dalai Lama as a modern bodhisattva. He always puts emphasis on the compassion in all his public talks.

– Guan Yin

Shiva, Nataraja

Nataraja means the king of dancers and actors. The iconography of the image is the Shaivite theology in a nutshell. The upper right hand has a beating drum, symbolizing the vibration and rhythm that creates the universe and the lower right hand (fear-not) represents the maintenance of the world. Upper left hand with fire represents destruction and also subsequent regeneration. The lower left hand represents concealment from jiva, the individual soul so it can experience samsara and its pleasures and sorrows. The right foot is crushing the individual ego and the raised left foot represents blessing leading to release fom the illusory bonds of the world. The ring surrounding the frame represents samsara, the phenomenal universe.

– March 18, 2024

Ardhnarishwara

Shiva is the absolute consciousness which is aware and autonomous. The external world already exists in his consciousness and represents his nature. Shiva wants to recognize himself so brings forth the external world that was already in his consciousness. Then Shiva intentionally obscures his consciousness and becomes Jiva (individual soul) and plays around in the external world. When he has his fill he tries to realize his true nature and due to grace of Shiva (who is himself but hidden due to his own obscuration) he becomes Shiva again. Then he wonders what he was meditating about. He was always Shiva and basically it was a process of remembering.

In the Vedanta as in Shankara, the external world is illusion (Maya) but not to the Shaivites, as Shiva is real and so is his creation (Shakti). Shiva and Shakti, in essence, are not different from each other. Shiva is Shakti and Shakti is Shiva. Or we can say he is half-man and half-woman. That is the concept of Ardhnarishwara: The Lord who is half man and half-woman.

Om Namo Shivaya.

– March 20, 2024

Source: Self-Realization in Kashmir Shaivism by Swami Lakshmanjoo.

PS: I have used the pronoun 'he' but could have used 'she' as well. Shiva is male and Shakti is female and both are the same.

His Form

He has no form but all forms are his.
He has no home but all homes are his.
He has no name but all names are his.
He does no work but all works are his.

All the wealth belongs to him but he owns nothing.
All the world thinks of him but he is beyond thought.

He is never born but all births are his.
He never dies but all deaths are his.

He never spoke a word but all words are his.
He never lifted a pen but all written words are his.

How do we bow at his feet when he has no feet?
How do we bow to him when all feet are his?

– March 22, 2024

PS: This is my primitive understanding of the Hindu Vedanta philosophy. It describes the paradoxical nature of Brahman, the ultimate reality in Vedanta. I personally don't completely subscribe to any established philosophy. Like Emerson, I don't claim to be consistent. Emerson haughtily said: Foolish consistency is a hobgoblin of little minds.

More on His Form

A friend suggested that this has been said before and he is absolutely right. It has been said many times. For example Tulasidas said it his RamCharitManas 400 years ago. In Balkand Shiva explains formless Brahman to Parvati this way:

बिनु पद चाहि सुनै बिनु काना
कर बिन कर्म करंज बिधि नाना
आनन रहित सकल रस भोगी
बिनु बानी बक्ता बड़ योगी
तन बिनु परस नयन बिनु देखा
ग्रहै घ्राण बहन बास। असेषा
अति सब भाँति अलौकिक करनी
महिमा जासु जाए नहिं बरनी

He walks but has no feet
Hears but has no ears
Has no hands but performs many deeds
Has no body but touches everything
Smells everything but has no nose
He does all these marvelous things
He is utterly beyond description.

– March 24, 2024

Trimurti

Trimurti is a sculpted image in the Elephanta caves near Mumbai(formerly Bombay) India. It represents Hindu Trinity of Brahma east face), Vishnu(Center) and Mahesh(west face). Brahma is the creator God, Vishnu, the protector ans Mahesh(also called Shiva) the destroyer. Theoretically all three Gods are at equal footing but Brahma got a short shrift some how as he is rarely worshipped. As for as I know there is one temple devoted to Brahma in Pushkar, Rajasthan, India. It might have been different in past. When Buddha achieved enlightenment, he thought it could mot be taught. He was then visited by Brahma and Indra, the king of gods(also called Shakra). They beseeched him to teach and he complied.

Sometimes the image is supposed to represent three aspects of Shiva, the creator, protector and destroyer.

– March 25, 2024

From the Womb of Maya

Buddha is born from Maya's womb.
Diamond is but a shiny piece of coal.
A great gurgling energetic flowing river Ensues from the hard rocks of mountain.
Only one who has enjoyed the comforts of the world Can renounce it all and be called an Yogi.
Only a sinner like Ratnakar can be redeemed And become the great sage Valmiki
Who wrote the first great poem When he was chagrined at the senseless killing
Of a bird who was mating.
Narayan was called a great savior when A dying man called his son
Who he had named Narayan.
A king of elephants was saved by the Lord Vishnu
Because the elephant called him to be saved From the clutches of a crocodile.
And a flash of lightning bursts forth The darkest clouds.

– 29 March, 2024

Proper Attire for the Lord's Court

What attire one should wear to the good Lord's court
Is the question.

The Christian priest recommends suit and tie with polished shoes
For men and a modest dress or a longish skirt with a modest top
For women.
There should be no hint of any sensuality in the clothes.
I suppose The Good Lord must be sexless.
And on no account one should cover his/her head.

In some Hindu temples, men must wear a Dhoti and
Women must not wear any European clothing.
A covered head would be nice but not mandatory.

In a Sikh Gurudwara, your head must be covered.
I guess an open head is an anathema to the good Lord.

While pondering on these dress rules
I was hit upon a novel idea.
One must go the Lord just the way
The great one sent us here.
Which means entirely in nude.
We must lead our body and soul bare.

Nothing is hidden from the good Lord any way
He knows us in its entirety.
We must check in our clothes at the door
And enter his abode in total humility
And surrender and commune with divine in total honesty.
I don't know if any church, temple, mosque or Gurudwara
Would allow it but if you think my idea has merit
You should fight non-violently of course
To spread and promote my vision.

– April 3, 2024

The Universal Enchantress

Maya (with both a's long) is the universal enchantress of Hindu mythology and sacred lore. She is the supreme Goddess often identified with Nature (prakriti), also called Devi or Shakti, the consort of Shiva, the absolute consciousness. In fact Shiva and shakti are not separable. Shiva is Shava (a corpse) without Shakti. It is also said that Maya or Shakti is this entire universe. The saint poet Tulasidas of seventeenth century says:

> गो गोचर जहँ लगि मन जाई, सो सब माया जानहु भाई।
>
> (The senses and whatever they perceive and what lies within the reach of mind is all Maya.)

Etymologically, the word Maya is related to "measure." It comes from the root "maa" that means to measure or lay out the plan as of a building or picture. By extension, then it means to create or shape or display. Thus it is the creative force of the universe.

In Hindu mythology all principal deities are males but their consorts represent their Shakti (power) are female. A deity's Shakti is a manifestation of his Maya or creative force. Thus Shiva's shakti is Parvati, Brahma's Saraswai and Vishnu's Lakshmi etc.

In Devi Bhagavata Purana written in third century CE, Devi says:

"All that is seen is I, myself. There is existent nothing other than is eternal.'

Canto 01, Chapter 15.

It appears that Devi does not need a male consort. She is self-sufficient.

Devi Bhagavata is some six hundred years older than the Vaishnava Bhagavat and is sometimes referred to as the original Bhagavata.

This view that Shakti is all that there is held by Shaktas evidently. But this seems a minority view. Most sources have an apparent duality between Shiva and Shakti; Purusha and Prakriti; Brahman and Jiva.

Let us get back to the role of Maya as an enchantress. I will illustrate it with a story.

Once upon a time, the great sage Narada who could travel anywhere with the speed of mind, went to visit the great lord Vishnu. After exchanging formalities, Narada said, "I have practiced many austerities and I think I can't be fooled by your Maya. Would you please demonstrate your Maya to me?" Vishnu tried to dissuade Narada but he will not take no for an answer. Vishnu said, "Narada, let us get out of this milky ocean and walk somewhere to talk." Off they went in sweltering summer heat. After some time Vishnu said, "Son, I am so tired and thirsty. Would you please go to that hut over there and get me some water. I will wait here." Narada went to the hut and knocked. A very beautiful young woman answered the door and welcomed him in. Introduced him to her parents. Everyone was pleasant to him and Narada was head over heels in love. In due course they married. Narada took care of the land, cattle and farming. Twelve years went by. He had a young son too. Then a great flood came. All his family his in-laws, wife and son were all swept away, Narada was totally distraught and fell unconscious. When he came to senses, there was no flood and no village and The Lord Vishnu was bending over him and asking, "Narada where is my water? I have been waiting here for half an hour."

In Shankara's Vedanta Maya is treated as a World-Illusion. Only reality is Brahman. So one has to tear the bonds of illusion and realize Brahman. Real here means something that is everlasting.

Tantra does not believe Maya or Shakti to be illusion. Shiva is real so how his Shakti can be unreal. The thing to do is to see Shiva in his Shakti,the visible universe. We are all Shivas who have deliberately obscured our nature to enjoy nature or Shakti and then realize the eternal union of Shiva and Shakti which is the great purpose of life.

It is an extensive subject and my talent is limited. So I will stop here.

I have extensively consulted two books by Heinrich Zimmer: "Myths and Symbols in Indian Art and Civilization" and "Philosophies of India," to write this brief essay.

I am including an image here Devi, the Mahamaya instructing Baby Vishnu in her secrets.

– April 4, 2024

More about the Enchantress

I missed some important information about the great Devi in the first post. Hence this supplementary post.

One of the most famous epithets of her is Mahishasur Mardini I.e. the killer of the buffalo demon Mahisha.

Once upon a time, a demon named Mahisha tormented the world. He defeated Devas and drove them out of the heaven. He spread a reign of terror in the three worlds. To overcome him all the devas and Brahma, Vishnu and Shiva combined their energies. These energies solidified in the form of Devi Chandika riding a ferocious line. Indra gave her his thunderbolt, Shiva his trident and so on.

Chandika went and challenged him to fight. Mahisha was entranced by this fierce but beautiful countenance and offered to marry her. Devi said she would marry him if he defeats her in the battle. Alas for the demon, this didn't happen. After a long and fierce battle, the demon was slain. All devas offered their gratitude and applauded her. These verses of prayers, accolades and other virtues of Devi, constitute what is called Devi Mahatmya or Chandi Path. In many hindu temples and homes, the ritual reading of the Mahatmya takes place in autumn Navaratris (Nine Nights) and is concluded on the tenth day. The festival of Durga Puja is celebrated with great fanfare especially in Bengal, Assam and Orissa.

– April 5, 2024

Markandeya

The time is between two eons. Pralay, the deluge has taken place. The great God Vishnu has swallowed the world. He is lying on a giant snake, named Ananta (the endless) in the cosmic waters. The world with all its potentialities is within him. A great sage named Markandeya is wandering inside the god and is pleased to see that people in all walks of life are following their dharma and perfect harmony reigns. Suddenly Vishnu yawns and Markandeya slips out of his mouth into chaotic primeval waters. Markandeya sees a luminous bluish boy lying on a leaf of a banyan tree. The child says, "Markandeya, come to me. Don't be afraid, my child." Markandeya takes offence in being addressed so casually. After all he is a venerated rishi honored even by Devas. The child says, "Markandeya, I am the supreme lord Vishnu, the creator, maintainer, and destroyer of all things. I am Brahma, Vishnu and Mahesh. I do all this by my yoga-maya. The child yawns again and Markandeya is sucked into his mouth and resumes his pleasant life inside god once again.

This myth is related in the Mahabharata in the book of forest, Shrimad bhagavatam (12th Canto) and other Puranas.

– April 9, 2024

Kaliya Mardan

When Krishna was 7-8 years old living with his foster parents Nanda and Yashoda in Vrindavan on the shore of the river Yamuna, also called Kalindi. A heavily poisonous snake by the name Kaliya took up the residence in the river. Any living creature approaching the bank of the river died. So potent was Kaliya's venom. Krishna wanted to protect his folks from Kaliya so he climbed on a tree and jumped into the river where Kaliya was. Multi-fanged Kaliya encircled boy Krishna and started crushing him. Krishna's older half-brother Balrama saw this and reminded Krishna of his divinity. Immediately Krishna was energized and started racing on the fangs of Kaliya. The snake got bloodied and fatigued. He also realized Krishna was no ordinary boy. He prayed Krishna for mercy as he was only doing what is natural for a snake as ordained by Krishna himself, the lord of nature. Krishna asked him to leave the populated areas and move to the ocean where he will not endanger the lives of his folks. The snake complied.

– April 12, 2024

The Origin of Lingam (Lingobhava)

As is known to most people Lingam represents the generative male power in the creation I.e. the phallus of Lord Shiva. But there is more to the story as we shall see.

This story is told in the Lingapurana amongst other places. First I heard it from Prof. Douglas Renfrew Brooks, then of the University of Rochester in a Sanskrit course I took from him around 1997. Here with the story.

Imagine a time after deluge(Pralay) and before the new creation(Sristi), Vishnu is floating around on the giant snake Ananta in the primeval waters. He sees another luminous being, riding his golden swan(Hamsa). He is Brahma with four resplendent heads. the progenitor of the universe. He asks Vishnu who he is and where did he come from. Brahma identified himself as Prajapati, the lord and originator of all beings. Vishnu says to the contrary that he has created and destroyed this universe many times. While they are debating thus, a towering pillar of light, Lingam, appears before them. It is growing rapidly in infinite space. Brahma flies up on his hamsa to to discover its upper end whereas Vishnu plunges down (reminiscent of his Boar incarnation) to find its lower end. Meanwhile the lingam keeps growing in both directions.

Presently the side of lingam burst open revealing the divine form of the Lord Shiva. He proclaimed himself to be the origin of both. The image here shows Shiva, Hara(who destroys or takes away all) in the middle, with Vishnu on his right(west) and Brahma on his left(east). Heinrich Zimmer dates this image to be from the thirteenth century. The myth itself is much older.

– April 14, 2024

Six Paramitas of Buddhism

(An underlined vowel is long).

First a bit of etymology:

Para = Other shore across from the Samsara, the ocean of coming and going.

Paramita = One who has gone to the other shore.

Paramita = A quality required of one who qualifies to get to the other shore.

Now the six Paramitas or perfections as they are often called.

1. **Generosity (Dana):** There are three requirements in this Paramita:
    i. Being generous to all without exception
    ii. Everything you possess can be given away without regard to what you will do afterwards
    iii. No expectation of any gain in return for your generosity.
2. **Morality (Shila):** Ahimsa, ethical behavior etc.
3. **Patience (Kshanti):** Forbearance, Stoicism in face of grief, pain pr loss.
4. **Energy (Virya):** To move ahead enthusiastically to do good.
5. **Meditation (Dhyana):** Concentration, one-pointedness.
6. **Wisdom (Prajna):** Realization of Truth.

Prajna paramita is visualized as a goddess in this image.

– April 19, 2024

Lilith

As is well-known Lolita by Vladimir Nabokov is a modern classic. I have tried to read it many times but for one reason or other always quit in the middle. Usually I get lost in many literary allusions that I don't know about. Recently I started to give it another try. On page 21 of the paperback edition of the book I have, the abominable narrator of the story Humbert Humbert expresses a preference for Lilith as compared to Eve. Now I know nothing about Lilith. But thanks to sites like Google and Wikipedia, you can find out anything you want.

So here are a few things I found out about Lilith. Interestingly Bible doesn't even mention Lilith. But references about her begin to appear in Jewish sources starting about 5th century B.C.

Apparently God created Adam and Lilith in the garden of Eden. They were supposed to be on equal terms but Adam wanted to boss her around but she would have none of it. So eventually she was banished from Eden for disobeying Adam. Then God saw Adam's loneliness and as per biblical account had a deep sleep fall upon him and created Eve from one of his ribs. As Eve was created from a rib of Adam, she was subservient to Adam which pleased both Adam and God.

Many later writers pick it up, give the story more flesh and blood along with many interpretations.

In Kevin R. Given's 'Last Rites' Lilith along with the Egyptian goddess Sekhmet and Hindu goddess Kali form a female trinity bent on destroying mankind.

In C.S. Lewis's The Chronicles of Narnia, the White Witch is a descendant of Lilith.

In Vipin Das's Malayalam novel, 'Anahi', Lilith is a fallen angel who revolted against God and was banished from Heaven for eternity.

In C.S. Moore's 1940 story, 'Fruit of Knowledge' she is part of love triangle with Adam and Eve. Eve eats the forbidden fruit as a result of manipulations by Lilith in an attempt to discredit her and regain Adam's love.

There are many many more authors, movies and TV shows featuring Lilith.

– May 3, 2024

Jewish Eschatology

I am treading here on unfamiliar grounds. I will appreciate any corrections or comments.

In chapter 37 of the Book of Ezekiel, Ezekiel has a vision of dry bones. Roughly here is what he sees. Guided by the hand of God, he arrives in a valley of dry bones. God instructed him to take some dry bones and asked Ezekiel to Prophesy that these bones shall live. God put flesh, sinews, tendons and skin on the bones and a lifeless body of a person came into being. God blew a breath into this person and lo and behold here was a live human. This is the classic image of physical resurrection.

In early Jewish theology, there is no concept of soul or spirit. As I understand, on judgement day in indefinite future, dead will be resurrected from their bones and God will judge them to go to eternal heaven or hell.

The idea of soul and afterlife enters Judaism between 6th and 4th century BC, influenced by Greek and/or Persian tradition. Idea of all good God and all bad Devil also comes from Zoroastrian theology in Persia.

– May 6, 2024

A Postscript to Jewish Eschatology

I neglected to mention that when Jesus was resurrected on the third day after his crucifixion, it has to the kind of bodily resurrection described in my post. It is because his tomb was empty and disciples saw him as he was at the time of crucifixion.

An evangelical colleague of mine found it absolutely thrilling that his bones will be gathered and made to appear before God. He was also a creationist.

To this day, many traditional Muslims and Christians subscribe to the notion of physical resurrection on the Judgement Day, whenever that may be.

A jewish friend thinks that I have deviated from the standard jewish practice and wants me to read a book he suggested. I stick to my guns and claim that I have quoted correctly from the book of Ezekiel. It is of course possible that in the course pf over 2000 years jewish philosophical thinking has evolved and is now substantially different from what it once was.

– May 7, 2024

Garden of One Thousand Buddhas

There is a Buddhist spiritual site near Arlee, Montana with this name. The site is within the Flathead Indian Reservation in Lake County, Montana. The monument itself occupies seven hundred and fifty sq, ft. and surrounding garden is spread across ten acres of land.

Buddhist Center is in the tradition of Nyingma School of Tibetan Buddhism.

One thousand hand-cast Buddhas are positioned around the central figure of Yam Chemo, the great mother, the manifestation of the perfection of wisdom. She is a form of Lord Avalokiteshwarw like Chinese Guan Yin.

(Courtesy of Wikipedia)

– May 11. 2024

Some Thoughts about Kamban and Tulsidas

Here are two quotes about the humility expressed by the two poets.

Kamb Ramayana Translated by P.S. Sundaram

Bal Kand

One thing I would say to those expert In trinal Tamil – verse, song and play – A critic's ear is ill-attuned to the words of a madcap or a devotee. Will children's sketches of rooms and halls Scratched on a floor annoy an artist? Should my poor and foolish poem irk those well-trained in making verse?

Ram Charit Manas by Tulsi Das (Gita Press Gorakhpur)

Bal Kand

For this I find not the least resources, while I am dull of mind and intellect, my ambition is right royal. Even though my intellect is exceedingly mean, my aspiration is pitched too high; while I crave for nectar, I have no means in this world to procure even butter-milk. The virtuous will forgive my presumption and listen to my childish babbling with interest. When a child prattles in lisping accents, the parents hear it with a mind full of delight.

Kamban lived from 1180 CE to 1250 CE. Tulsidas lived fom 1543(?) - 1623 CE. He published Ram Charit Manas in 1574 CE (We know because he states so in the text itself) during the reign of Akbar.

Note how similar they are in humility asking the scholars to excuse their inferior efforts and accept it any way. Kamban lived about 350 years before Tulsidas. In Kamban's work, Rama is not aware of his divinity, just as in Valmiki Ramayana. Tulsidas, on the other hand is much influenced by Adhyatma Ramayana, now believed to be composed in 15th century. In Adhyatma Ramayana, Rama is fully aware of his divinity just as Tulsidas is. Adhyatma Ramayana also introduces the notion of shadow Sita (Chhaya Sita) which Tulsidas also adopts.

The subject of telling about these two great poets and devotees of Rama is huge. I hope to write more about it at a later date.

– June 2, 2024

Vishnu Mathur

I received a very sad news today of passing of a longtime friend, Vishnu Mathur, today.

We affectionately called him Bhai Sahab. Bhai Sahab was a learned man, a physicist by profession, an author of a textbook one Quantum Mechanics. He was also a great lover of Hindustani classical music, a respected Tabla player and an authority on ragas for people like me who are not conversant with music but just love to hear it.

He often recommended to his friends like me the pieces of Hindustani music which we would enjoy. He freely shared his expertise on music.

Bhai Sahab was a gentle soul with never a bad word for any one. Moderate in his tastes and habits, he was admired by all who knew him. He frequently housed visiting Indian musicians and played Tabla for them in their concerts. Mamta Bhargava is a well-known Indian singer in nearby Buffalo. Mathur Sahab routinely played Tabla for her until quite recently.

Mathur Sahab lived by himself even in his advanced age. When he turned ninety about a year ago, his daughters didn't want him to live him alone and moved him to Madison, Wisconsin. Unfortunately he had a fall and had severe head injuries. He succumbed to these injuries.

Dear Bhai Sahab, you are gone but we, who are your admires and friends, will greatly miss you.

– June 26, 2024

A Guide for Living

Expect nothing and you will never be disappointed.
Don't be attached to anything or anyone and you will never grieve.
Be compassionate to all without any attachment.
Don't try to always have the last word and you will be happier and calmer.
Debate never changes anyone's mind so avoid debates as much as possible.
Be gentle but not to a fault.
Be agreeable without being a pushover.
Follow the old adage to put yourself in others' shoes.
Use words such as please, thank you, sorry and have a good day
Frequently and both you and receiver of these words will be happy.
Be considerate without being condescending.
Above all don't take yourself too seriously.
All that we see, feel and experience is Maya that is cosmic illusion
Ephemeral and impermanent.
So enjoy your play as long as you can.

– June 29, 2024

Pain

When you have pain in your body or soul
It is good to remember that you are more
Than the pain you have.
Pain conditions your behavior
That is true but it doesn't define you.
Now if you are a self-realized person
You have pain but you don't suffer.
For ordinary folks it's not possible
But they too can try not to focus on the pain
But distract themselves from it by actions
Such as listening to music they like
A book they enjoy, commune with friends
And loved ones.
If you are a writer, write.
If you like gardening, engage in gardening.
If you are a carpenter, make something.
Anything to get your mind off the pain is good.
Remember like everything pain will also pass.
Above all keep a balance and think of
All the blessings you can still enjoy.
Nature, sky, clouds, the sun, moon and stars
Flowers, birds and bees and people
Are there to amuse you and please you.
Don't give way to fear and loneliness
And soon you will heal and be whole again.

– July 6, 2024

Pain, Again

Pain saps your spirit
Sinks it low and keeps it there
Unless you actively work to lift it up.
It may not soar it high but let it not sink.
You really have to pull yourself
By your bootstraps as they say.

I am reminded of Dylan Thomas urging
His father, "Do not go gentle into that good night.
Rage, rage against the dying of the light."
Albeit, my situation is less dire.
I don't face death at least not yet.

Work till you are afloat if not swimming.
Don't let your spirit sag.
Do something, anything
As if Your very survival is at risk
Because it is.

Pain is insidious.
Some say you have to befriend it.
It doesn't work for me.
I am always fighting it
And keep hoping against hope
That I will overcome it somehow.

That's what keeps me going.
Without hope, I think I will die
Or will be as good as dead.
I want to live till I am really dead.

– July 9, 2024

Self-Understanding

How much do we understand ourselves?
One might think quite well
But I know from my own experience
That it will be a delusion.
All I know how I would I react to a situation
Depends on if I have faced A similar situation before.
If I did then more or less I know my reaction from memory.
Faced with an unforeseen situation, I am not
At all sure, I can predict how I will react.

To give an example, very recently
I found myself in a very morose mood.
First I thought it was due to a disturbing health news.
But upon further thinking, I realized I had known
This for a few days.
So why didn't I feel this way earlier.
Then I thought of an unpleasant phone conversation
And some not so great email exchanges with a close relative.
I thought I was over it but bad mood continued.
When I realized by the process of elimination
That this must be the reason.
Gradually my mood lifted to normal.
I am still not one hundred percent sure
That this was it.

Perhaps some people know their minds well
But I am not one of those people.
I am just a perfectly ordinary un-enlightened old fool
Who can't fathom his own mind.

– July 11, 2024

Tragic Love Story of Kacha and Devayani

This Hindu mythological tale is prior to the Churning of Ocean and delivery of Amrita (the elixir of life} to Devas(gods) and its denial to Asuras(demons). At that time both devas and asuras were subject to death. Now asura's preceptor Shukracharya knew Sanjivani Vidya by which he could bring dead asuras back to life. Brihaspati, the preceptor of devas wanted to know this Vidya so he could bring dead devas back to life. To this end he recruited his own son Kacha to go to Shukracharya and become his disciple.

Shukracharya was glad to accept Kacha as his disciple but knowing that Kacha was a son of Brihaspati, asuras were not. Kacha studied diligently and also became friendly with Shukracharya's daughter Devayani. Actually Devayani fell in love with Kacha. Kacha and Devayani frolicked together but never did anything improper.

Asuras were apprehensive that Kacha may somehow learn the Sanjivini Vidya so one day when Kacha was out gathering firewood they attacked and killed him. They cut up his body and fed it to jackals. When Kacha didn't home even after sunset, Devayani asked her father to do something. Shukracharya by his power of Sanjivani Vidya, was able to summon Kacha who told them what had happened.

Asuras were now even were more determined than ever to kill Kacha. This time they killed Kacha, cremated him and mixed his ashes in Shukracharya's wine which he drank. When Kacha didn't return, Devayani was extremely worried. Shukracharya tried to deter her but she will not take no for an answer.

Shukracharya invoked Sanjivani Vidya and Kacha spoke from his tummy telling what had happened. Now Devayani was in a quandary. She didn't want to lose neither her father nor Kacha. So the agreement was reached that Shukracharya will teach Kacha Sanjivani Vidya while he was in his stomach. Kacha will tear Shukracharya's stomach from inside and then Kacha will revive Shukracharya.

So that's what happened but Kacha refused to marry Devayani. He claimed that as he came out of Shukracharya's stomach, he is like Shukracharya's son. Thus Devayani is like his sister.

Devayani was furious and cursed him that he will forget Sanjivani Vidya when he most needs it. Kacha counter cursed that she will never be able to wed a Brahmana. Kacha's curse turned out to be true as Devayani married Yayati, a Kshatriya king. I couldn't find out what happened to Kacha fom the forces available to me.

Note the irony in the story. If asuras didn't try so hard kill Kacha, he and so devas wouldn't have learned Sanjivani Vidya.

– July 22, 2024

Old Age Dreams

When you are old and I am by any definition of the word
What do you dream of in the security of your subconscious?
You might think a person of advanced age might dream
Of all the horrors that old age might bring
Such as wheel chair, senior home, disability, old age diapers
And God knows what else.

But you may be surprised to learn that such is not the case.
I dream of my graduate student days, not really carefree.
I think of the girls I failed to ask out
The good times I rarely had
Of the research problems I couldn't solve.

I dream of the sandy beaches pristine and pure
With girls I never dared to ask out.
I think of a few friends I partied with.
I dream of graduate students as insecure as me.

The time was late sixties and early seventies.
If you don't get a PhD, you will consider yourself a failure
And if you did, there were no jobs to be had.
Demand for math, buoyed by the sputnik age had petered out.
And some friends who had graduated were pumping gas.
But in spite of all this, this was the happiest time of my life
Except that I didn't know it.
I was young and had a fair sense of adventure.
I was hardened by adversities back home
And didn't easily quit.

I used to think that the best time of my life
Was when I was in my forties, settled in my profession
With a good sense of what I could and couldn't do
With a loving wife and two little girls.

Yes, it was a good life but surprisingly
That's not why dream of.
I dream of my salad days as a young immigrant
In a foreign culture with all the disadvantages that came with it.

– July 27, 2024

Rabindranath Tagore

Tagore was one of the greatest poet, novelist, essayist, musician and beloved personalty of Bengal. He is affectionately called Guru deva all across India and Bangladesh. He died on August 7, 1941. "Ekla Cholo Re" is one of his greatest songs. Here is a rendering of the song by well-known singer of yore, Kishor Kumar. Enjoy:

https://www.youtube.com/watch?v=Pmzvr3aZXQc

Please copy the URL in your browser and enjoy.

– August 9, 2024

Remembrances and forgettances

Remembrances and forgettances are major themes in Indian literature and mythology. Examples abound.

After the universe is dissolved, Vishnu is lying on serpent Shesha (literally the remainder) and dreaming of the new universe, he would create. Later, remembering this dream, he creates the universe.

In Kalidasa's most famous play, Shakuntala, Dushyanta's forgettance of Shakuntala, drives all action of the play.

After Vishnu in the form of a boar lifts the Earth up from the primordial waters, he forgets that his job is done and goes on a rampage. Indra has to kill the boar so Vishnu can reacquire his divine form.

When Sita is brought to Rama after killing of Ravana, he refuses to accept her, gods appear including Rama's father Dasharatha and tell Rama that he is an incarnation of Vishnu, he does not accept the preferred divinity and claims he is just Rama, eldest son of Dasharatha.

Hanuman lives with Sugriva, totally unaware of his great powers until at the time when Sugriva sends him to search for Sita. Jambavan reminds Hanuman of his great prowess and Hanuman acquires his massive form and flies over the ocean to Lanka.

In Tantric theology, the good lord (Shiva in this case), in the form of a Jiva, deliberately forgets his divine nature and this forgettance or ignorance (Maya) is the Creatrix of the whole creation.

Dasharatha forgets the boons he offered to the queen Kaikeyi and pays for it with his life in the end.

– August 15, 2024

Dharma

What sustains us is Dharma, so the scriptures say.
Faith sustains faithful, so faith is their Dharma.

Who do not have faith in a personal deity
Are not sustained by faith
So their Dharma is not faith.

They have to look deeply into their soul
To see what moves them.
They trust science and reason
So partly that is their Dharma.

But the universe is a truly magical
And mysterious place.
Faith trivializes this mystery
By anthropomorphizing and calling this mystery God.

Reasonable people can acknowledge this mystery
And be in its awe and realize how puny
And trivial we are in the scheme of things.

But then again We are the only species
-Or so we think-
That tries to grasp
This wonder and majesty.

So our Dharma is
To be reasonable and scientific.
We have to tamper our reason
With compassion and care
And also be humble
Before this awesome and wondrous
Universe that we are privileged to inhabit.

– August 18, 2024

Krishna Janmashtami 2024

Time to celebrate your birthday is upon us
Dear Krishna, the loveliest of all incarnations.
We remember you in so many ways.
In arts, literature, paintings, folk stories and
In all spheres of human activities.

You were a delightful child to Nand and Yashoda, your foster parents.
Butter thief, flute player and demon killer even as a child.
All the gopis of Vrindavan were charmed by you
And pined for you when you left for Mathura
As a teen age boy.
You killed Kamsha, your tyrant uncle
And freed your parents from his terrible bondage.

You never came back to sere how gopis
Were suffering in your absence.
You sent Uddhav to console them.
Uddhav tried to teach gopis to worship
The formless God but gopis would have none of it.
Uddhav was drowned in gopis' ocean of devotion
And returned flummoxed by selfless devotion of gopis.

This part of you Krishna is totally forgotten
As you become charioteer of Partha in the Mahabharata war.
As Partha Sarathi you preach Gita to Partha.
You imparted the immortal wisdom
To faint-hearted Arjuna in the midst of a battlefield.

In the battlefield of our lives, O Krishna,
We are still guided by your timeless teachings.
So many modern people like Sri Aurobindo,
Mahatma Gandhi and Lokamanya Tilak
Have been guided by your teaching to do our duty

Faithfully but not feel entitled to the fruits of our action.

In my humble way, I have tried to follow your teaching
Not always successfully and not always well.
I leave it all Ito providence per your advice.
In all humility, I salute you Krishna.

– August 24, 2024

Krishna's Birthday

Dear Krishna, today we are celebrating your birthday.
And we earnestly seek your help.
As you know, dear Lord, your sphere of activity
Has broadened and now it includes
The United States of America,
The richest nation on Earth.

In your time, dear Krishna
You fought evil demons called asuras.
The greatest asura of our times
Is a man called Donald Trump.
From now on we will call him Trumpasura.
Trumpasura is an arrogant liar, sinner and a convicted felon.
It is strange that a felon is not allowed to vote
But he can run for president,
This is a strange paradox of American law.

His opponent is Kamala Devi Harris
A child of an Indian mother and Jamaican father.
She is an able lady and uniquely qualified
To hold the highest office in the nation.

But against her is Trumpasua's great wealth
And support of tech billionaires of Silicon Valley
Whom Trumpasura has offered tax cuts.

Dear Krishna, in your time you had Yoga-Maya
The magic of yoga.
Nowadays it is Silicon Valley technology.
Dear Lord, if your Yoga-Maya
Is still potent, please help Kamala win the election.
I pray to you in earnest humility
To grant this wish to help this nation
And the whole world

From the evil designs of Trumpasura.

– August 26, 2024

PS: This is a translation of my Hindi poem, "कन्हैया का जन्मदिन". I have translated it or my readers who don't know Hindi. Posted on September 17.

King Prithu

In Sanskrit the earth is known as Prithivi. The name comes from the name of King Prithu.

To start with the beginning, there was a king named Vena in the dynasty of well-known Hindu icon: Dhruva. Dhruva was so great that the star Polaris is named after him. The king Vena was a tyrannical king. He did not follow scriptures, insisted that people should worship only him. Under his rule there were famines, disasters and tyranny all around. The sages in kingdom took the unusual step of doing something about it. With their Brahmanic Power (Brahma-Teja), they killed Vena. Vena's mother had his body embalmed and preserved.

Now with no king in-charge, things were even worse than before. The sages churned the arm of the dead king Vena and out came Prithu, a lovely divine boy. Prithu had a sign of Sudarshan Chakra on his arm. So it was prophesied that he would be a Chakravarti Samrat I.e. a universal leader.

Prithu set out to make sure that his land was capable of sustaining land. With his bow, he flattened parts of earth to become more arable and capable of sustaining the population. The Earth requested Prithu to tread gently and treat her as his daughter. Prithu agreed.

That is how the earth came to be known as Prithivi, the daughter of Prithu.

– September 1, 2024

Trumpasura vs. Kamala Devi Round 1

Devas and asuras have been fighting for ever.
It is aware between protectors and predators.
This story was repeated on September 10, this year.
There was a debate between Trumpasura and Kamala Devi.
It was such a weird debate to watch.
Kamala baited Trump and he took all the baits.
Kamala totally trounced him.
Trump was reduced to lamely defending his record.
While Kamala won the debate hands on.

Kamala kept smiling and laughing
And Trump kept making ugly faces
Making his ugly countenance even uglier.
He kept on repeating his falsehoods
Which has become second nature to him.

Trump never looked at the public watching the debate
He Just kept looking at the mike.
After all he cares only for himself.
He repeats his admiration for dictators
Like Putin and Orb'an.
And does not give a hoot for democracy.

I think Trump is the single most danger
To Amrican democracy.
Just look at the list of things
He has promised to do on the first day
He comes back to power.
Vote for Kamala and tell Trump
To pack up his baggage, Go home to Maralago
And take shelter in the bosom of Melania
If she still wants you after your dastardly acts.

– September 18, 2024

The Story of Nahusha

King Nahusha of Kosala was an ancestor of Dasharathi Rama. He was a great and virtuous king who had performed several horse sacrifices. When Indra killed the demon Vritra who had encircled all the waters of the world and the people were dying of hunger and thirst as there were no rains, every one rejoiced. But Vritra was a Brahmin and Indra had to run and hide from Brahma-hatya, Brahminicide incarnate. Indra hid somewhere in the ocean waters.

Svarga needed a king and illustrious Nahusha was requested by Devas to be their king in the absence of Indra. For a while Nahusha ruled as a good king and performed all his duties faithfully. But as time passed he became arrogant and a bully. Devas wanted to get rid of him but how?

Nahusha was becoming more and more intolerable. He figured that all things in Svarga belonged to him including Indra's wife Shachi. He approached Shachi and asked to be her paramour. Shachi asked for some time. She approached Brihaspati and Brihaspati devised plan that will undo Nahusha. He told Shachi to ask Nahusha to visit her as a great king in a palanquin carried by the seven sages, called Saptarishis. One of the seven sages was Rishi Agastya who was of short stature. He was having trouble carrying the load with other rishis who were taller. Nahusha admonished Agastya saying: sarpa, sarpa and kicked him, Now sarpa also means snake. Agastya was livid and cursed Nahusha to fall and become a snake. Nahusha while falling asked when his curse would end. Agastya told him when he meats with Pandavas in the Dvapar Yuga after he converses with Yudhishthira.

Indra came back to Svarga and performed requisite Yajnas to be freed from the sin of killing a Brahmin.

Nahusha's reign was in Treta Yuga. In Dvapar Yuga, when Pandavas were dwelling in the forest, Bhima had gone hunting. When Bhima did not return for a long time, Yudhishthira and other Pandavas went to look for Bhima. They found Bhima helplessly bound in the coils of a huge snake who was poised to eat him. Yudhishthira asked Nahusha for substitute food and let Bhima go but Nahusha said that he has to eat at whoever he finds this hour of the day. Nahusha introduced himself and told his story and agreed that If Yudhishthira answers some questions to his satisfaction, he might relent and let Bhima go.

Yudhishthira answers all the questions to Nahusha's satisfaction. Then Yudhishthira asks Nahusha some questions. After this scholarly dialog, Nahusha relents and let Bhima go. Right at that moment Nahusha is released from his curse and ascends to Svarga.

– September 22, 2024

The Magical Universe

What ails the soul of a modern man
I think I have a clue.
We have lost the capacity to wonder.
Stand in awe of the magical universe
Like the people of Veda did.
They sang beautiful songs in praise of
The dawn, the goddess of dawn
In intricate rhymes and sophisticated meters.
Many so called primitive tribes
Still have it. They sing and dance
In a magical universe denied us by our progress,
Science and technology.

To us the universe is not magical and mysterious
Everything can be explained by science.
But it indeed is not so.
Can you explain the beauty of a flower
By directing it?
Can you explain the beauty of a sunset
By describing scientific reasons for its occurrence?

We need to develop again the sense of wonder,
The awe of our magical universe
And also that we are also magical creatures
Just like all other magical beings
That inhabit mother earth
Which indeed is the wonder of all wonders
The only place in the universe as far as we know
Inhibited by sentient beings.

– September 23, 2024

Jaratkaru

Jaratkaru is a famous rishi in the Mahabharata. As the epic explains it is the combination of 'jara' and 'karu'. Karu means a monstrous body and Jara means consumption. A monstrous body reduced by consumption I.e. by ascetic practices. Jaratkaru becomes well-known for his spiritual powers. Once while traveling in the nether levels he saw some people hanging on to a precipice supported by some plants. On inquiry he finds out that they are his own ancestors trying to avoid going to hell. All because Jaratkaru is the last in their line and if he has no progeny, no body will perform shraddhas and the ancestors will surely fall to hell.

Jaratkaru promised he will marry but he still has his own conditions. He will marry a virgin who also has the same name as his and must marry him willingly, not forced by any one. If she ever displeases him, he will leave.

Meanwhile Vasuki, the king of Nagas(snakes but with a shape-shifting ability) was looking for a groom for his sister Jaratkaru, also called Manasa. It had been prophesied that Jaratkaru's son will prevent Nagas from total destruction in a future Naga Yagna to be performed by the king Janamejaya, a descendent of the Pandavas. Meanwhile Rishi Jaratkaru was praying and trying frantically to find a bride. Eventually Vasuki meets the rishi and a wedding takes place.

While Jaratkaru and his wife were living in a forest as rishis normally do, one early morning the rishi was sleeping on his wife's lap. It was time for his daily rituals. Manasa was in a jeopardy as to what to do. If she does not wake him up, he may be angry for missing the rituals. If she does wake him he may be angry because she woke him up. She decides to wake him up and predictably he is angry and ready to leave. Before leaving he assures Manasa that she is pregnant.

A little earlier Arjuna's grandson Parikshita was the king at Hastinapur. He was a just and mighty king. One day, Parikshita got lost in a forest while hunting. He found an ashram where a rishi was sitting in profound meditation. The king enquired him where he was but rishi couldn't hear him in deep samadhi. The king got angry and put a dead snake around rishi's neck. When rishi's son Shringi came back to the ashram after picking roots and fruits for their meal, he was outraged by this insult to his father. He cursed that the perpetrator of this crime will die of a snake bite seven days from now. When the rishi came out of his samadhi, he was not at all pleased. He scolded his son for his rash action. He said Parikshita was a good and righteous king and didn't deserve this punishment.

Now the curse came true and Parikshita was bit by a famous Naga, Takshaka by name and Parikshita died. Now Takshaka was a friend of Indra, the king of devas so Takshaka was beyond the limits of justice. It helps to have friends in high places then as well now. Parikshita's son Janamejaya was just a little boy when this happened. When Janamejaya grew up and became the king he learned of this story.

Janamejaya was furious and was determined to punish the Nagas. He decided to commit a Naga Yagna. In this yagna, a huge fire was built and several powerful Munis (same as rishis) chanted invoking the names of Nagas. The mantras I.e. the chants were so powerful that the invoked Naga had to fly into the fire pit.

While this was ongoing, Astika, the son of rishi Jaratkaru and Manasa was grown up and heard of this wholesale destruction of Nagas. He came to the Yagna and impressed the king Janamejaya by his wit and learning. He was pleased to offer Astika a wish. Astika asked for the cessation of Naga Yagna. Thus Astika saved Nagas from a wholesale destruction. By the way just before the rite was stopped Takshaka's name was invoked so he was saved just in the nick of time.

The Mahabharata says that any body who reads or hears this story will have no fear from Nagas. The famous festival of Naga Panchmi is celebrated on the fifth day of the bright half of the Shravana month of the Hindu calendar. On this day, milk is offered to the snakes. When I was a child, well over sixty years ago, snake charmers did a heavy business on Naga Panchami by bringing snakes to the families who offered milk to the snakes and a fee to the charmer. I don't know if the custom still endures.

– September 29, 2024

Shringi Rishi

Once upon a time there was a rishi named Vibhandaka totally immersed in ascetic practices. His asceticism gave him tremendous occult powers so that Indra, the king of gods became afraid that Rishi was after his throne. So he sent a heavenly Apsara to break his taapas. After seeing this heavenly damsel, Rishi spilled his seed which was eaten by a doe. In due time the doe gave birth to human male child but with a horn on his head. Remember dear readers, we are in a land of math mixed with real events so we can't tell where one begins and other ends.

This boy born of a human and a deer was named Shringi because of the horn on his head. His father brought him up to be a fierce ascetic and he did not even know of the presence of fair sex. He virtually had no contact with any human other than his father.

Mean while in the nearby kingdom of Anga, there was a famine as it had not rained in several years due to a curse that had fallen on the king, due to some misdeeds of him. The only way, the curse could be averted if the king could bring this innocent and totally sinless Shringi rishi to the kingdom, according to the Brahmans of the king's court.

The king devised a clever plan in consultation with his ministers and leading Brahmins.

The king got the most beautiful courtesan of the court and settled her on a float with all the amenities and servants. The float docked on a river bank close to the ashram of Rishi Vibhandaka.

Now one day, when Rishi Vibhandaka was away from the ashram, the courtesan made her move. Armed with beautiful flowers, delicious foods and drinks, silks and other good things of life, she went to meet Shringi rishi. As is customary, Shringi rishi offered to wash her feet and offered fruits and roots that forest dwellers eat. He of course took her to be a rishi visiting his ashram. She said in her devotional practice, feet were not washed. She offered Rishi all the fine things to eat. She danced around and hugged Rishi making sure that her bosom touched him. She played around, danced and made merry to the great delight of young rishi. Then she left before Vibhandaka could come back.

When Vibhandaka came back to the ashram, he found his son greatly disturbed and unhappy. He told Vibhandaka how a rishi kumar(young rishi) had visited and how much he had enjoyed his company and things he had brought. He described how the guest was decked with flowers and had these delightful growths on his chest and how he danced and sung. He wanted to see him again. Rishi told his son that he was a rakshasa and his company will be disastrous for his ascetic practice.

Vibhandaka searched for the elusive courtesan but did not succeed. Meanwhile, the courtesan made her move and visited Shringi rishi and invited him to her ashram. She brought him to her float and took off to the capital of Anga. There Shringi rishi was given a palatial house to live in and all luxuries were provided. Rishi now learned of the fair sex and other worldly things. The king's daughter Shanta fell in love with Rishi and they were married. Of course, the famine was over and rains returned to the kingdom.

Rishi Vibhandaka put two and two together and took off for Anga's capita. King's spies learned of his departure and they got in motion. They provided sumptuous guest houses on his journey and took care of all his needs. So by the time he reached the capital, he had mellowed. When he visited his son and daughter-in-law, and saw how happy they were. He blessed their union and left for his ashram.

This same Shringi rishi, was invited by the king Dashraatha to conduct the yagna which resulted in the birth of Rama and his half-brothers.

– October 5, 2024

Dussehara 2024

Dussehara is on October 12 this year. It is celebrated all over India but especially in Bengal and Karnataka. It celebrates the victory of good over evil.

There are two different mythological stories associated with it.

The story that is prevalent where I grew up is the killing of demon Ravana by Rama, an avatar of Lord Vishnu. I grew up in Kanpur, Uttar Pradesh. So in much of North India, except Bengal, part of Bihar and Odisha, we celebrate the victory of Rama over Ravana. There are big melas(fairs) and huge crowds gather to see a huge effigy of Ravana burnt in a bonfire. I remember watching great throngs gathering to watch this event. In my village and nearby villages, people visited each other and greeted with Pans(spiced Betel leaves). I don't know how widespread is this practice. Many people also record the prices of common goods like sugar, salt, food grains, pulses and other everyday items.

There is a bird called Nila-Kantha, literally blue-throated bird. It is supposed to be auspicious to see this bird on Dussehara. I should note that Lord Shiva has a blue throat because when the poison came out as a result of the churning of the ocean, Shiva drank it so the living creatures will not be poisoned and suffer a horrible death. His throat is blue because tha's where the poison is stored.

Dussehara is also called Vijayadashami or Durga Puja. Vijaya means victory and Dashami is the tenth day of a fortnight. The festival falls on the tenth day of the bright fortnight of Kwar, month of the Hindu calendar.

The other mythological story celebrates the victory of Goddess Durga over the buffalo demon Mahishsura. Mahisha means buffalo and asura means demon.

Mahishasura practiced austerities for many years to please Lord Brahma. Eventually Brahma appeared and offered to grant him a boon. Mahisha wanted to be immortal but that is one thing Brahma can't grant. Any body who is born must die. Mahisha then gave a long list of people: gods, men, gandharvas, demons who would not be able to kill him. In his list he neglected to mention women. Lord Brahma said: So be it.

Mahishasura became arrogant and insufferable. He conquered the three worlds and began his reign of terror. All gods including the trinity of Brahma, Vishnu and Shiva were worried. All the gods then put all their energies together and created a woman who was more powerful than any body in the entire universe. This was the Goddess Durga.

Durga challenged Mahishasura for a battle. Durga was extremely pretty and full of grace. Mahisha fell in love with her and proposed a marriage. Durga said if he defeats her in battle, she will marry him. Unfortunately, he was killed so this one-sided love story remained unfinished.

The three worlds heaved a sigh of relief and rejoiced.

– October 11. 2024

Prison of Sadness

We are sad when we don't get our way.
We are sad when we don't accept
The way things are.
We are sad when we want life to be different
Than what it is but don't see a
Way to change it.

A physical prison keeps you locked in.
You can't easily break out
And if you do, you are a fugitive from law
And even if you some how make another
Life for you, you can get caught
And may be in worse trouble than before.

Sadness is a mental prison is of your own making
And may be even worse than a prison
Of brick and mortar.
A prison of our negative mental feelings
Are like fetters on our feet
And keep us bound and captive.

It is best to break these bonds
With mental resolve.
Either accept your situation
Or make every attempt to break free.

Be of good cheer.
Smile and let that smile get bigger and broader.
If you smile, world smiles with you.
If you cry no body cries with you.
People have enough of their own worries
To worry about yours.

– October 12, 2024

A Perspective on My Life

As I am getting old, I have been taking stock of my life.
Things that I have not done.
It occurred to me that I have
Never lived a care-free
Devil may care type of life
With bravado and spirit soaring high.
Then I realized that would not be me
But altogether a different type of person.

Only bravado I had was to get the highest
Marks in a class I was taking.
This was also a necessity
Education was my ticket out of my little village
And I had to win scholarships to fund my education.

I never played sports
Or, ran for any office during school or collage.
I only received academic distinctions.
Became infatuated with books and
Got myself educated in many things
Not related to my areas in academics.

I Lost faith in any personal deity
And became an agnostic early in my life
But learned all I could about religions
Not just mine but others too.

I have lived the life I chose to live with no lingering regrets.
It has been a reasonably happy life
With some painful bumps early on.
I have tried to treat my fellow humans
As in the classic motto with charity towards all
And malice towards none.

– October 22, 2024

Deepavali 2024

This year Deeepavali or Diwali falls on November 1, according to Hindu Calendar. It is the most popular of Hindu festival and is celebrated more or less in all of India. The word literally means a row of lamps.

It is collection of holidays,lasting for five consecutive days. The first day is Dhan Teras which celebrates the appearance of the physician Dhanavantari from the celebrated churning of the ocean in Hindu mythology. I don't know how he really figures in the celebration. What I remember is that on the day of Dhan Teras(13th day of the dark fortnight in the month of Kartik), we discarded any broken pots and bought at least one new one.

The next day is Narak Chaturdashi. It celebrates the killing of the demon Narakasura by Krishna. We light a lamp by the gutter, presumably to guide Narakasura on his way to nether lands.

Fifteenth day is the dark night, Amavasya when Rama returned to Ayodhya with wife Seeta and brother Lakshmana after a long eventful exile of fourteen years. All of Ayodhya was lit by bright lights to celebrate Rama's homecoming. We celebrate by lighting hundreds of little clay oil lamps, all over the house. I remember the tremendous excitement with which we kids accomplished the task. There also was an associated Puja, performed by my father. Prasad was parched rice called layya and kneel, sugary batasha's and other sweets. It is also a tradition amongst Hindus and Sikhs to visit friends and relatives with Diwali sweets.

Next day is the start of New business year. Most businesses have switched to the western calendar but traditionalists still commemorate the day and consecrate their account books with sacred symbols, Hindu Swastka(卐), as one of them. Swastka is a symbol of universal well-being. Business offices are also decorated with sacred symbols.

The last day of the celebration is Bhai Dooj. On this day, sisters anoint the foreheads of their brothers with a holi Tika (sort of a vertical mark) and feeding the brother with a piece of sweetmeat. The brother promises the sister to protect her from any harm. Brothers travel far to meet the sisters on this occasion. My sister always sent me a Tika by mail while she was alive.

This, in brief, is how my family celebrated Diwali. Admittedly it is a bare bones account. I have purposely refrained from any detailed mythological yarns.

– October 27, 2024

Humans vs. Animals

We, humans pride ourselves on our knowledge
Of good and bad, moral or immoral, right or wrong.
That puts us at a higher level than the rest of creation
We like to believe.

But is it really so?
Except humans, all animals live their lives
Without guilt or shame.
They grieve or rejoice but do not suffer as we do.
We are ridden with guilt, shame and
Other dualities mentioned above.
An animal lives its life
And when end comes, seeks a corner
To lay its head on and die.

We on the other hand are burdened with
Existential angst. We worry if it is the end
Of our existence or we survive and have
A life after we die.

So we have come up with the ideas of God
And Devil, Karma and reincarnation, Angels,
Saint and sinners, Buddhas, Messiahs,
Incarnations and what not.

We have devised rituals of all kinds
Christening, confirmation,
Weddings, Bar Mitzvah, funerary rites
And myriads more.

We write books
And then claim they are divine
And believe in what they say
As much as to kill those

Who don't believe.
There is no comparable despicable
Activity that animals engage in.

All these things hinge on our
Notion of self-importance.
Christians talk of an immortal soul
Hindus call it Self and Buddhists deny a Self.
But even then focus is on Self.

An animal does not give a hoot about self.
Don't you think that makes it freer than you.
An animal has no self-importance
And is free of notions of good and evil.

An animal is FREE in a sense
That we never are.
So if you insist on a hierarchy,
You have to put dumb animals
Higher than us miserable
Self-important beings.

– October 31, 2024

DK PRINTWORLD